KEVIN P. RAY

ART & BUSI-NESS

TRANSACTIONS IN ART
& CULTURAL PROPERTY

Cover design by Tahiti Spears/ABA Design

Printed in the United States of America.

20 19 18 17 16   5 4 3 2 1

ISBN: 978-1-63425-669-8

e-ISBN: 978-1-63425-670-4

For Joe and for my parents,
whose patience appears to know no bounds.

And for Father R. Stephen Almagno,
a dear friend, mentor, and colleague,
whose scholarship and commitment to
learning and culture have provided a powerful inspiration.

CONTENTS

ACKNOWLEDGMENTS

This book would not have been possible without the guidance and support of many people, in conversations and e-mails. I deeply appreciate their comments, questions, and musings. All faults, errors, and mistakes, however, are solely my own. I would like to extend my deepest thanks to Prof. Patty Gerstenblith, Deborah and Larry Hoffman, Prof. Stephen Urice, Robert Morrison, Amy Parenti, Jane C.H. Jacob, Judith Prowda, Tom Christopherson, Lucian Simmons, Steven Zick, Paul Provost, Andrew Augenblick, Lawrence Shindell, Judith Pearson, Prof. Francesco Francioni, Prof. Riccardo Pavoni, Prof. Federico Lenzini, Prof. Holly Flora, Rebecca Woan, Hillary Bauer, Jacqueline Chezar, Diego Figueroa, Mudita Chawla, Prof. Maureen Collins, Lubna El Gendi, Barbara Rea, Prof. Leila Sadat, Prof. Karen Tokarz, and to my colleagues Diane Vuocolo, Nancy Peterman, Carla Greenberg, Elizabeth Hodgman, Troy Eid, and John Voorhees.

INTRODUCTION

Art and cultural property[1] are global phenomena, crossing both physical and conceptual borders. The art market is similarly expansive. Traditional art transactions—sales through dealers, galleries, and auction houses—have been experiencing a significant increase, reflected, to some degree, in recurring headlines trumpeting record prices at auction. However, these traditional types of transactions are only part of the picture. As art has gained greater acceptance as a quasi-asset class for investment, buoyed by an often rising global market, art is appearing in a variety of transactions that expand the traditional dealer-gallery-auction house sale form. Art transactions increasingly include many art-secured lending, securitization, and commercial transactions. The presence of art in these transactions is frequently novel to the parties involved, who may be unfamiliar with the unique issues and challenges of the art world. Insurance plays a more significant role in art transactions than it has in the past, including title insurance. In addition, freeports allow collectors to store art in secured, climate-controlled facilities and also to receive the benefit of the freeports' tax-deferred status.

We frequently speak of *centers* of the art world, assuming that the same centers are centers both of art production and of the art trade. In the 17th century, we would have spoken of Rome as the center of the art world. In the 19th century, it would have been Paris. To a great extent, these were understood to be centers of both artistic production and the art trade. Artists travelled to Rome to study and to work, as later they would travel to Paris, and later still to New York. However, while the old art centers continue in their importance and vitality, artistic production is now far more geographically diverse.

Similarly, the centers of the art trade are also becoming more dispersed. For decades, there were two great centers, the *entrepôts* of New York and London. Both cities remain enormously influential and are certainly the principal centers for secondary sales through the major auction houses of Sotheby's and Christie's. However, art fairs are proliferating, and they bring together galleries from the world over in a circuit of sales and events in Maastrict, Basel, London, New York, Miami, Los Angeles,

1 For convenience, I will use the term "art" to mean both art and cultural property, except where the discussion requires that distinctions between art and cultural property be made.

Chicago, and elsewhere. The expanded list of art centers is not restricted to Europe and the United States. Mexico, Argentina, Brazil, Qatar, the United Arab Emirates, and China have all experienced significant increases in art transactions. The liberalization of many emerging economies and changing patterns of global wealth distribution and concentration have had a profound effect on the global art trade, including the newer types of art transactions.

Sometimes, a highly publicized incident, such as the contest over the fate of the Detroit Institute of Arts, the bankruptcy of the Salander O'Reilly Gallery or Ace Gallery, or the forgery scandal that felled venerable Knoedler & Company, focuses public attention on art transactions (sales, art-secured loans, bankruptcy, etc.). These incidents highlight the importance of having the right types of knowledge and advice when dealing with art. Financial stress or insolvency can motivate a collector to sell or leverage objects or an institution to restructure or dissolve. The insolvency of a museum donor or of an art gallery can have reverberations throughout the world of lenders, trade creditors, and others. Even the intent of a donor can be changed or undone. The set of issues—which include domestic and cross-border restrictions on trade in (and sometimes even ownership of) certain types of art—are essential elements that parties to a wide variety of transactions need to be able to recognize and address. However, as the disputes over appraisals and methods of valuing art in the Detroit Institute of Arts case and the disagreements among experts in the Knoedler & Company cases over the provenance and authentication of paintings show, the processes and conclusions of art expertise can be simultaneously complex and contingent.

This book is not intended to be exhaustive. No book on so diverse a subject could be. Rather, what I have tried to do is to provide an introduction to what people need to know when entering into transactions that involve art. In several instances, I use certain complex subjects as something like case studies, where those subjects touch on multiple issues and perspectives within a broad topic. The Parthenon sculptures, for example, embody many of the conflicting perspectives, interests, and changing legal and ethical principles that arise in connection with archaeological and ethnographic objects; the controversies over the cultural affiliation of Kennewick Man and the Paris auctions of Hopi and Navajo sacred and ceremonial objects exemplify the challenges involved with indigenous cultural heritage that have only begun to be addressed in domestic and international law; the interactions over a decade or more among gallerists, collectors, artists' estates and foundations, scholars, provenance researchers, and materials analysts over the authenticity of a group of paintings that were sold by or through the well-respected gallery Knoedler & Company offer insight into the problem of accurate and inaccurate information in art transactions; the tension between regulators, dealers, museums, and collectors over the regulation of ivory, particularly antique ivory, is not only interesting in itself, but provides a point of entry to an understanding of how laws protecting endangered species can have an impact on art transactions; and the story, told through multiple cases over several decades, of the looting by the Nazis of public and private art collections not only helps one to understand what issues are involved with stolen and looted art, but these cases have themselves been integral in the ongoing development of domestic and international law in this area. In each of these subjects, the general and the particular are closely linked.

It is my hope this book will be of interest and use to artists, collectors, museum and art trade professionals, finance professionals, fund managers, wealth advisors, investors in art securitizations, family office professionals, and insurance professionals, as well as attorneys.

CHAPTER 1

Art and Cultural Property in the Law

A. What Is Art?

"Our fine arts were developed, their types and uses were established, in times very different from the present, by men whose power of action upon things was insignificant in comparison with ours. But the amazing growth of our techniques, the adaptability and precision they have attained, the ideas and habits they are creating, make it a certainty that profound changes are impending in the ancient craft of the Beautiful. In all the arts there is a physical component which can no longer be considered or treated as it used to be, which cannot remain unaffected by our modern knowledge and power. For the last twenty years neither matter nor space nor time has been what it was from time immemorial. We must expect great innovations to transform the entire technique of the arts, thereby affecting artistic invention itself and perhaps even bringing about an amazing change in our very notion of art."

—Paul Valéry[1]

"Ideas alone can be works of art; they are in a chain of development that may eventually find some form. All ideas need not be made physical."

—Sol LeWitt[2]

---

1 Paul Valéry, *Pièces sur L'Art, 1931, Le Conquete de l'ubiquite*, quoted in Walter Benjamin, *The Work of Art in the Age of Mechanical Reproduction*, in ILLUMINATIONS 223–24 (Harry Zohn trans., 1968).

2 Sol LeWitt, *Sentences on Conceptual Art*, in ART AND ITS SIGNIFICANCE: AN ANTHOLOGY OF AESTHETIC THEORY 691 (Stephen David Ross ed., 3rd ed. 1994).

"The conventions of art are altered by works of art."

—Sol LeWitt[3]

"A work of art is the unique result of a unique temperament. Its beauty comes from the fact that the author is what he is. It has nothing to do with the fact that other people want what they want. Indeed, the moment that an artist takes notice of what other people want, and tries to supply the demand, he ceases to be an artist, and becomes a dull or an amusing craftsman, an honest or a dishonest tradesman. He has no further claim to be considered as an artist. Art is the most intense mode of Individualism that the world has known."

—Oscar Wilde[4]

"There really is no such thing as Art. There are only artists."

—E. H. Gombrich[5]

1. Objects and Contexts

This book is about how art is treated, and what role it plays, in many different kinds of transactions (sales, leases, loans, etc.). Therefore, it concerns itself primarily with the *legal* status of art. Still, it is essential to consider the conceptual constructs that undergird what we believe art is because those concepts inform how art is understood and treated in the law. Thoughtful people over many centuries have attempted to understand what art is and what role art and the artist have in a society, and those centuries of analyses are a critical background to how we answer these questions today.

---

[3] *Id.*

[4] Oscar Wilde, THE SOUL OF MAN UNDER SOCIALISM 11 (2012).

[5] E.H. Gombrich, *On Art and Artists*, *in* THE ESSENTIAL GOMBRICH: SELECTED WRITINGS ON ART AND CULTURE 65 (Richard Woodfield ed., 1996).

"What is art?" It seems to be a simple enough question.[6] Histories of western art[7] often begin with cave paintings[8] or the *Woman of Willendorf*[9] and identify a progression to the present day, reasoning by abduction to an understanding of what art is. Many artists, though, particularly in the modern and contemporary period, have rejected attempts to define art as limiting and illegitimate. Art critics, art theorists, and art historians take differing approaches to the question. The art trade, on the other hand, takes a pragmatic and largely object-focused approach to art, in which art is a tangible object embodying the creative expression of one or more individuals in traditionally recognized media (i.e., drawing, painting, prints, sculpture, metalwork, ceramics, and textiles). However, even this definition is continuously challenged and stretched, both by contemporary artistic practice and by changes in individual and institutional collecting.

The materials and subject matter of art are continuously changing—including *readymades* (manufactured or found objects, such as Duchamp's *Fountain,* a porcelain urinal that the artist exhibited in 1917),[10]

---

[6] Some have said that the question has no answer. Philosopher of aesthetics Morris Weitz, in an influential 1956 essay, *The Role of Theory in Aesthetics,* declared that art is not truly definable, that it is instead a philosophically open category. "[T]he very expansive, adventurous character of art," Weitz wrote, "its ever-present changes and novel creations, makes it logically impossible to ensure any set of defining properties." Morris Weitz, *The Role of Theory in Aesthetics, in* THE PHILOSOPHY OF ART: READINGS ANCIENT AND MODERN 183–92 (Neill et al. eds., 1995).

[7] Two of the most prominent histories of art used in American art history courses are GARDNER'S ART THROUGH THE AGES: A GLOBAL HISTORY (15th ed., 2016, first published in 1926) and JANSON'S HISTORY OF ART: THE WESTERN TRADITION (8th ed., 2015, first published in 1962). Many consider the concept of the art historical survey that sets out an established canon to be outdated. This anti-canonical view was incorporated into the most recent revision of Janson. *See* Randy Kennedy, *Revising Art History's Big Book: Who's In and Who Comes Out?* N.Y. TIMES, March 7, 2006, *available at* http://www.nytimes.com/2006/03/07/arts/design/07jans.html?pagewanted=all.

[8] The oldest known cave paintings (at least 35,400 years old) are believed to be located on the Indonesian island of Sulawesi. *See, e.g.,* Jo Marchant, *A Journey to the Oldest Cave Paintings in the World,* SMITHSONIAN MAGAZINE, January 2016, *available at* http://www.smithsonianmag.com/history/journey-oldest-cave-paintings-world-180957685/?no-ist. As Cynthia Freeland has noted in her book ART THEORY: A VERY SHORT INTRODUCTION (2001), not only is art conceptualized and understood differently in different cultures and times, but the concept of "art" may not apply at all. She writes that: "The practices and roles of artists are amazingly multiple and elusive. Ancient and modern tribal peoples would not distinguish art from artifact or ritual. Medieval European Christians did not make 'art' as such, but tried to emulate and celebrate God's beauty. In classical Japanese aesthetics, art might include things unexpected by modern Westerners, like a garden, sword, calligraphy scroll, or tea ceremony."

[9] The *Woman of Willendorf* (also known as the *Venus of Willendorf*) is a stone statuette of a female figure believed to have been made between 28,000 and 25,000 BCE. The figure was discovered in 1908 at a Paleolithic site near the Austrian village of Willendorf. It is housed in the collection of the Naturhistorisches Museum Vienna. *See* https://www.wien.info/en/sightseeing/museums-exhibitions/top/museum-natural-history.

[10] *See* http://www.tate.org.uk/art/artworks/duchamp-fountain-t07573.

conceptual art,[11] performance art,[12] appropriation art,[13] kinetic art,[14] and art in an ever-expanding array of new media[15] (not only digital art and video art,[16] but art that uses technologies themselves, particularly social media, as medium, subject, or muse).[17]

Even the working assumption that art is a tangible object is itself only tentative, because much art of the last century has made a deliberate break with traditional notions of art as a static image fixed at a moment in time. Performance art in its various manifestations (by such artists as Marina Abramovic,[18] Joseph Beuys,[19] Bruce Nauman,[20] Nam June Paik,[21] and Yoko Ono[22]) is emblematic of this change, not only by introducing movement and sound (as much video art does as well), but also by refusing the requirement that art be fixed in a stable medium. The fleeting quality and impermanence of such works are both part of the artist's medium and part of the work's message. However, not all performance artists are satisfied to have a work vanish once the performance has ended. Some sell photographic or video documentation of the performance. Others, like Abramovic, preserve a performance through reperformance.[23]

---

[11] *See, e.g.,* the entry for "Conceptual Art" in *The Art Story, available at* http://www.theartstory.org/movement-conceptual-art.htm.

[12] *See, e.g.,* the entry for "Performance Art" in *The Art Story, available at* http://www.theartstory.org/movement-performance-art.htm.

[13] *See, e.g.,* Museum of Modern Art, *Appropriation, available at* https://www.moma.org/learn/moma_learning/themes/pop-art/appropriation.

[14] *See, e.g.,* the entry for "Kinetic Art" in *The Art Story, available at* http://www.theartstory.org/movement-kinetic-art.htm.

[15] *See, e.g., New Media, available at* http://www.newmediaart.eu.

[16] For more information about digital and video art, see *Video Data Bank, available at* http://www.vdb.org.

[17] *See, e.g.,* An Xiao, *Always Social: Social Media Art (2004-2008)*, HYPERALLERGIC, June 14, 2010, *available at* http://hyperallergic.com/6644/social-media-art-pt-1; Ben Davis, *'Social Media Art' in the Expanded Field*, ARTNET, *available at* http://www.artnet.com/magazineus/reviews/davis/art-and-social-media8-4-10.asp (alluding to Rosalind Krauss's 1979 essay *Sculpture in the Expanded Field*, OCTOBER 30–44 (Spring 1979).

[18] For more information about Serbian performance artist Marina Abramovic (1946–), see the website of the Marina Abramovic Institute, *available at* http://www.mai-hudson.org.

[19] For more information about German artist Joseph Beuys (1921–1986), see the Beuys entry on the website of the Museum of Modern Art, *available at* http://www.moma.org/collection/artists/540.

[20] For more information about American artist Bruce Nauman (1941–), see the Nauman entry on the website of the Museum of Modern Art, *available at* http://www.moma.org/collection/artists/4243.

[21] For more information about Korean-American artist Nam June Paik (1932–2006), see the website of the Nam June Paik Estate, *available at* http://www.paikstudios.com.

[22] For more information about Japanese-American multimedia artist Yoko Ono (1933–), see the Imagine Peace website, *available at* http://imaginepeace.com.

[23] Carol Kino, *A Rebel Form Gains Favor. Fights Ensue*, N.Y. TIMES, Mar. 10, 2010, *available at* http://www.nytimes.com/2010/03/14/arts/design/14performance.html.

Still others, like Tino Sehgal,[24] license the right to perform a work. The idea of preserving a performance—whether by authorized reperformance or licensed rights to perform—remains controversial, with many performance artists regarding attempts to preserve or monetize performances as betrayals of the purpose and nature of performance art itself.

2. Mimesis from Plato to Tracey Emin

Western discussions of art and aesthetics typically begin with Plato (427–347 BCE) and his view that art is by its nature representational or mimetic. Art as mimesis continues to be influential. Aristotle[25] and the later Greek Neo-Platonists, like Plotinus,[26] reinterpreted Plato's position, as did medieval Christian philosophers.[27] Mimesis was radically re-envisioned

---

24 For more information about the British artist Tino Sehgal (1976–), see the Sehgal entry on the website of the Guggenheim Museum, *available at* http://www.guggenheim.org/new-york/exhibitions/past/exhibit/3305.

25 Plato's student Aristotle (384–322 BCE) agreed that art is fundamentally mimetic, but he disagreed with Plato on the source of the artist's imitation. For Aristotle, the artist was not concerned with representing objects in their particularity, but with representing things and, even more, persons in their ideal form. The artist was concerned with representing ideal reality. *See Art and Its Significance* at 35. Aristotle describes three types of production: (1) by nature; (2) by skill or artistry (*techne*), of which there are two forms—production by design and production to an end; and (3) that form of production that brings into being from nonbeing (*poesis*). Art is concerned with this final category, bringing something into being. For Aristotle, the artist imitates the ideal and improves upon the mere particulars of objects in the world.

26 Plotinus (ca. 204/5–270 CE) refined Plato's concept of the Forms to provide for a single, unified, and transcendent "One," which was the "Good." Under Plotinus's system, "Beauty" is an aspect of the Good and is a manifestation of the unity that is the One. The beauty of objects and of nature are manifestations—indeed, symbols—of Beauty, and thus are manifestations or symbols of the Good. However, in Plotinus's system, artworks are higher than natural objects, which are imperfect and incomplete. Art perfects nature in service of Beauty, so that artworks are symbols of the greater cosmic harmony. *See* PHILOSOPHIES OF ART AND BEAUTY: SELECTED READINGS IN AESTHETICS FROM PLATO TO HEIDEGGER 140–141 (Albert Hofstadter & Richard Kuhns eds., 1976).

27 In the Medieval period, the concept of art continued the influence of Platonic and Aristotelian views of art, as interpreted through Christian philosophers, chief among them St. Augustine (354–430 CE) and St. Thomas Aquinas (1225–1274 CE). Medieval aesthetics drew upon the Neoplatonic view that the world was a manifestation or symbol of a higher celestial truth, God. But for Augustine, the visual symbols of art and nature present a risk of sensual allure, drawing an individual away from contemplation of the eternal through a fascination with surfaces and sensual pleasures. Reason is what leads man to God and right action, and so the senses must be approached with caution, tempered and guided by reason. Augustine observes that "in the pleasure of those senses (vision and hearing), what pertains to reason is that in which there is a certain rhythmic measure." PHILOSOPHIES OF ART AND BEAUTY at 175, quoting Augustine, *De Ordinare*, Chapter Eleven, para. 33. Aquinas reintroduced and reinterpreted the relation between the visible, the beautiful, and the eternal. For Aquinas, "allegory was a logical way to understand how God is present in the world. Each thing in the world could be a sign from God." ART THEORY at 28. In medieval aesthetics, God creates light, of which the Good and the Beautiful are emanations. Through Beauty, color texture and structure are apprehended. *See, e.g.*, John Haldine, *Medieval Aesthetics*, *in* THE ROUTLEDGE COMPANION TO AESTHETICS 26 (Berys Gaut & Dominic McIver Lopez eds., 3rd ed. 2013). Within this understanding of the nature of art, the relation of man to God is represented through the forms of painting and sculpture, but also significantly through architecture and stained glass.

by Renaissance artists and philosophers, who elevated the status of the artist from technician and craftsman to genius and creator.[28] Understanding of art's mimetic role changed again in the late 17th and 18th centuries as the Enlightenment took hold, and science and rationalist philosophy challenged previous understanding of the relation of art to the natural world,[29] followed by Romanticism's focus on artistic genius, the emotional content

---

[28] Renaissance artists and philosophers reconceived both the status of the artist, elevating the artist from technician and craftsman to genius and creator, and the nature of artistic mimesis. In his 1436 treatise, *On Painting* (*Della Pittura*), Leon Battista Alberti (1404–1472) reasserted the preeminence of mimesis as the foundation of the artist's practice, stating that "there should be no visual difference between looking at a painting or looking out a window at what the painting shows. Thus a successful portrait should be indiscernible from seeing the subject of the portrait looking at us through a window." Arthur C. Danto, WHAT ART IS (2013) at 1. But the Renaissance view of the nature of art was part of a broader philosophical program of rediscovery and reinvention of ancient art and thought that developed in the Platonic Academy in Florence, led by Marsilio Ficino (1433–1499), under the patronage of Cosimo de Medici. For Ficino, the universe is created in beauty, with each of its parts similarly created in beauty. The human form, represented in art, was a perfected form of nature. As Ficino wrote to Giovanni Cavalcanti, "[t]he beauty of bodies does not consist in the shadow of materiality, but in the gracefulness of form, not in the hidden bulk, but in a kind of luminous harmony, not in an inert and stupid weight, but in a fitting number and measure. Light, gracefulness, proportion, number, and measure which we apprehend by thought, vision, and hearing [are the beautiful]. It is toward these that the true ardor of the genuine lover strives." PHILOSOPHIES OF ART AND BEAUTY, at 203–204. Ficino's philosophy provided the foundation of Renaissance humanism, and his close friendship with Alberti influenced the older scholar's work. For both Ficino and Alberti, "harmonies shared by the body and music are manifestations of the harmonies of the soul. Beauty in body and matter is determined by beauty in mind or *mens*, that part of the mind directed toward *intellectus divinus*, and beauty is made manifest in mind by the *lineamenti*, the lines of the mind which are distinguished from matter. Beauty is the internal perfection of the *intellectus divinus*, which is the Good, which is a perfect harmony called *concinnitas*. Ornament is not beauty, but rather a physical complement to beauty." John S. Hendrix, *Alberti and Ficino*, SCHOOL OF ARCHITECTURE, ART, AND HISTORIC PRESERVATION FACULTY PUBLICATIONS (2012, Paper 25), *available at* http://docs.rwu.edu/saahp_fp/25.

[29] While the Enlightenment did not reject the prior conception of art entirely, the rise of rationalism and the status of science required a different relationship between art and the world. Mimesis remained central to understanding of art, but the artist's use of nature changed significantly. Gotthold Lessing (1729–1781) broke with prior ages' conception of art as a link in the transcendence of nature toward the eternal. He declared that "I should prefer that only those be called works of art in which the artist had occasion to show himself as such and in which beauty was his first and ultimate aim. None of the others, which betray too obvious traces of religious conventions, deserves this name because in their case the artist did not create for art's sake. . . but his art was merely the handmaid of religion, which stressed meaning more than beauty in the material subjects it allotted to art for execution." Lessing, Gotthold & Ephraim, *Laocoon* (Ch. 1), quoted in Paul Guyer, *18th Century German Aesthetics*, THE STANFORD ENCYCLOPEDIA OF PHILOSOPHY (Edward N. Zalta ed., Spring 2014), *available at* http://plato.stanford.edu/archives/spr2014/entries/aesthetics-18th-german. Others turned to classical art for inspiration and found there art's ideal. The importance of form as a defining element of the concept of art was foregrounded in the work of Johann Joachim Winckelmann (1717–1768), who, with his HISTORY OF ART OF ANTIQUITY (GESCHICHTE DER KUNST DES ALTERTHUMS) (1764), spurred the era's passion for antiquity and what would become neoclassicism. For Winckelmann, in its imitation of nature, art is to take beauty as its subject and its purpose. It should, he advises, "always seek out what is natural for the forms of beauty, and should avoid, as much as is possible, all that is violent, because even the beauty in life can become displeasing through forced gestures." Johann Joachim Winckelmann, *On the Capacity for the Sentiment for the Beautiful in Art, in* ESSAYS IN THE PHILOSOPHY AND HISTORY OF ART, VOL. I, xlvi, in Paul Guyer, *18th Century German Aesthetics*, THE STANFORD ENCYCLOPEDIA OF PHILOSOPHY 28 (Edward N. Zalta ed., Spring 2014), *available at* http://plato.stanford.edu/archives/spr2014/entries/aesthetics-18th-german.

of art, and questions of the relation of art to the sublime. The mid-19th century saw the rise of the artistic academy, with a focus not only on mimetic representation but on realism. Science and technology spurred an important reassessment of the nature of art and mimesis, not only with the rise of lithographic and other advanced mechanical processes of reproduction but more crucially with photography, with its ability to reproduce the world with seeming exactness. In the late 19th century, the role of mimesis in the definition of art was even more radically called into question, beginning a movement that continues to the present day. However, in a sense, art is still in a prolonged discourse with Plato.

For Plato, the artist reproduces the appearance of objects from the visible world. However, art and its mimetic nature is part of a Platonic theory on the nature of knowledge and how (and why) a person may (or should) lead a just life. That theory entails a hierarchy of values. In the *Republic*, Plato addresses the broad question of why a person should be just through a series of dialogues between Socrates and a gathering of companions on the nature of the ideal state. In the course of that discussion, they consider the nature and role of art. Because Plato views justice as "an ideal order, in the state and in the individual soul, governed by reason," the question is what role art has in that ideal order.[30]

Because for Plato a work of art is mimetic, it is a representation of something that exists in the visible, tactile, everyday world. However, objects in the world are themselves iterations of eternal, nonphysical ideas (the Forms), which are the true, primary states of existence. Knowledge and understanding are gained from the apprehension of these eternal, unchanging Forms. Objects in the world are imperfect copies of those Forms. They are mutable, certainly, unlike the Forms, but more importantly they are particular examples of their Form and are therefore partial and incomplete. If knowledge is to be gained by contemplating the Forms, contemplating objects in the world will introduce error and misunderstanding.

An artwork, for Plato, is in an even more inferior position because, being a representation of an object that is itself merely a representation of a Form, it is twice-removed from eternal truth and even more likely to introduce imperfection and error. The example of the hierarchical problem of art as knowledge that Plato gave in Book X of the *Republic* has

---

30 ART AND ITS SIGNIFICANCE: AN ANTHOLOGY OF AESTHETIC THEORY, Stephen David Ross, ed., 8 (3rd ed. 1994).

influenced discussions of the nature of art for millennia. His example is of a bed. "Beds," Socrates states:

> Are of three kinds, and there are three kinds of artists who superintend them: God, the maker of the bed, and the painter . . . God, whether from choice of from necessity, made one bed in nature and one only; two or more such ideal beds neither have been nor ever will be made by God.
>
> Why is that?
>
> Because even if He had made but two, a third would still appear behind them which both of them would have for their idea, and that would be the ideal bed and not the two others. . . . God knew this, and He desired to be the real maker of a real bed, not a particular maker of a particular bed, and therefore He created a bed which is essentially and by nature only one. . . . And what shall we say of the carpenter—is he not also the maker of the bed?
>
> Yes.
>
> But would you call the painter a creator and maker?
>
> Certainly not.
>
> Yet if he is not the maker, what is he in relation to the bed?
>
> I think, he said, that we may fairly designate him as the imitator of that which the others make.[31]

Art is merely an imitation of a particular, imperfect object, and the artist does not produce work from an apprehension of the Form itself. In a witty response to Plato's metaphor of the bed as art, several artists in recent decades have incorporated elements or entire actual beds into their work. Robert Rauschenberg, for example, in 1955, produced *Bed*,[32] one of his earliest "combines" (in which he incorporated found objects into his paintings); it included a pillow and a worn blanket. Rauschenberg's challenge to the Platonic view of art was highlighted by critic Arthur C. Danto, who observed that "Robert Rauschenberg wrote in the catalog of *Sixteen Americans* at the Museum of Modern Art in 1955 that 'a pair of socks is no less suitable to make a painting with than wood, nails, turpentine, oil, and fabric.' He used a quilt, Coca-Cola bottles, automobile tires, and stuffed animals in his art. Bringing reality into art, when reality had been

---

[31] *Id.*

[32] *See* https://www.moma.org/learn/moma_learning/robert-rauschenberg-bed-1955.

what art was to represent, changed the way people thought of art."[33] Rauschenberg is not alone. Tracey Emin, for example, produced *My Bed* (1998),[34] which presents her own, unmade, unkempt bed, and draws the Platonic trope of the artist-made bed into the context of the postmodern examination of artistic experience, perspective, and, most of all, self-presentation.

3. Formalism and After

From the late 19th century to the present day, art theory and art practice have expanded dramatically. Art theories have emphasized form in a variety of ways, including, early in the 20th century, that articulated by Clive Bell, in which he stated that "the one quality common to all works of visual art" is "significant form."[35] By "significant form," Bell meant lines and colors combined in a particular way, certain forms and relations of forms [that] stir our aesthetic emotions.[36]

Others have looked to the effect that a work of art has on its viewer, the aesthetic experience of the work. Monroe Beardsley, for instance, in *The Aesthetic Point of View* (1982), insisted that an artwork is "either an arrangement of conditions intended to be capable of affording an experience with marked aesthetic character or (incidentally) an arrangement belonging to a class or type of arrangements that is typically intended to have this capacity."[37] Benedetto Croce, however, emphasized the creator's side of this experiential equation, stating instead "works of art exist only in the minds that create or recreate them."[38] Martin Heidegger, though, pointed out a certain necessary circularity in the artist's relation to the artwork. "On the usual view," he observed:

> the work arises out of and by means of the activity of the artist. But by what and whence is the artist what he is? By the work; for to say that it is the work that first lets the artist emerge as a master of his art. The artist is the origin of the work. The work is the origin of the artist.

---

[33] Arthur C. Danto, What Art Is 20 (2013).

[34] *See* http://www.saatchigallery.com/artists/artpages/tracey_emin_my_bed.htm.

[35] Clive Bell, Art 3 (1913).

[36] *Id.*

[37] Michael Wreen, *Beardsley's Aesthetics*, The Stanford Encyclopedia of Philosophy (Edward N. Zalta ed., Winter 2014), *available at* http://plato.stanford.edu/entries/beardsley-aesthetics.

[38] Philosophies of Art and Beauty: Selected Readings in Aesthetics from Plato to Heidegger 567 (Albert Hofstadter & Richard Kuhns eds., 1976).

> Neither is without the other. Nevertheless, neither is the sole support of the other. In themselves and in their interrelations artist and work are each of them by virtue of a third thing which is prior to both, namely that which also gives artist and work of art their namely—art."[39]

So, in Heidegger's view, the concept of art stands apart from and is prior to either the individual artist or the individual artwork. Where Gombrich states that art in the abstract does not exist but comes to exist only through the actions of artists, Heidegger finds the particular activity of the artist to be defined by the concept in which the artist works. The conceptual framework makes the artist's action and the artwork perceptual.

Still other theorists, like George Dickie, Janet Wolff, and Arthur C. Danto, have extended this prior concept to examine the ways in which "art-world" institutions (galleries, museums, critics) shape not simply the making and reception of art at any given point in time, but also confer (or deny) legitimacy on artworks by articulating those qualities regarded as essential to any artwork. They do not, however, agree on how this process occurs. In this view in its broadest form, an object is a work of art only if the art-world institutions declare it to be so.

Danto inaugurated what has come to be called the institutional theory of art in an influential 1964 essay, *The Artworld*, in which he considered the questions raised by Andy Warhol's Brillo box sculptures. The challenge was to understand why and how one object could be designated as being art and a seemingly identical object could be designated as not-art. In looking at *Brillo Boxes*, Danto observed:

> What in the end makes the difference between a Brillo box and a work of art consisting of a Brillo Box is a certain theory of art. It is the theory that takes it up into the world of art, and keeps it from collapsing into the real world object which it is (in a sense of *is* other than that of artistic identification). Of course, without the theory, one is unlikely to see it as art, and in order to see it as part of the artworld, one must have mastered a good deal of artistic theory as well as a considerable amount of the history of recent New York painting.[40]

---

[39] Martin Heidegger, *The Origin of the Work of Art*, *in* BASIC WRITINGS 143 (2008).
[40] Arthur C. Danto, *The Artworld*, 61 THE JOURNAL OF PHILOSOPHY 581 (1964).

Dickie picked up on Danto's observation, elaborating on it in his 1974 book, *Art and the Aesthetic*. For Dickie, "[a] work of art in the classificatory sense is (1) an artefact (2) a set of the aspects of which has had conferred upon it the status of candidate for appreciation by some person or persons acting on behalf of a certain social institution (the artworld)."[41]

The institutional theory of art, however, is not the end of art theory. Danto himself later distanced himself from the institutional theory. His concern instead was to define the essence of art—"the necessary and sufficient conditions for something to fall under [the] concept."[42] Viewing the history of art, particularly art since Duchamp, Danto perceived a process by which modernist art challenged art's definition—subtracting aspects (beauty and ugliness, for instance) until art's essence was revealed, ironically, through the expansion of art to encompass potentially anything. "What made essentialism *seem* impossible," Danto concluded, "was the condition of ultimate pluralism, since works of art had outwardly so little in common."[43] Every artwork, he held, has two essential qualities: (1) it is *about* something, which is a form of representation, but it is not necessary that such representation be mimetic or reflect the world (this element could be stated as "the artist has a thesis"), and (2) the artwork *embodies* that thesis.

Nelson Goodman, in *Languages of Art*, looked instead at what he saw as the contingency of art—that an object may be an artwork at one moment, in one context, and yet not an artwork in another. Goodman thought that the seemingly simple question which we began—"what is art?"—was perhaps not the right question at all. Rather, Goodman thought that "part of the trouble lies in asking the wrong question—in failing to recognize that a thing may function as a work of art at some times and not at others. In crucial cases, the real question is not 'What objects are (permanently) works of art?' but 'When is an object a work of art?'—or, more briefly, . . . 'When is art?'"[44]

Across two and a half millennia, the simple question "What is art?" has been asked and answered many times and in manifold ways. Efforts to say what art is have often trailed behind artists' actual practice. As we will see, that is no less true when the law attempts to provide an answer.

---

41 George Dickie, Art and the Aesthetic 34 (1974).

42 Arthur C. Danto, *The End of Art: A Philosophical Defense*, 37 History and Theory 129 (1998).

43 Arthur C. Danto, *The End of Art: A Philosophical Defense*, 37 History and Theory 128 (1998).

44 Art and Its Significance: An Anthology of Aesthetic Theory 244 (Stephen David Ross ed., 3rd ed. 1994).

B. Defining Art in the Law

In the broadest sense, the law does not define (or even really attempt to define) what art is. After all, if philosophers over a span of several millennia have not reached consensus on how art is to be defined, what chance do lawyers, judges, legislators, and agency administrators have? But, like the art trade, the law has no choice but to address the question of what art is, out of sheer pragmatic necessity. The law must address art as it pertains to the rights of individuals, groups, or entities relating to, variously, contract rights, property rights (both tangible and intangible), and Constitutional rights (freedom of expression being chief among them). Nevertheless, there is no single definition of art that operates across the full spectrum of legal applications to art. Instead, the law understands art in different and discrete ways depending on which set of legal structures are being brought to bear, with quite different approaches applying when art is being considered under copyright law versus customs law or tax law or contract law or the First Amendment. In each of these areas, legal understanding of what art is (or is not) is guided, at least to some degree, by the broader concepts of what art is common to an era. Also, legal understandings of art change over time, usually when confronted with something new or different from what has previously been accepted as (or assumed to be) art.

While law encounters art in nearly every practice area, the question of a *definition* of art arises most intensively in two areas: (1) customs classifications and (2) copyright and intellectual property. Because copyright is so central to most aspects of art and art law, I will discuss the issues arising in defining art in customs classifications first, and discuss how art is defined in copyright more extensively in the following chapter, which addresses intellectual property more broadly.

Where copyright traces the parameters of what art is in order to establish the relative rights of parties within a framework of providing incentives for artists to create new work, the driving policy behind United States customs and tax law treatment of art lies in a policy of more favorable treatment for art. In the 19th century, as a new nation with a desire to establish itself as a cultural center on a par with the old nations of Europe, the United States encouraged the importation of art. American art museums were, with few earlier exceptions, established in the late

19th century,[45] and their collections have been built by policies encouraging donations of art from private collectors. This approach is advanced by two methods: (1) giving collectors a fair market value tax deduction for charitable donations of art, and (2) making imported art exempt from customs duties. Some of the most dramatic and even shocking legal discussions of what art is (and is not) come from customs cases, where one conception of art (typically older and outdated) clashes with contemporary art practice.

The most frequently mentioned customs case involving the determination of whether an object was an artwork is the U.S. Customs Court's 1928 decision in *Brancusi v. United States.*[46] In 1926, Brancusi shipped 20 sculptures, including *Bird in Space*, from Paris to New York for exhibition at the Brummer Gallery. Although Article 1704 of the 1922 Customs Act allowed sculptures to enter the United States free of customs duties, customs officials in New York refused to recognize *Bird in Space*—an elongated, abstract piece cast in bronze—as a sculpture and instead classified it as "kitchen utensils and hospital supplies," which subjected the work to a 40 percent customs duty (approximately $240 at that time). Brancusi appealed.

In its defense, the customs office relied upon a 1916 customs decision, *United States v. Olivotti & Co.*,[47] in which the court had affirmed the classification of "manufactures of marble" and not "sculptures" for a marble font, seats, and other objects sculpted by a recognized Italian sculptor. The *Olivotti* court had observed that "a work is not necessarily sculpture because artistic and fashioned by a sculptor," and went on to define sculpture as:

> that branch of the free fine arts which chisels or carves out of stone or other solid material or models in clay or other plastic substance for subsequent reproduction by carving or casting, imitations or natural objects, chiefly the human form, and represents such objects in their true proportions of length, breadth, and thickness, or of length and breadth only.[48]

---

[45] For a history and discussion of the creation of American art museums, *see* KARL E. MEYER, THE ART MUSEUM: POWER, MONEY, ETHICS (1979). For a history of the different approaches taken in the creation of European art museums, *see* Carole Paul ed., THE FIRST MODERN MUSEUMS OF ART: THE BIRTH OF AN INSTITUTION IN 18TH AND 19TH CENTURY EUROPE (2012).

[46] Brancusi v. United States, T.D. 54,428 (U.S. Cust. Ct. 1928).

[47] U.S. v. Olivotti, T.D. 36,309 (U.S. Ct. Cust. App. 1916).

[48] *Id.* at 48.

The question for the *Brancusi* court, then, was whether an abstract, nonrepresentational work could be classified as a sculpture, and by extension, as a work of art. Brancusi's witnesses at trial included photographer Edward Steichen and sculptor Jacob Epstein. Accepting the *Olivotti* court's view that art must be representational, the customs service's attorney focused his questioning on the sculpture's title. Of Epstein, he asked:

> **Q.** When you say someone represented a bird, does that (Exhibit 1) represent a bird to you?
>
> **A.** To me it is a matter of indifference what it represents.
>
> **Q.** In so far as that piece of sculpture is concerned, in appealing to the aesthetic taste, it does not make any difference what it represents?[49]

The court agreed with Brancusi, holding that "under the evidence that it is the original production of a professional sculptor and it is in fact a piece of sculpture and a work of art according to the authorities above referred to."[50]

After *Brancusi*, customs law abandoned the narrow representationalism demanded by *Olivotti*. By 1958, we find a more sophisticated statement of the realities of the art world:

> Modern suggestive art does not portray things in their natural form, but merely portrays objects in such form, sometimes distorted or incomplete, as will be suggestive of the idea which is to be conveyed. . . . These innovations by modern artists seem to be in harmony with the tendency of the times, and it is the kind of art which possesses such elements of eccentricity that holds the stage today. It has its friends and enemies, but the enemies of suggestive sculpture and painting all agree that it is art, has artistic merit, when done by a good artist, but contend that it is not as good from an artistic standpoint as realistic art.[51]

It is easy to laugh at what in the present day seems to be nothing but blind philistinism in the customs official failure to acknowledge abstract art as art, and to sneer at the narrow definition of sculpture the *Olivotti*

---

[49] Quoted in Daniel McClean & Armen Avanessian, *Trials of the Title: The Trials of Brancusi and Veronese*, in THE TRIAL OF ART 49 (Daniel McClean ed., 2007).

[50] *Id.* at 53.

[51] Ebeling & Reuss Co. v. U.S., 40 Cust. Ct. 387, 393–394 (U.S. Cust. Ct. First Div. 1958).

court articulated. However, *Olivotti* was one in a succession of decisions that attempted to draw a line between fine art and applied or merely decorative art. It is a distinction that is still made, although with greater and greater difficulty as artists draw upon popular culture and the decorative arts for inspiration, subject matter, and media. In the late 19th and early 20th centuries, however, the distinction between fine art (the "free fine arts") and applied art (what we would describe today as craft or design) was accorded greater weight, and that was reflected in the law as well.

The fine art/applied art distinction was at times made categorically, as in designating stained glass/painted glass windows to be applied, not fine, art.[52] In other instances, however, customs courts looked to the studio processes used in the production of the work, typically requiring the active involvement of the artist (the "hand of the artist"), not mechanical processes, in rendering a fine art object. This requirement that the work be made by the artist's own hand was applied to a marble vase,[53] carved alabaster pedestals,[54] and china and earthenware figurines.[55] The distinction between fine art and applied art has persisted. Pop art uses this dichotomy, incorporating the subject matter and methods of advertising and popular culture. Pop artists often reject the privileging of the hand of the artist, preferring instead the smooth, brushless surface of mechanical production. In other circumstances, however, an object that would otherwise be entitled to a fine art customs classification and exempted from customs duty could nevertheless be transformed into an object imported for industrial use and subject to applicable applied art customs duties by virtue of the use to which the object was to be put once imported. In *United States v. J.E. Bernard & Co., Inc.*, an original oil painting was denied free entry because the purpose of the painting being imported was solely for use as a magazine illustration. The court concluded that the painting was not entitled to a fine art classification "by reason of the fact that it was concededly purchased and imported for the sole purpose of being reproduced and used as the front cover of a magazine."[56]

Lest we look too smugly at the preconceptions of the past, it is important to acknowledge the disconnect even today between artistic practice and legal categories and frameworks. Nowhere is this more surprising than

---

52 U.S. v. Perry, 146 U.S. 71, 72–73 (1892).

53 U.S. v. Baumgarten & Co., T.D. 32,052 (U.S. Ct. Cust. App. 1911).

54 Lazarus, Rosenfeld & Lehmann v. U.S., T.D. 32,247, 510–511 (U.S. Ct. Cust. App. 1912).

55 Wm. S. Pitcairn Corp. v. U.S., 39 C.C.P.A. 15, 36 (U.S. Ct. of Cust. & Pat. App. 1951).

56 U.S. v. J.E. Bernard & Co., Inc., 33 C.C.P.A. 166, 168 (U.S. Ct. Cust. & pat. App. 1946).

in a recent dispute over the importation into the United Kingdom of several works by the American artists Dan Flavin and Bill Viola. Flavin was a minimalist sculptor who is best known for light sculptures using fluorescent tubes.[57] Bill Viola is an American artist known for his video installations.[58]

In 2006, the London gallery Haunch of Venison imported six video works by Viola and a fluorescent tube installation by Flavin. The six Viola works were *Catherine's Dream, 2002*; *Man of Sorrows* and *Witness, 2001*; two editions of *Catherine's Vow, 2002*; and *Mater, 2001*. The Viola works consisted of DVDs, DVD players, monitors, and speakers. The Flavin work, titled *Six Alternating Cool White/Warm White Flourescent Lights Vertical and Centered, 1973*, consisted of six fluorescent lighting tubes, their fixtures, and instructions. Both artists' works were shipped disassembled.

Under U.K. customs law, sculptures may be imported free of customs duty and subject to a lower VAT rate of 5 percent. The HM Revenue and Customs Office (HMRC) determined that the disassembled Flavin and Viola works were not classifiable as sculptures. Rather, HMRC classified the Flavin work as "chandeliers and other electrical ceiling or wall lighting fittings excluding those of a kind used for lighting public open spaces or thoroughfares—other," and the Viola works as "image projectors, other than cinematographic; photographic (other than cinematographic) enlargers and reducers—other image projectors." HMRC further determined that the disassembled works were subject to both customs duties and to the highest VAT rate of 20 percent, which amount would be calculated based upon the works' assembled values as artworks.

The gallery appealed, and the tax and duties tribunal reversed the HMRC's determination. The court stated that "[i]t stretches the objective characteristics principle too far to say that a work of art is no longer a work of art if it is dismantled for transportation."[59] However, the matter did not end there. In a widely criticized ruling, the European Commission reversed the tribunal's decision, stating that the disassembled artworks could not be classified for customs and VAT purposes as sculptures, but must be classified as their constituent parts.

The Commission rejected the gallery's claim that the Viola work is a sculpture and questioned whether it was art at all. The regulation stated that

---

[57] *See* http://www.guggenheim.org/new-york/collections/collection-online/artists/bios/704.

[58] *See* http://www.billviola.com.

[59] Haunch of Venison Partners Ltd. v. Her Majesty's Commissioners of Revenue and Customs, LON/2006/7090 and LON/2007/7055, 2008 WL 5326820, *7 (London Tribunal Centre Dec. 11, 2008).

the disassembled Viola video installation is not a sculpture "as none of the individual components or the whole installation, when assembled, can be considered a sculpture. The components have been slightly modified by the artist, but these modifications do not alter their preliminary function of goods of Section XVI. It is the content recorded on the DVD which, together with the components of the installation, provides for the 'modern art.'"[60] In so holding, the Commission ignored that tribunal's more sophisticated observation that "[i]f someone obtained a copy of one of the DVDs and played it on ordinary equipment that would not be a Viola work any more than a reproduction or a copy of an original painting would be that painting."[61]

In its rejection of the gallery's claim that the Flavin work is a sculpture, the Commission waxed metaphysical, concluding that "it is not the installation that constitutes a 'work of art' but the result of the operations (the light effect) carried out by it."[62] By contrast, the tribunal's decision evinced an understanding of the interplay between the "light effect" and the means of producing that effect:

> Flavin works use ordinary lighting components (though of high quality) but the artist specified exactly what had to be used and how it had to be installed. . . . Some of the works will have light fittings attached to boards of other suitable structures and the lights themselves are taken out of the structures for transportation. The Flavin estate supplies replacement components when required. The works are accompanied by detailed instructions drawn up by the artist. Clearly authenticity is an important issue in the case of the Flavin works because they use mainly or even entirely replaceable parts. The work's provenance and the artist's instructions in an original form are therefore important. Mr. Flavin also adopted a policy of never supplying a duplicate of the certificates of authenticity which he supplied when he sold a work, so that authentic copies could not be made. The works are dismantled for transport when required and must be put back together as instructed by the artist.[63]

---

60 Commission Regulation (EU) No. 731/2010 of 11 August 2010 concerning the classification of certain goods in the Combined Nomenclature.

61 Haunch of Venison Partners Ltd. V. Her Majesty's Commissioners of Revenue and Customs, LON/2006/7090 and LON/2007/7055, 2008 WL 5326820, *2 (London Tribunal Centre Dec. 11, 2008).

62 Commission Regulation (EU) No. 731/2010 of 11 August 2010 concerning the classification of certain goods in the Combined Nomenclature.

63 Haunch of Venison Partners Ltd. V. Her Majesty's Commissioners of Revenue and Customs, LON/2006/7090 and LON/2007/7055, 2008 WL 5326820, *2 (London Tribunal Centre Dec. 11, 2008).

The law has moved piecemeal in its approach to art, asking specific questions and venturing discrete answers, both determined by the particular legal discipline. As with aesthetic theory, legal understanding of art lags behind contemporary artistic practice, and is often more retrospective than forward-looking.

CHAPTER 2

Intellectual Property

For the collector, it is often an unwelcome surprise to discover that in acquiring an object, one acquires the physical object alone. Copyright and other intellectual property rights typically remain with the artist unless they are specifically assigned to the collector (or another party).

The source of United States intellectual property law is Article I, Section 8, Clause 8 of the United States Constitution, which states that "[t]he Congress shall have Power . . . (8) To promote the Progress of Science and useful Arts, by securing for limited Times to Authors and Inventors the exclusive Right to their respective Writings and Discoveries."[1] The Supreme Court analyzed the policy behind this clause as follows:

> The economic philosophy behind the clause empowering Congress to grant patents and copyrights is the conviction that encouragement of individual effort by personal gain is the best way to advance public welfare through the talents of authors and inventors.[2]

Of the three forms of intellectual property—patent, trademark, and copyright—copyright is the most relevant to art. Patent, traditionally, has played little or no part, while trademark plays a small role. A brief primer on those aspects of intellectual property law that are most essential to art law is provided in this chapter.

A. Copyright

In Anglo-American law, the first copyright law was the Statute of Anne,[3] enacted in 1710, which recognized and protected the exclusive economic rights

[1] U.S. CONST. art. I, § 8, cl. 8.
[2] Mazer v. Stein, 347 U.S. 201, 219 (1954).
[3] 8 Ann. c. 21.

of authors in their writings. The right was initially vested in the author, but the publishing practice at the time typically meant that authors received a single lump-sum payment and transferred their copyright to the publisher. The statute's protections did not extend to engravings. Thus, in 1734, Parliament enacted the Engravers' Copyright Act,[4] also known as Hogarth's Act, after William Hogarth, who refused to publish his popular engravings until such protection was given. His series of engravings, *A Harlot's Progress* and *A Rake's Progress*, were enormously popular and frequently pirated.

Congress has enacted successive copyright acts, of which two have relevance today.[5] The Copyright Act of 1909 applies to works created before January 1, 1978; it provides for a 28-year term, renewable for a second 28-year term (subsequently extended for a total maximum aggregate term of up to 95 years). The Copyright Act of 1976,[6] which replaced the Copyright Act of 1909, applies to works created after January 1, 1978; it provides for a term of the life of the author plus 70 years. The latter act was enacted in association with U.S. adherence to the Berne Convention for the Protection of Literary and Artistic Works of 1886 (the "Berne Convention").[7] The extended copyright protection is consistent with that of the European Union.[8]

1. Copyright Requirements

Under the Copyright Act, to qualify for copyright protection, a work must (1) fall within the copyrightable subject matter,[9] (2) be fixed in a tangible medium of expression,[10] and (3) be an original work of authorship.[11]

Section 102(a) of the Copyright Act provides that:

> Copyright protection subsists . . . in original works of authorship fixed in any tangible medium of expression, now known or later developed,

---

4 8 Geo.2 c. 13.

5 The full text of both the Copyright Act of 1909 and the Copyright Act of 1976 (17 U.S.C. § 101, *et seq.*) are *available at* http://www.copyright.gov/title17/. *See also* Melville B. Nimmer & David Nimmer, Nimmer on Copyright (2012); Jane Ginsburg, Robert Gorman & R. Anthony Reese, Gorman, Ginsburg and Reese's Copyright (8th ed. 2011).

6 Unless the context requires otherwise, hereinafter I refer to the Copyright Act of 1976 simply as the "Copyright Act."

7 *See* Berne Convention for the Protection of Literary and Artistic Works, Sept. 9, 1886, *available at* http://www.wipo.int/treaties/en/text.jsp?file_id=283698.

8 Council Directive 93/98/EEC of October 29, 1993, harmonizing the term of protection of copyright and certain related rights, 1993 O.J. (L 290/9).

9 17 U.S.C. § 102(a).

10 17 U.S.C. § 102(a).

11 *See, e.g.*, Burrow-Giles Lithographic Co. v. Sarony, 111 U.S. 53 (1884).

> from which they can be perceived, reproduced, or otherwise communicated, either directly or with the aid of a machine or device. Works of authorship include the following categories: (1) literary works; (2) musical works, including any accompanying words; (3) dramatic works, including any accompanying music; (4) pantomimes and choreographic works; (5) pictorial, graphic, and sculptural works; (6) motion pictures and other audiovisual works; (7) sound recordings; and (8) architectural works.

However, copyright protects *expression* only, not the underlying concept or idea.[12] This is set out in Section 102(b), which states that: "[i]n no case does copyright protection for an original work of authorship extend to any idea, procedure, process, system, method of operation, concept, principle, or discovery, regardless of the form in which it is described, explained, illustrated, or embodied in such work."

For purposes of the Copyright Act, a work is fixed in a tangible medium of expression when:

> its embodiment in a copy or phonorecord, by or under the authority of the author, is sufficiently permanent or stable to permit it to be perceived, reproduced, or otherwise communicated for a period of more than transitory duration. A work consisting of sounds, images, or both, that are being transmitted, is "fixed" for purposes of this title if a fixation of the work is being made simultaneously with its transmission.[13]

The requirement of fixation is particularly important with performance art and other transitory forms, which do not qualify for copyright protection unless they are recorded or reduced to some form of notation.

The question of whether a work is original for purposes of qualifying for copyright protection is a more problematic question, but it should be noted that "originality" for copyright purposes should not be confused with uniqueness or novelty. For copyright originality, the bar is not set high. The U.S. Supreme Court has stated that to qualify for copyright protection, a work must show some creativity or element that is not obvious.[14]

---

12 17 U.S.C. § 102(b).
13 17 U.S.C. § 102(a).
14 *See* Feist Publications, Inc. v. Rural Telephone Service Co., 499 U.S. 340 (1991).

At least one court has suggested that a higher degree or originality is required for derivative works to qualify for copyright protection.[15]

2. Formal Requirements

Under the Copyright Act of 1909, which applies to works created prior to January 1, 1978, three formal steps were required for copyrights to be enforceable: (1) a copyright notice had to be affixed to the published work or a work offered for sale,[16] (2) the copyright had to be registered with the U.S. Copyright Office,[17] and (3) two copies of the best edition of the work had to be deposited with the U.S. Copyright Office.[18]

3. Exclusive Rights

The essence of copyright is that it gives to the copyright holder the exclusive right to control and exploit the copyrighted work in specific ways. These exclusive rights are set out in Section 106 of the Copyright Act giving the holder the right to: (1) reproduce the work, (2) create derivative works,[19] (3) distribute the work, (4) perform the work, and (5) display the work.[20]

4. First Sale Doctrine

The first sale doctrine is a limitation on the copyright holder's right to control distribution of a copyrighted work. While Section 106(3) of the

---

15 *See* Gracen v. The Branford Exchange and Metro-Goldwyn Mayer, 698 F.2d 300 (7th Cir. 1983).

16 Copyright notice has not been required for unpublished works. For more information about the notice required for copyrights in works of visual art (required under the 1909 Copyright Act, but not under the 1976 Copyright Act), *see* U.S. Copyright Office, *Copyright Notice* (Circular 3), *available at* http://copyright.gov/circs/circ03.pdf.

17 For more information about the procedures for registration of copyrights in works of visual art (under both the 1909 and 1976 Copyright Acts), *see* U.S. Copyright Office, *Copyright Registration for Pictorial, Graphic, and Sculptural Works* (Circular 40), *available at* http://www.copyright.gov/circs/circ40.pdf.

18 For more information about the deposit requirements for works of visual art, *see* U.S. Copyright Office, *Mandatory Deposit of Copies or Phonorecords for the Library of Congress* (Circular 7D), *available at* http://www.copyright.gov/circs/circ07d.pdf.

19 A derivative work is "a work based upon one or more preexisting works, such as a translation, musical arrangement, dramatization, fictionalization, motion picture version, sound recording, art reproduction, abridgment, condensation, or any other form in which a work may be recast, transformed, or adapted. A work consisting of editorial revisions, annotations, elaborations, or other modifications which, as a whole, represent an original work of authorship, is a 'derivative work.'" 17 U.S.C. § 101.

20 17 U.S.C. § 106.

Copyright Act reserves to the copyright holder the exclusive right to "distribute copies . . . of the copyrighted work to the public by sale or other transfer of ownership, or by rental, lease, or lending,"[21] that right is limited by section 109(a), which codifies the first sale doctrine, and which provides that "the owner of a particular copy . . . lawfully made under this title . . . is entitled, without the authority of the copyright owner, to sell or otherwise dispose of the possession of that copy."[22] The first sale doctrine has long been a feature of U.S. copyright law.[23] In the context of art, where a work may exist in a single copy or a limited number of copies, once the artist has sold an artwork/copy, the artist no longer controls any future sales of that artwork/copy. The first sale doctrine has been qualified in certain circumstances. The Visual Artists Rights Act (VARA) (discussed in Section 6(c) below),[24] for example, restricts an owner's right to modify an artwork in a manner that is prejudicial to the artist's reputation.

5. Infringement and Registration

Unauthorized use of a copyrighted work that violates any of the copyright holder's exclusive rights constitutes infringement of that copyright. A copyright holder asserting a claim that one or more of the exclusive rights granted to the holder by the Copyright Act has been violated must show (1) that the holder does, in fact, have a valid copyright in the allegedly infringed work, and (2) that the allegedly infringing party copied protected elements of the work or otherwise violated the holder's exclusive rights.

Although the Copyright Act of 1976 does not require registration of the work with the U.S. Copyright Office for copyright protection to inhere, registration is required before the copyright holder may bring an action for infringement.[25] In the context of art and cultural property, the most important defense to infringement is *fair use*. The defense of fair use is discussed in detail in Section A.6(b).

---

21 17 U.S.C. § 106(3).

22 17 U.S.C. § 109(a).

23 *See, e.g.*, Quality King Distributors, Inc. v. L'anza Research Int'l, Inc., 523 U.S. 135, 152 (1998) (stating that "for at least a century the 'first sale' doctrine has played an important role in American copyright law.").

24 17 U.S.C. § 106A.

25 The United States Copyright Office has published a brief guide to copyright registration for artworks, titled *Copyright Registration for Pictorial, Graphic, and Sculptural Works* (Circular 40, rev/09/2015), *available at* http://www.copyright.gov/circs/circ40.pdf.

6. Defining Art in Copyright Law

One of the best-known warnings against legal (and more particularly, judicial) imposition of personal taste in the definition of art came in a 1903 case that involved the question of whether posters advertising a circus could be protected by copyright.[26] Justice Oliver Wendell Holmes, Jr., cautioned:

> It would be a dangerous undertaking for persons trained only to the law to constitute themselves final judges of the worth of pictorial illustrations, outside of the narrowest and most obvious limits. At the one extreme some works of genius would be sure to miss appreciation. Their very novelty would make them repulsive until the public had learned the new language in which their author spoke. It may be more than doubted, for instance, whether the etchings of Goya or the paintings of Manet would have been sure of protection when seen for the first time. At the other end, copyright would be denied to pictures which appealed to a public less educated than the judge. Yet if they command the interest of any public, they have a commercial value—it would be bold to say that they have not an aesthetic and educational value—and the taste of any public is not to be treated with contempt.[27]

Despite Justice Holmes's admonition against imposing one's own taste and values in drawing the line between art and nonart, taste and value judgments continue to insert themselves into legal discussions of art, even in Justice Holmes's own decision in *Bleistein*. Considerations of how art is defined for purposes of copyright are of three types: (1) whether a work may be copyrighted (the issue Justice Holmes was addressing in *Bleistein*), (2) whether an artist's use of preexisting copyrighted work is a permitted fair use of that work, and (3) whether a work is entitled to protection of the artist's rights of integrity and attribution (what are termed "moral rights").

a. Copyrightability

In *Bleistein*, which was decided under an earlier, more restrictive version of the Copyright Act (which explicitly referred to "fine art"), the open

---

[26] Bleistein v. Donaldson Lithographing Co., 188 U.S. 239 (1903).

[27] *Id.* at 239, 251–252.

door through which value judgments entered was the statutory threshold for a work to qualify for copyright protection. As noted earlier, in order to qualify for copyright protection, a work must be (1) original and (2) fixed in a tangible medium of expression.[28] However, the Copyright Act excludes ideas, procedures, processes systems, methods of operation, concepts, principles, and discoveries.[29] *Expression* can be protected, but the underlying concept cannot. Therefore, a painter's rendering of a landscape can be protected by copyright, and the painter can then prevent others from copying the artist's rendering. However, the artist cannot prevent another artist from producing that artist's own version of the same landscape (subject). A problem arises in situations where the subject of a work is so specific that it can only be represented in one way, and so the subject and its representation are said to merge. Under copyright law's merger doctrine, if there is only one way to represent a subject, then representations of that subject cannot qualify for copyright protection.[30] Courts have applied the merger doctrine to some simple forms of artistic expression.[31]

In *Bleistein*, the defendant, who was accused of copying the poster artist's work, argued that the subject of the poster was commonplace and so should not be protected by copyright. The Court distinguished between a merged subject/expression and the circumstance where two artists separately make works of the same subject. Justice Holmes wrote:

> [E]ven if [the figures in the circus poster] had been drawn from the life, that fact would not deprive them of protection. The opposite proposition would mean that a portrait by Velasquez or Whistler was common property because others might try their hand on the same face. Others are free to copy the original. They are not free to copy the copy. . . . The copy is the personal reaction of an individual upon nature. Personality always contains something unique. It expresses its singularity even in handwriting, and a very modest grade of art has in it something irreducible, which is one man's alone. That something he may copyright unless there is a restriction in the words of the act.[32]

---

[28] 17 U.S.C. § 102(a).
[29] 17 U.S.C. § 102(b).
[30] William S. Strong, The Copyright Book: A Practical Guide 15 (6th ed. 2014).
[31] *Id.*
[32] *Id.* at 250.

At least within the frame of copyright, Justice Holmes articulates an understanding of art built on expression. It is not, however, the expression of Wordsworthian emotion experienced by the artist and communicated to the viewer. Instead, it is an expression of the artist's personality. The Court wrote:

> The copy is the personal reaction of an individual upon nature. Personality always contains something unique. It expresses its singularity even in handwriting, and a very modest grade of art has in it something irreducible, which is one man's alone. . . . The least pretentious picture has more originality in it than directories and the like, which may be copyrighted.[33]

However, Justice Holmes linked this expression of the artist's personality to the artist's training and effort, noting that:

> The amount of training required for humbler efforts than those before us is well indicated by Ruskin. "If any young person, after being taught what is, in polite circles, called 'drawing,' will try to copy the commonest piece of real work,—suppose a lithograph on the title page of a new opera air, or a woodcut in the cheapest illustrated newspaper of the day,—they will find themselves entirely beaten."[34]

In his dissent, however, Justice Harlan disagreed with the Holmesian view of artistic expression, insisting instead on a categorical distinction - a distinction between fine art and applied art. For Justice Harlan:

> [I]f a chromo-lithograph, or other print, engraving, or picture has no other use than that of a mere advertisement, and no value aside from this function, it would not be promotive of the useful arts, within the meaning of the constitutional provision, to protect the "author" in the exclusive use thereof, and the copyright statute should not be construed as including such a publication, if any other construction is admissible. . . . It must have some connection with the fine arts to give it intrinsic value.[35]

---

33 Bleistein v. Donaldson Lithographing Co., 188 U.S. 239, 250 (1903).
34 *Id.*
35 Bleistein v. Donaldson Lithographing Co., 188 U.S. 239, 300–301 (1903).

In a late 19th-century decision, *Burrow-Giles Lithographic Company v. Sarony*, 111 U.S. 53 (1884), the Supreme Court considered whether a photographic studio portrait could contain sufficient creativity to qualify for copyright protection. The Court noted:

> [I]t is said that an engraving, a painting, a print, does embody the intellectual conception of its author, in which there is novelty, invention, originality, and therefore comes within the purpose of the constitution in securing its exclusive use or sale to its author, while a photograph is the mere mechanical reproduction of the physical features or outlines of some object, animate or inanimate, and involves no originality of thought or any novelty in the intellectual operation connected with its visible reproduction in shape of a picture. That while the effect of light on the prepared plate may have been a discovery in the production of these pictures and patents could properly be obtained for the combination of the chemicals, for their application to the paper or other surface, for all the machinery by which the light reflected from the object was thrown on the prepared plate, and for all the improvements in this machinery, and in the materials, the remainder of the process is merely mechanical, with no place for novelty, invention, or originality. It is simply the manual operation, by the use of these instruments and preparations, of transferring to the place the visible representation of some existing object, the accuracy of this representation being its highest merit. This may be true in regard to the ordinary production of a photograph, and that in such case a copyright is no protection.[36]

The Court contrasted the subject of the photograph—in this instance, Oscar Wilde, although the subject could have been a building, a landscape, or any other existing object—with the active creative engagement and contribution of the photographer. Against the accusation that a photograph could not be copyrighted because it was a mere mechanical process of recording objects, the Court found that the photographer made the photograph "entirely from his own original mental conception." [37] He posed Wilde and arranged his model's costume and setting, the light and shade, and Wilde's expression. This activity on the part of the photographer set his work apart from an ordinary, merely mechanical, and therefore

---

[36] Burrow-Giles Lithographic Company v. Sarony, 111 U.S. 53, 59–60 (1884).

[37] *Id.* at 55.

passive photograph. As then-Judge Alito, writing for the Third Circuit in *Southco, Inc. v. Kanebridge Corp.*, commented:

> [W]hile a painting or engraving is an expression of ideas in the artist's mind, a photograph is a bit of objective reality. Where, as in the Oscar Wilde portrait, the photographer poses the subject, the photographer may exercise creativity in arranging the bit of reality to be captured by the photo, but the photograph itself is not expression.[38]

Contrary to what many who snap photographs may assume, some photographs—what the *Burrow-Giles* court identified as "ordinary" photographs—may lack sufficient creativity to satisfy the Copyright Act's requirements. In *Oriental Art Printing, Inc. v. Goldstar Printing Corp.*, [39] the court was asked to determine whether photographs of food included in a restaurant menu were protected by copyright. A competing printer had used the photographs in its own work, as if they were stock photographs. The photographs at issue showed the restaurant's menu items, depicting them exactly as they appeared when served. In finding that the photographs were not entitled to copyright protection, the court stated "this is the rare case where photographs contained in plaintiffs' work lack the creative or expressive elements that would render them original works subject to protection under the Copyright Act." [40] Unlike the crafted image of Oscar Wilde, these menu photographs presented to the court lacked "any artistic quality."[41]

In re Trade Mark Cases, 100 U.S. 82, 94 (1879), the court denied copyright to symbols and devices used to identify goods in commerce (which are covered instead under trademark) because they were not "founded in the creative powers of the mind" as compared to "original designs for engravings, prints, etc."[42]

b. Fair Use

Currently, the forefront of legal definitional and conceptual struggles surrounding art arises out of appropriation art. In appropriation art,

---

[38] Southco, Inc. v. Kanebridge Corp., 390 F.3d 276, 284 (3d Cir. 2004)—opinion by Circuit Judge Alito.

[39] Oriental Art Printing, Inc. v. Goldstar Printing Corp., 175 F.Supp.2d 542 (S.D.N.Y. 2001).

[40] *Id.* at 547.

[41] *Id.*

[42] *In re* Trade Mark Cases, 100 U.S. 82, 94 (1879).

an artist uses others' preexisting works (frequently drawn from popular culture) and incorporates those preexisting works into the artist's own work.[43] The legal debate on appropriation art turns on the question of the minimum level of transformation of the preexisting work that is required in order to allow the copying of work without infringing the right of the prior artist. The slightly differing definitions of "appropriation" offered by the Museum of Modern Art (MOMA) and the Tate highlight this problem. For MOMA, appropriation "is the intentional borrowing, copying, and alteration of preexisting images and objects."[44] The Tate on the other hand states that appropriation "refers to the practice of artists using pre-existing objects or images in their art with little transformation of the original."[45]

In several recent cases involving works by the artists Jeff Koons and Richard Prince, courts have been faced with the question of whether an artist's appropriation of another's work is sufficiently creative or transformative to qualify as a statutorily-sanctioned fair use. Koons is an American artist who appropriates objects from popular culture. In 1988, Koons exhibited *String of Puppies*, a polychromed porcelain sculpture of a man and woman seated on a bench, holding eight puppies in their arms, as part of his Banality Show at the Sonnabend Gallery. Three of the four copies of *String of Puppies* sold for an aggregate amount of $367,000. The sculpture was adapted from a photograph by Art Rogers, which Koons had purchased in what he described as a "very commercial, tourist-like card shop."[46] Rogers brought suit against Koons for copyright infringement, and Koons argued that his appropriation of the photograph was within the fair use exception, which permits the use of works protected by copyright based upon four factors: (1) the purpose and character of the use, (2) the nature of the copyrighted work, (3) the amount and substantiality of the work used, and (4) the effect of the use on the market value of the original.[47] Koons argued that his use of the photograph was permitted because it was social satire or parody. His purpose, the court summarized, was to show that "mass production of commodities and media

[43] *See* Museum of Modern Art, *MOMA Learning: Pop Art, available at* https://www.moma.org/learn/moma_learning/themes/pop-art/appropriation.

[44] *Id.*

[45] *See* Tate, *Appropriation, available at* http://www.tate.org.uk/learn/online-resources/glossary/a/appropriation.

[46] Rogers v. Koons, 960 F.2d 301, 305 (2d Cir. 1992), *cert. denied*, 506 U.S. 934, 113 S.Ct. 365, 121 L.Ed.2d 278 (1992).

[47] *Id.* at 308.

images has caused a deterioration in the quality of society" and that he incorporates "these images into works of art to comment critically both on the incorporated object and the political and economic system that created it."[48] The court, however, insisted that fair use requires that a satire or parody must comment on the work being used, not more generally on society or social issues. The court noted that "even given that 'String of Puppies' is a satirical critique of our materialistic society, it is difficult to discern any parody of the photograph 'Puppies' itself."[49] The court concluded that "[t]he copying was so deliberate as to suggest that defendants resolved so long as they were significant players in the art business, and the copies they produced bettered the price of the copied work by a thousand to one, their piracy of a less well-known artist's work would escape being sullied by an accusation of plagiarism."[50]

Several other of Koons's sculptures from the Banality Show (*Wild Boy and Puppy*, which appropriated the *Garfield* comic strip character Odie,[51] and *Ushering in Banality*, appropriating Barbara Campbell's photograph *Boys with Pig*[52]) and a painting from his *Easyfun-Ethereal* series (*Niagara*, which appropriated part of an Andrea Blanch photograph that appeared in an *Allure* magazine advertisement for Gucci sandals[53]) were also the subject of copyright infringement suits. The court concluded:

> When, as here, the copyrighted work is used as "raw material" . . . in the furtherance of distinctive creative or communicative objectives, the use is transformative. . . . The test for whether "Niagara's" use of "Silk Sandals" is "transformative," then, is whether it merely supercedes the objects of the original creation, or instead adds something new, with a further purpose or different character, altering the first with new expression, meaning, or message.[54]

A more recent, and controversial, decision by the Second Circuit, *Cariou v. Prince*,[55] revisited the parameters of what constitutes an artist's "transformative" use of preexisting copyrighted material. Artist Richard

---

48 *Id.* at 309.
49 *Id.* at 310.
50 *Id.* at 303.
51 United Features Syndicate v. Koons, 817 F. Supp. 370 (S.D.N.Y. 1993).
52 Campbell v. Koons, No. 91 Civ. 6055(RO), 1993 WL 97381 (S.D.N.Y. April 1, 1993).
53 Blanch v. Koons, 467 F.3d 244 (2d Cir. 2006).
54 Blanch v. Koons, 467 F.3d 244, 253 (2d Cir. 2006).
55 Cariou v. Prince, 714 F.3d 694 (2d Cir. 2013).

Prince appropriated several photographs from the photographer Patrick Cariou's book *Yes Rasta* and incorporated them into a series of his own paintings and collages, the *Canal Zone* series. The district court had found in Cariou's favor, holding that Prince's appropriation infringed Cariou's copyright in his photographs, and ordered the infringing works to be turned over to Cariou to be destroyed.[56] On appeal, however, the Second Circuit looked at the 30 Prince works side by side with Cariou's photographs and concluded that 25 of Prince's images "have a different character, give Cariou's photographs a new expression, and employ new aesthetics with creative and communicative results distinct from Cariou's."[57] The court regarded the appropriation artist's transformation of the preexisting work as determinative, finding that an appropriation was fair use and added something new to the prior work "with a fundamentally different aesthetic."[58] The Second Circuit remanded the case to the district court to determine whether the remaining five *Canal Zone* works were fair use; however, the parties reached a settlement before the district court could make that determination.[59]

The *Cariou* court's analysis, with its emphasis on transformativeness as the central determinant of fair use, has been controversial and was explicitly rejected by the Seventh Circuit in *Kienitz v. Sconnie Nation LLC.*[60] In *Sconnie Nation*, the court held instead that the effect of a use on the market for the preexisting work determines whether a use is fair use, "whether the contested use is a complement to the protected worm (allowed) rather than a substitute for it (prohibited)."[61]

In 2011, while he was appealing the district court's decision, Prince engaged in a more complete appropriation, offering for sale 500 nearly duplicate copies of the 1951 first American edition of J. D. Salinger's novel *The Catcher in the Rye*. The only differences between the first edition and the Prince version was that Prince replaced Salinger's name on the dustjacket, title page, and elsewhere with his own. The book's colophon notes, "This is an artwork by Richard Prince. Any similarity to a book is coincidental and not intended by the

[56] Cariou v. Prince, 784 F.Supp.2d 337 (S.D.N.Y. 2011).

[57] Cariou v. Prince, 714 F.3d 694, 708 (2d Cir. 2013).

[58] *Id.*

[59] Brian Boucher, *Landmark Copyright Lawsuit Cariou v. Prince is Settled*, ART IN AMERICA, Mar. 18. 2014, *available at* http://www.artinamericamagazine.com/news-features/news/landmark-copyright-lawsuit-cariou-v-prince-is-settled/.

[60] Kienitz v. Sconnie Nation LLC, 766 F.3d 756 (7th Cir. 2014).

[61] *Id.* at 758.

artist."[62] As with Warhol's *Brillo Boxes*, Prince's *Catcher in the Rye* challenges the distinction between art and its subject. Where one ends and the other begins seems to hinge not only on minute factual distinctions but on legal concepts of copyright and the blurred line between permissible and impermissible use. In his blog, Prince described the *Catcher in the Rye* project:

> There would only be two changes to the book. The first, substituting my name for Salinger's. The second, doubling the price. (Actually there was a third change . . . sort of. We removed the author's photograph from the back cover. We had heard when the book first came out Salinger didn't like his portrait on the book and made sure the publicity picture never appeared on the second and all subsequent editions. Hey, if he didn't like it . . . we didn't either.[63]

The Salinger estate did not sue Prince, but a controversy did arise from Prince's appropriation of others' Instagram photographs, enlarged, modified with comments by Prince, and printed on canvas, for his *New Portraits* show at the Gagosian Gallery in late 2014.[64] Instead of suing for copyright infringement, one group whose photographs were appropriated by Prince, SuicideGirls, instead sold prints of the images Prince had used for $90 (instead of the $90,000–$100,000 Prince's works commanded); however, in two separate cases, photographer Donald Graham and makeup artist Ashley Salazar have brought actions against Prince and Gagosian Gallery for infringement.[65]

c. Moral Rights

Copyright law also struggles with definitions of art in the context of moral rights, or *droits moral*, which are comprised of two distinct rights or

---

[62] Kenneth Goldsmith, *Richard Prince's Latest Act of Appropriation: The Catcher in the Rye*, POETRY FOUND (Apr. 19, 2012), *available at* http://www.poetryfoundation.org/harriet/2012/04/richard-princes-latest-act-of-appropriation-the-catcher-in-the-rye/.

[63] *See* http://www.richardprince.com/contact/.

[64] *See* http://www.gagosian.com/exhibitions/richard-prince--september-19-2014.

[65] Hannah Ghorashi, *$90 vs. $90,000: SuicideGirls Are Selling Their Richard Prince Appropriated Photos*, ART NEWS (May 27, 2015), *available at* http://www.artnews.com/2015/05/27/90-vs-90000-suicidegirls-are-selling-their-richard-prince-appropriated-instagram-photos/; Eileen Kinsella, Outraged Photographer Sues Gagosian Gallery and Richard Prince for Copyright Infringement, ArtNet Nets (Jan. 4, 2016), *available at* https://news.artnet.com/market/donald-graham-sues-gagosian-richard-prince-401498; Julia Halperin, Instagram Model and Makeup Artist Sues Richard Prince Over Copyright Infringement, The Art Newspaper (Aug. 26, 2016), *available at* http://theartnewspaper.com/news/news/instagram-model-and-makeup-artist-sues-richard-prince-over-copyright-infringement/.

concepts: (1) the right for an artist to be acknowledged as the author or creator of a work (known as the "right of attribution") and (2) the right for an artist to control alterations or modifications of the artist's work and to prevent its destruction (known as the "right of integrity"). In other countries, however, moral rights are more expansive and include (1) the right of disclosure (*droit de divulgation*) and (2) the right to withdraw from publication or to modify (*droit de retrait ou de repentir*).[66] The United States does not presently recognize the *droit de divulgation* or the *droit de retrait ou de repentir.* Rather, the right of attribution and the right of integrity are incorporated into U.S. copyright law by the Visual Artists Rights Act (VARA),[67] which was enacted in 1990. VARA exclusively applies to works of visual art, which it defines as follows:

- A painting, drawing, print, or sculpture (in a single copy or in a limited edition of 200 or fewer copies, signed and consecutively numbered by the artist)
- A sculpture, in multiple cast, carved, or fabricated sculptures (in 200 or fewer copies, signed and consecutively numbered by the artist)
- A still photographic image produced for exhibition purposes only, existing in a single copy (in an edition of 200 or fewer copies, signed and consecutively numbered by the artist). [68]

However, the statute excludes from the definition of "work of visual art" posters, maps, gloves, charts, technical drawings, diagrams, models, applied art, motion pictures and audiovisual work, books, magazines, newspapers, periodicals, databases, electronic information services, electronic publications or similar publications, merchandising items or advertising, promotional, descriptive, covering, or packaging materials or similar publications, works made for hire, and works that are not copyrightable.[69]

While there have been few decisions issued under VARA, courts interpreting VARA have had to grapple with the question of whether a particular work falls within the definition of "work of visual art." The results

---

[66] JUDITH PROWDA, VISUAL ARTS AND THE LAW: A HANDBOOK FOR PROFESSIONALS 102–103 (2013).
[67] 17 U.S.C. § 106A (1990).
[68] 17 U.S.C. § 101.
[69] 17 U.S.C. § 101.

have been mixed. In *Phillips v. Pembroke Real Estate, Inc.*,[70] a sculptor who had made sculptures for Boston's Eastport Park, a public sculpture garden, sought to prevent the manager of that sculpture garden from altering the work. Phillips created 27 sculptures in bronze and granite and designed stone walls, granite paving stones, and landscape design elements. A few years later, the park manager wished to modify the park and hired a landscape architect to redesign the park. Phillips brought suit under VARA to prevent the modification of his work in the park, arguing that the entire design was a single integrated whole, designed specifically for the site, and could not be altered without destroying the work's integrity. Phillips explained:

> If any sculptures are moved or removed, the spirit, integrity and character of [the] installations will be destroyed. . . . [because] the meaning and purpose of the art derives in large part from its physical locations. . . . [E]ven if the sculptures and stonework are rebuilt elsewhere someday, the artwork will never be the same as [I] intended it to be, and as it currently exists.[71]

The district court agreed with Phillips that VARA's definition of "work of visual art" extended to integrated works of art and determined that most (but not all) of Phillips's work in the park was a single integrated work of visual art.[72] While the district court held that VARA protects site-specific art, it nevertheless found that VARA permits the removal of a site-specific work, stating that "an artist has no right to the placement or public presentation of his sculpture" under VARA.[73] Both Phillips and Pembroke appealed on the issue of whether VARA protects site-specific works.

The problem of relocating artworks that have been designed and made for a specific site was well known in the decades immediately preceding enactment of VARA, principally in the dispute between Richard Serra and the United States General Services Administration over the removal of his site-specific sculpture *Tilted Arc* from Foley Federal Plaza in Manhattan. This dispute, and the public discussion over it, contributed to the efforts at legislative reform that resulted in enactment of VARA. Serra opposed the removal, arguing that it violated his free expression and due

---

[70] Phillips v. Pembroke Real Estate, Inc., 459 F.3d 128 (1st Cir. 2006).
[71] *Id.* at 135.
[72] Phillips v. Pembroke Real Estate, Inc., 288 F.Supp.2d 89, 98 (D.Mass. 2003).
[73] *Id.* at 100.

process rights. However, the Second Circuit rejected the artist's claim, stating that Serra's "lawsuit is really an invitation to the courts to announce a new rule, without any basis in First Amendment law, that an artist retains a constitutional right to have permanently displayed at the intended site a work of art that he has sold to a government agency. Neither the values of the First Amendment nor the cause of public art would be served by accepting that invitation."[74]

On appeal, the *Phillips* court acknowledged the precedent set by *Tilted Arc* in the genesis of VARA. The court, however, took exception with the district court's analysis of VARA's treatment of site-specific works, and the disagreement was, in large measure, based on a definitional disagreement on the nature of site-specific work. The First Circuit reasoned:

> By definition, site-specific art integrates its location as one of its elements. Therefore, the removal of a site-specific work from its location necessarily destroys that work of art. Here, the district court concluded that VARA recognized site-specific art as a type of integrated art, and then concluded that VARA treats site-specific art the same way that it treats other integrated art. However, a work of integrated art, unless it is a site-specific work, is not destroyed by removal from its location. . . . Either VARA recognizes site-specific art and protects it, or it does not recognize site-specific art at all.[75]

Looking to the plain language of VARA, observing that the statute does not expressly reference "site-specific art," the court concluded that VARA does not protect site-specific art.[76]

The First Circuit's reading of VARA's application to site-specific art was called into question by the Seventh Circuit in *Kelley v. Chicago Park District*.[77] Chapman Kelley, an artist who makes representational paintings using landscapes and flowers as his medium, objected to the Chicago Park Service's modification of a work he had created for Grant Park. The district court, citing and following the First Circuit's decision in *Phillips*, rejected Kelley's claim, stating that VARA categorically does not protect site-specific art. On appeal, the Seventh Circuit, in dictum, noted that VARA nowhere excludes site-specific art: "Nothing in the definition of a

---

74 Serra v. United States Gen. Serv. Admin., 847 F.2d 1045 (2d Cir. 1988).
75 Phillips v. Pembroke Real Estate, Inc., 459 F.3d 128, 140 (1st Cir. 2006).
76 *Id.* at 143.
77 Kelley v. Chicago Park District, 635 F.3d 290 (7th Cir. 2011).

'work of visual art' either explicitly or by implication excludes this form of art from moral-rights protection."[78] Moreover, the court stated:

> *Phillips's* all-or-nothing approach to site-specific art may be unwarranted. Site-specific art is not necessarily destroyed if moved; modified, yes, but not always utterly destroyed. . . . An artist's right of integrity can be violated in ways that do not implicate the work's location or manner of public presentation; site-specific art—like any other type of art—can be defaced and damaged in ways that do not relate to its public display.[79]

However, the court nevertheless denied Kelley's claim on a separate but still largely definitional ground—copyrightability. The court criticized the district court's finding that the work was a painting or sculpture, but that it lacked sufficient originality to qualify for copyright protection: "[T]he district court's conclusion misunderstands the originality requirement. . . . Despite its centrality to our copyright regime, the threshold for originality is minimal. . . . The requisite level of creativity is extremely low; even a slight amount will suffice. The vast majority of works make the grade quite easily, as they possess some creative spark."[80] Originality or creativity was not Kelley's challenge where copyright was concerned. Rather, the court reasoned, the problem lay in that "a living garden lacks the kind of authorship and stable fixation normally required to support copyright."[81]

With a nod to conceptual, kinetic, and multimedia artworks (including those that incorporate natural or living elements), the court acknowledged that mere variation and changeability in a work does not necessarily defeat copyright's fixation requirement. The court found sufficient fixation in Jaume Plensa's *Crown Fountain*[82] (which incorporates LED screens and changing video projections of faces), Alexander Calder's mobiles ("Although the aesthetic effect of a Calder mobile is attributable in part to its subtle movement in response to air currents, . . . the mobile itself is

---

[78] Kelley v. Chicago Park District, 635 F.3d 290, 306 (7th Cir. 2011).
[79] *Id.* at 307.
[80] *Id.* at 302.
[81] *Id.* at 303.
[82] *See* City of Chicago's Chicago Public Art Program, *Crown Fountain in Millennium Park, available at* http://www.cityofchicago.org/city/en/depts/dca/supp_info/chicago_s_publicartcrownfountaininmillenniumpark.html.

obviously fixed and stable."),[83] and perhaps Jeff Koons's *Puppy*[84] (in which "the artist assembled a huge metal frame in the shape of a puppy and covered it with thousands of blooming flowers sustained by an irrigation system within the frame").[85] In the context of a garden, the court distinguishes between the gardener's written or drawn plan (which is fixed and protected by copyright) and the actual physical garden (which is not fixed, nor is it authored, and so not protected by copyright). The court stated:

> [W]hen a landscape designer conceives of a plan for a garden and puts it in writing—records it in text, diagrams, or drawings on paper or on a digital-storage device, we can say that his intangible intellectual property has been embodied in a fixed and tangible "copy." This writing is a sufficiently permanent and stable copy of the designer's intellectual expression and is vulnerable to infringing copying, giving rise to the designer's right to claim copyright. The same cannot be said of a garden, which is not a fixed copy of the gardener's intellectual property. Although the planting material is tangible and can be perceived for more than a transitory duration, it is not stable or permanent enough to be called "fixed." Seeds and plants in a garden are naturally in a state of perpetual change; they germinate, grow, bloom, become dormant, and eventually die. This life cycle moves gradually, over days, weeks, and season to season, but the real barrier to copyright here is not temporal but essential. The essence of a garden is its vitality, not its fixedness. It may endure from season to season, but its nature is one of dynamic change.[86]

As with questions of fair use, moral rights can also be a ground on which artists' respective rights conflict. In 1964, Joseph Beuys gave a live art performance titled *Das Schweigen von Marcel Duchamp wird uberbewertet, 1964* (Marcel Duchamp's *Silence is Overrated*, 1964). The performance was televised but was not recorded. However, photographer Manfred Tischer made photographs of the performance, allegedly with Beuys's approval. Tischer's photographs remained unpublished until they were exhibited by the Museum Schloss Moylander in 2008.

---

83 *See* Alexander Calder Foundation website, *available at* http://www.calder.org/.
84 *See* Jeff Koons website, *available at* http://www.jeffkoons.com/artwork/puppy.
85 *Id.* at 305.
86 *Id.* at 305.

However, the Beuys estate objected to the exhibition and brought suit through the German artists' copyright collecting society, *Verwertungsgesellschaft Bild-Kunst*. The Regional Court of Dusseldorf (*Landgericht Dusseldorf*) held in favor of the Beuys estate, finding that Tischer's series of photographs violated Beuys's rights under German copyright law, which protects live art performances.[87] On appeal, the Higher Regional Court of Dusseldorf (*Oberlandesgericht Dusseldorf*) affirmed the lower court's ruling, holding that the photographs constituted an impermissible reworking or deformation of Beuys's performance.[88] The court observed that the photographs were not sufficiently different from the original unrecorded performance to satisfy the requirements to be a free adaptation of the work. The court also found there to be insufficient evidence of Beuys's authorization for the photographs to be taken.

The museum appealed to the German Federal Supreme Court (*Bundesgerichtshof*), which reversed the lower courts' rulings.[89] Judge Joachim Bernkaum described the matter as an "interesting and not very simple case."[90] The court held that Tischer's photographs did not infringe the Beuys estate's rights. In its decision, the court reproduced the entire 18-photograph series and concluded that the photographs were more than a simple representation of Beuys's performance. In an analysis that blended what in U.S. copyright law would be issues of fair use and the right of integrity, the court looked to the transformative nature of the photographs—how the series selected out moments from the performance, viewed from different angles and perspectives. The court acknowledged that the case involved determining the respective rights of two artists and that no bright line can be drawn between impermissible deformation and permissible transformation.

B. Artists' Resale Rights

The artist resale royalty right, which in Europe is often called the *droit de suite*, is a form of intellectual property right that allows primarily visual artists (who produce work in single objects or limited editions) with a right to receive a percentage of the purchase price when their works are

87 VG Bild-Kunst v. Museum Schloss MoylanderAZ: 12 O 255/09 (LG Dusseldorf Sept. 29, 2010).

88 VG Bild-Kunst v. Museum Schloss MoylanderAZ: I-20 U 171/10 (OLG Dusseldorf Dec. 30, 2011).

89 VG Bild-Kunst v. Museum Schloss MoylanderAZ: I ZR 28/12 (BGH May 16, 2013); *available at* http://dejure.org/dienste/vernetzung/rechtsprechung?Text=I%20ZR%2028/12.

90 *Beuys Witwe unterliegt vor BGH*, HANDELSBLATT (May 16, 2013), *available at* http://www.handelsblatt.com/panorama/kultur-kunstmarkt/streit-um-fotoserie-beuys-witwe-unterliegt-vor-bgh/8220192.html.

resold. The resale royalty's purpose is to allow artists to share in the increased value of their work over time. Each time a work is sold for a higher price than was originally paid for the work, a percentage of that sale price is required to be paid to the artist or the artist's estate or heirs. Typically, the resale royalty falls within copyright law (it is provided for in the Berne Convention, Art. 14ter),[91] and attempts to bring the visual artist's rights into closer alignment with the rights of authors and recording artists, where the right to receive royalties is not cut off at the time of the original sale of a work or a copy. Although the *droit de suite* originated in France, it has been widely incorporated into copyright law in Europe and elsewhere. Currently, more than 70 countries provide in some measure for a resale royalty.[92] However, it is not currently part of U.S. copyright law.[93]

The United States has considered—and rejected—a resale royalty several times.[94] In 1992, the U.S. Office of the Registrar of Copyrights, at the request of Congress, issued a report titled *Droit de Suite: The Artist's Resale Royalty*, which concluded that it would be premature to enact such a right because only approximately 30 countries at that time had such a right and the impact on the art trade was unclear. Many parties in the art trade voiced concern that imposing a resale royalty would burden the trade and result in sellers shifting their sales activities to locations outside of the United States that did not have a resale royalty.

In December 2011, bills were introduced in both houses of Congress titled the Equity for Visual Artists Act of 2011 (EVAA), as S.2000 and H.R.

---

91 *See* BERNE CONVENTION FOR THE PROTECTION OF LITERARY AND ARTISTIC WORKS, SEPT. 9, 1886, *available at* http://www.wipo.int/treaties/en/text.jsp?file_id=283698. As the U.S. Office of the Registrar of Copyrights has recently stated: "Because several countries opposed addition of the right at the 1948 Brussels conference, the resale right in Berne ultimately was made optional and reciprocal—Member States were not required to implement the right, but if they failed to do so their citizens could not benefit from the right in other countries. Thus, although the United States is a signatory to the Berne Convention, it is not required to implement *droit de suite* under its domestic copyright law. As a result of this omission, United States artists are prevented from recouping any royalties generated from the sale of their works in those countries that do have a resale royalty right." *See* RESALE ROYALTIES: AN UPDATED ANALYSIS, DECEMBER 2013 (the "2013 Report"), *available at* http://copyright.gov/docs/resaleroyalty/.

92 *See id.* (noting that "Today more than seventy foreign countries—twice as many as in 1992—have enacted a resale royalty provision of some sort to address this perceived inequality").

93 *See* Copyright Act, 17 U.S.C. 101 et seq., *available at* http://www.copyright.gov/title17/92chap1.html#101.

94 *See* Visual Artists' Residual Rights Act of 1978, H.R. 11403, 95th Cong. (1978); and Visual Artists Rights Amendment of 1986, S. 2796, 99th Cong. (1986). The 1986 bill was eventually enacted as the Visual Artists Rights Act of 1990 (VARA), but with the resale royalty provisions removed. However, VARA did direct the office to undertake a study on the feasibility of a resale royalty. That study was eventually published as the office's 1992 report, DROIT DE SUITE: THE ARTIST'S RESALE ROYALTY (the "1992 Report"), which concluded that the office was "not persuaded that sufficient economic and copyright policy justification exists to establish droit de suite in the United States." 1992 REPORT at 149.

3688, respectively.[95] The EVAA would have amended the Copyright Act to require a seller[96] to pay a resale royalty of 7 percent of the purchase price on objects sold at public auction for a purchase price of at least $10,000. That royalty would be divided between the artist and nonprofit art museums. Congress asked the Office of the Registrar of Copyrights to revisit and update its 1992 report, and in December 2013, the office issued its follow-up report titled *Resale Royalties: An Updated Analysis*.[97] In its updated report, the office reversed its prior opposition to enactment of a resale royalty right and supported the EVAA.[98] The report observed that

> Certain visual artists may operate at a disadvantage under the copyright law relative to authors of other types of creative works. Visual artists typically do not share in the long-term financial success of their works because works of visual art are produced singularly and valued for their scarcity, unlike books, films, and songs, which are produced and distributed in multiple copies to consumers. Consequently, in many, if not most instances, only the initial sale of a work of visual art inures to the benefit of the artist and it is collectors and other purchasers who reap any increase in that work's value over time.[99]

Without a resale royalty, the report noted, "the financial gains from the resale of [artists'] works inure primarily to third parties such as auction houses, collectors, and art galleries."[100]

In the United States, resale royalties received public attention in 1973, when artist Robert Rauschenberg took offense at the resale of his 1958 painting *Thaw* at auction for $85,000.[101] Collector Robert Scull had purchased the

---

95 The bills were introduced by Senator Herb Kohl and Congressman Jerrold Nadler. *See Resale Royalty Right*, Federal Register (Sept. 19, 2012), *available at* https://www.federalregister.gov/articles/2012/09/19/2012-23076/resale-royalty-right.

96 The EVAA imposes this obligation not directly on the seller per se, but on the party responsible for collecting the "money or other consideration."

97 2013 Report, *available at* http://copyright.gov/docs/resaleroyalty/.

98 *Id.* (noting that "The Copyright Office agrees that these factors place many visual artists at a material disadvantage *vis-à-vis* other authors, and therefore the Office supports congressional consideration of a resale royalty right, or droit de suite, which would give artists a percentage of the amount paid for a work each time it is resold by another party").

99 *Id.*

100 *Id.*

101 *See* Marion Maneker, *The Famous Rauschenberg Scull Shoving Match Didn't Go Down the Way You Think It Did*, Art Market Monitor (Sept. 2, 2013), *available at* http://www.artmarketmonitor.com/2014/09/02/the-famous-rauschenberg-scull-shoving-match-didnt-go-down-the-way-you-think-it-did/.

painting in the late 1950s for $900.[102] Rauschenberg's objection was that Scull alone benefitted from the increase in the painting's value brought about through the artist's efforts and growing reputation. Rauschenberg later asked Scull to purchase his new work at a comparable price.

An earlier effort to create a resale royalty took a contractual form and was promoted in 1971 by conceptual art dealer Seth Siegelaub; it was known as The Artist's Reserved Rights Transfer and Sale Agreement (the "Artist's Agreement").[103] The Artist's Agreement was a three-page agreement meant to be used on the first sale of an artist's work (either by the artist via a studio sale or through the artist's gallery or other agent), in which the buyer of the work agrees, among other things, to (1) notify the artist of any transfer of the work (including by inheritance, bequest, operation of law, or in the case of destruction of the work and payment of insurance proceeds); (2) pay the artist a 15 percent royalty of the appreciated fair market value of the work at the time of the transfer; (3) not allow any public exhibition of the work except with the artist's consent; (4) not intentionally destroy, modify, or change the work; and (5) consult with the artist on any repairs to be made to the work. A number of the rights granted to artists in the Artist's Agreement, particularly those moral rights (such as those concerning the integrity of the work), were later addressed by statute in the Visual Artist's Rights Act.[104] Kibum Kim, co-founder and director of the NEWD Art Show,[105] has advocated a reconsideration of the contractual approach to a resale royalty, writing that:

> Should we be in a position to make a choice between legislation and contractual agreements, I would argue that the contract is preferable by far. In contrast to the legislative option, which pits artists and collectors against each other in antagonistic positions, contracts that collectors agree to strengthen their relationships with artists and encourage collectors to be stewards of artists' works. Legislation only grants monetary royalties and does not cover exhibition-related rights, which, for some artists, are more important. The resale royalty being calculated

---

102 Roni Feinstein, *The Scull Collection*, ART IN AMERICA (June 4, 2010), *available at* http://www.artinamericamagazine.com/reviews/the-scull-collection/.

103 *See* http://www.primaryinformation.org/the-artists-reserved-rights-transfer-and-sale-agreement-1971/.

104 *See* https://www.law.cornell.edu/uscode/text/17/106A.

105 *See* http://www.newdartshow.com/.

> off the profit made from a sale in the [Artist's Agreement] makes it a more agreeable proposition for collectors (and is more fair) than legislative proposals, which call for royalties to be calculated off the sale price, meaning a collector would be liable even if she sells at a loss. Current proposed legislation would also paternalistically prohibit the artist from selling the rights, so that an artist could not sell future potential royalties for a lump sum in the present day, as musicians frequently do. And generally, as a flexible document, the artist can modify the terms of the contract.[106]

The idea of taking a contractual approach to an artist retaining a certain amount of control over how the artist's work may be displayed and transferred has had more prominence among conceptual artists for a number of years. "The estate of artist Sol LeWitt,"[107] as Daniel Grant has written, "has demanded that collectors who buy his works agree to seek its permission before selling to new owners. . . . Another artist, Hans Haacke,[108] asks buyers to sign a contract agreeing to pay him a royalty of 15% whenever they sell his work for a profit on the secondary market. And if buyers exhibit his work in 'a public venue, I want a say in the circumstances,' [Haacke] says."[109]

Kim pointed out that, under the ART Act, "'a work of visual art' is defined as 'a painting, drawing, print, sculpture, or photograph, existing either in the original embodiment or in a limited edition of 200 copies or fewer.' Under this definition, many of the works by the conceptual artists who inspired the [Artist's Agreement] would likely not be covered by [the ART Act]. Some of the most interesting artists working today, like Ryan Trecartin and Camille Henrot, may not be either."[110]

A flexible, contractual approach to resale rights has a growing appeal in some art circles. The company Level Rights,[111] for instance, provides a

---

106 Kibum Kim, *Could a Long-Forgotten Contract Settle the Artist Resale Royalties Debate?* HYPERALLERGIC (Jan. 5, 2015), *available at* http://hyperallergic.com/172688/could-a-long-forgotten-contract-settle-the-resale-royalties-debate.

107 *See* http://www.nytimes.com/2007/04/09/arts/design/09lewitt.html?pagewanted=all.

108 *See* http://www.nytimes.com/2014/10/24/arts/design/hans-haacke-gets-establishment-nod-of-approval.html.

109 Daniel Grant, *Fine-Art Sales Often Come with Strings Attached*, THE WALL STREET JOURNAL, April 12, 2015, *available at* http://www.wsj.com/articles/fine-art-sales-agreements-often-come-with-strings-attached-1428894129.

110 Kibum Kim, *Could a Long-Forgotten Contract Settle the Artist Resale Royalties Debate?* HYPERALLERGIC (Jan. 5, 2015), *available at* http://hyperallergic.com/172688/could-a-long-forgotten-contract-settle-the-resale-royalties-debate.

111 *See* http://www.levelrights.com/.

platform for establishing what it terms a negotiated resale right (NRR).[112] The NRR, Level Rights explained, "allows artists to choose whether or not to participate, it enables galleries to receive a share of the resale proceeds, and, any holder may transfer the resale right for value."

One state, California, provided for a resale royalty until that statute (the California Resale Royalties Act, or the CRRA) was struck down on Constitutional and Copyright Act preemption grounds.[113] The CRRA established a resale royalty of 5 percent of the purchase price, but only if all of the following conditions were met: (1) the artist was a U.S. citizen or California resident for at least 2 years at the time of the sale; (2) the seller was a California resident or the sale occurred in California; (3) the object was a work of "fine art"; (4) the object sold for a purchase price higher than what was originally paid for it; and (5) the purchase price was at least $1,000.

In 2011, several artists and their heirs filed class action complaints against Sotheby's, Inc., and Christies, Inc., alleging violation of the CRRA. The plaintiffs alleged that the auction houses had "sold works of fine art at auction but failed to pay the appropriate resale royalty provided for under the CRRA."[114] The auctions in question had been held in New York. The auction houses filed a joint motion to dismiss the complaints and urged the court to strike down the CRRA on the grounds that the statute (1) violates the dormant Commerce Clause of the U.S. Constitution, (2) effects a taking of private property in violation of the U.S. and California constitutions, and (3) is preempted by the Copyright Act.

The United States District Court for the Central District of California agreed with the auction houses, holding that the CRRA violates the dormant Commerce Clause "*per se*," finding that "the CCRA explicitly regulates applicable sales of fine art occurring wholly outside California."[115] The court considered whether the CCRA's extraterritorial reach could be severed from the statute, preserving the unoffending provisions. Despite the CCRA's inclusion of a severability provision, the court examined the statute's legislative history, finding that the California legislature explicitly

---

112 *See* http://www.levelrights.com/how.html.

113 California Resale Royalties Act, Cal. Civ. Code § 986 (the CRRA), *available at* http://leginfo.ca.gov/cgi-bin/displaycode?section=civ&group=00001-01000&file=980-989.

114 Estate of Graham v. Sotheby's Inc.; Sam Francis Foundation v. Christie's, Inc., Case Nos. 2:11-cv-08604-JHN-FFM (Sotheby's), 2:11-cv-08605-JHN-FFM (Christie's), 860 F.Supp.2d 1117 (C.D. Cal. 2012).

115 *Id.* at 1124.

contemplated and intended for the statute to have extraterritorial reach.[116] The court concluded that to sever the extraterritorial provisions of the CCRA from the remainder of the statute would result in the court impermissibly rewriting in a manner directly contrary to the legislature's intent. "Were the court merely to sever the extraterritorial provisions of the statute," the court reasoned, "it would create a new law that the legislature clearly never intended to create."[117] The court concluded that it had no choice but to strike down the entire statute.

The artists appealed the decision to the United States Court of Appeals for the Ninth Circuit, and requested that the appeal be heard by the full panel of nine judges sitting *en banc* (rather than a three-judge panel, which would normally hear such an appeal). On August 29, 2014, the Ninth Circuit asked the parties to submit further briefing on whether a conflict exists among existing Ninth Circuit decisions as to the applicability of the United States Supreme Court's holding in *Healy v. Beer Inst.*, 491 U.S. 324 (1989), in which the Court struck down a Connecticut statute that required out-of-state beer distributors to affirm that their prices charged to Connecticut wholesalers were no higher than prices charged to wholesalers in other states, because the statute had "the impermissible practical effect of controlling commercial activity wholly outside Connecticut."

The possible conflict that the Ninth Circuit asked the parties to brief was between its prior holdings in *Rocky Mountain Farmers Union v. Corey*, 730 F.3d 1070, 1101 (9th Cir. 2013) (stating that "the dormant Commerce Clause holds that any 'statute that directly controls commerce occurring wholly outside the boundaries of a State exceeds the inherent limits of the enacting State's authority.'")[118] and *Ass'n des Eleveurs de Canards et d'Oies du Quebec v. Harris*, 29 F.3d 937, 951 (9th Cir. 2013) (in which the court had held that "the [Supreme] Court has held that *Healy* . . . [is] not applicable to a statute that does not dictate the price of a product and does not 't[ie] the price of its in-state products to out-of-state prices.'").[119]

The United States Court of Appeals for the Ninth Circuit, *en banc*, issued a long-awaited decision in a suit brought by a group of artists against several major auction houses,[120] upholding, but narrowing, the district court's

---

116 *Id.* at 1226.

117 *Id.*

118 Rocky Mountain Farmers Union v. Corey, 730 F.3d 1070, 1101 (9th Cir. 2013).

119 Ass'n des Eleveurs de Canards et d'Oies du Quebec v. Harris, 29 F.3d 937, 951 (9th Cir. 2013).

120 Estate of Graham v. Sotheby's, Inc.; Sam Francis Foundation v. Christie's, Inc., 860 F.Supp.2d 1117 (C.D. Cal. 2012).

decision for impermissibly regulating out-of-state conduct. Because it was enacted in 1976, the CRRA has been the only artist's resale royalty statute in the United States, and remains so, applying now exclusively to sales occurring within California. The economic impact of this California-only 5 percent resale royalty will likely be felt immediately, as California-based sellers weigh the convenience of a local sale against out-of-state sales.

While the district court struck down the whole of the CRRA, finding that the out-of-state sales regulation could not be severed from the remainder of the CRRA, the Ninth Circuit narrowed that holding, striking only the clause that imposed the resale royalty on out-of-state sales. On the question of whether the clause regulating out-of-state sales could be severed, allowing the rest of the CRRA to stand, the district court had found that the legislative history of the CRRA showed that the legislature had considered and abandoned a version of the bill that would have only regulated sales within California. The court noted that "the legislature endorsed the CRRA's extraterritorial reach, despite the fact that California's Legislative Counsel [former Stanford law professor John Merryman] advised both Assemblyman Sieroty and then-Governor Brown, in opinion letters, that the bill 'would constitute an undue burden on interstate commerce in contravention of the Federal Constitution in its application to sales which occur outside the State of California.'"[121]

On the question of whether that portion of the CRRA applied the resale royalty to out-of-state sales, the Ninth Circuit was unanimous in holding that it facially violated the dormant Commerce Clause and was therefore unconstitutional.[122] The Ninth Circuit was also unanimous in holding that the offending provision could indeed be severed from the rest of the CRRA, but the Ninth Circuit was divided on the extent of the portion to be severed. The CRRA provided that the 5 percent resale royalty would apply if "the seller resides in California or the sale takes place in California."[123] The majority severed "the seller resides in California," leaving the in-state sales provision ("the sale takes place in California") in effect.

Because the district court struck down the whole of the CRRA, it never reached the auction houses' remaining arguments against the CRRA—namely, that it (1) effects an unconstitutional taking of private property

---

121 Estate of Graham v. Sotheby's, Inc.; Sam Francis Foundation v. Christie's, Inc., 860 F.Supp.2d 1117, 1126 (C.D. Cal. 2012).

122 Sam Francis Foundation v. Christie's; Estate of Graham v. Sotheby's, Case Nos. 12-56067, 12-56058, 12-56077, 2015 WL 2059003, *2 (May 5, 2015).

123 Cal. Civ. Code § 986(a).

and (2) is preempted by the federal Copyright Act of 1976. The Ninth Circuit noted that "[w]e return this case to the three-judge panel for its consideration of the remaining issues. We leave to the panel's discretion the decision whether to address those issues on the merits or to remand them for the district court's determination in the first instance."[124]

On April 11, 2016, the district court issued its decision on the remaining issues, finding that the CRRA is preempted under the Copyright Act, because (1) the CRRA stands in conflict with the first sale doctrine codified in 17 U.S.C. § 109(a), which prohibits copyright holders from exercising downstream distribution control of their products" (conflict preemption), and (2) the plaintiffs' claims "are independently preempted under the express preemption clause of 17 U.S.C. § 301(a) because they are not qualitatively different from garden-variety copyright claims."[125]

The U.S. Copyright Office, in both its 1992 and 2013 reports, acknowledged that state resale royalty statutes violate the Copyright Act's first sale doctrine.[126] Leading copyright treatises have also noted that the first sale doctrine presents a strong challenge to resale royalty statutes.[127] As the Copyright Office has noted, there is no constitutional bar to Congress modifying the first sale doctrine to provide for a resale royalty right. [128]

---

[124] *Id.* at *5.

[125] Estate of Graham v. Sotheby's, Inc., Case Nos. CV-11-08604-MWF-FFM, CV-11-08605-MWF-FFM, CV-11-08622-MWF-PLA, 2016 U.S. Dist. LEXIS 53079, *3-4 (D.C.D. Cal. April 11, 2016).

[126] Office of the Registrar of Copyrights, Resale Royalties: An Updated Analysis 59 (2013) ("In the 1992 Report, the Copyright Office acknowledged that '[i]mplementation of the royalty would require qualification of the First Sale Doctrine' and suggested that such a law could amount to an 'abandon[ment] of well-settled principles of free alienability in Anglo-American property jurisprudence.'").

[127] *See, e.g.*, 2 Nimmer on Copyright 8C.04 (rev. ed. 2013); 2 William F. Patry, Copyright Law and Practice 1129 n. 235 (1994) ('[T]he [resale royalty] right clearly conflicts with 109 of the Copyright Act, which generally exhausts the copyright owner's rights with respect to a particular copy once that copy is lawfully distributed.').

[128] *Id.* at 59 ("Should Congress conclude that [considerations in favor of establishing a resale royalty] warrant qualification of the first sale doctrine, there would be no constitutional bar to such action. As a general matter, Congress has broad authority 'to determine the intellectual property regimes that, overall, in that body's judgment, will serve the ends of the [Copyright] Clause.'").

CHAPTER 3

Cultural Property

A. Definition and Development

Although "art" is a familiar, if highly complex, concept, "cultural property" is far less familiar. It can include both tangible cultural property and intangible cultural property (i.e., cultural narratives, songs, dances, and traditional knowledge). In the present context, it chiefly refers to tangible cultural property.

The term has developed as a legal, anthropological, sociological, and museological concept, recognizing that a more encompassing term was required to address rights and protections relating to not only art, but many other types of objects as well. The term "cultural property" (as well as the term "cultural heritage") recognizes that many objects that are collected, studied, and exhibited are not created primarily with their artistic or aesthetic aspects in mind. Many objects produced by ancient societies were not created as aesthetic objects but were primarily designed for ritual, religious, or other cultural uses. In the contemporary world, this is frequently also true of objects produced by and in many contexts, and is notably true for native and indigenous societies. Nevertheless, many such objects have tremendous aesthetic appeal, and have been acquired and exhibited by many nonnative collectors and museums—a practice that in recent decades has given rise to tensions and protests. Many "cultural property" objects are what are called ethnographic objects, which are expressive of a culture or cultural practice. In some instances, these objects have a sacred value to the society that produces them; they are not intended to be objects of commerce. Frequently, the concept of personal ownership does not apply to such objects, which are held by the society—not only its present-day members, but its ancestors and future generations.

Some of these objects are only to be viewed or used by certain persons and in specific contexts. Some such objects are regarded as having a close connection to spirits or ancestors, even embodying those spirits or ancestors. As a result, the removal of these objects from their specific cultural context is forbidden. This has been true, for instance, of certain Hopi and Navajo objects that have been sold at Parisian auctions in recent years, over the protests of the Hopi and Navajo nations.

Not all cultural property is sacred. Cultural property includes the types of objects that we typically regard as art—those that are created within the context of the art world, intended to be owned and collected and exhibited. It also includes antiquities, books, manuscripts, scientific collections, collections of books or archives, monuments of architecture, groups of buildings, and archeological sites.

The term *cultural property* was first used in an international instrument in the 1954 Convention for the Protection of Cultural Property in the Event of Armed Conflict.[1] The Hague Convention definition is quite expansive and includes both movable and immovable cultural property. For purposes of the Hague Convention, *cultural property* means:

> (a) movable or immovable property of great cultural importance to the cultural heritage of every people, such as monuments of architecture, art or history, whether religious or secular; archaeological sites; groups of buildings which, as a whole, are of historical or artistic interest; works of art; manuscripts, books and other objects of artistic, historical or archaeological interest; as well as scientific collections and important collections of books or archives or of reproductions of the property defined above; (b) buildings whose main and effective purpose is to preserve or exhibit the movable cultural property defined in subparagraph (a) such as museums, large libraries and depositories of archives, and refuges intended to shelter, in the event of armed conflict, the movable cultural property defined in subparagraph (a); [and] (c) centers containing a large amount of cultural property as defined in subparagraphs (a) and (b), to be known as "centers containing monuments." [2]

1 Convention for the Protection of Cultural Property in the Event of Armed Conflict, May 14, 1954, 249 U.N.T.S. 240 (1954) (the "Hague Convention").

2 *Id.*

The Hague Convention applies specifically during periods of armed conflict. The 1970 United Nations Educational, Scientific and Cultural Organization (UNESCO) Convention on the Means of Prohibiting and Preventing the Illicit Import, Export and Transfer of Ownership of Cultural Property[3] expanded the protection afforded to cultural property to peacetime as well. Because the 1970 UNESCO Convention is addressed specifically to movable cultural property, its definition of cultural property is the most influential and relevant for cultural property in the kinds of transactions discussed in this book. For the 1970 UNESCO Convention, *cultural property* means:

> property which, on religious or secular grounds, is specifically designated by each State as being of importance for archaeology, prehistory, history, literature, art or science and which belongs to the following categories: (a) Rare collections and specimens of fauna, flora, minerals and anatomy, and objects of palaeontological interest; (b) property relating to history, including the history of science and technology and military and social history, to the life of national leaders, thinkers, scientists and artists and to events of national importance; (c) products of archaeological excavations (including regular and clandestine) or of archaeological discoveries; (d) elements of artistic or historical monuments or archaeological sites which have been dismembered; (e) antiquities more than one hundred years old, such as inscriptions, coins and engraved seals; (f) objects of ethnological interest; (g) property of artistic interest, such as: (i) pictures, paintings and drawings produced by hand on any support and in any material (excluding industrial designs and manufactured articles decorated by hand); (ii) original works of statuary art and sculpture in any material; (iii) original engravings, prints and lithographs; (iv) original artistic assemblages and montages in any material; (h) rare manuscripts and incunabula, old books, documents and publications of special interest (historical, artistic, scientific, literary, etc.) singly or in collections; (i) postage, revenue and similar stamps, singly or in collections; (j) archives, including sound, photographic and cinematographic archives; (k) articles of furniture more than one hundred years old and old musical instruments.[4]

---

[3] Convention on the Means of Prohibiting and Preventing the Illicit Import, Export and Transfer of Ownership of Cultural Property, Nov. 14, 1970, 823 U.N.T.S. 231 (1972), reprinted in 10 I.L.M. 289 (1970) (the "1970 UNESCO Convention").

[4] *Id.*

The norms and legal regimes that structure and govern the ownership of and trade in much cultural property have undergone tremendous change since 1970, and they remain highly fluid. Significant shifts have occurred in both the recognition and enforcement of national ownership laws[5] and restrictions on export and import of certain classes of cultural property,[6] and in international agreements restricting the transfer of certain classes of materials.[7] Transactions in cultural property generally, and archaeological or excavated objects specifically, are evaluated in and scrutinized differently than they were in the past.

The Hague Convention and the 1970 UNESCO Convention lay out principles and procedures for, on the one hand, the safeguarding and protection of cultural property during times of armed conflict (the Hague Convention) and, on the other, the suppression of looting and the illicit export of cultural property (the 1970 UNESCO Convention). While the Hague Convention is highly important in the regulation and protection of cultural property in times of war, it has little relevance to the art trade and to the kinds of transactions discussed here. The 1970 UNESCO Convention, on the other hand, has had a profound effect on the art trade, including on how and what collectors collect.

B. The 1970 UNESCO Convention

The genesis of the 1970 UNESCO Convention reflects persistent tensions between market countries (those countries that are important centers of the art and cultural property trade, both selling and collecting, many of which are former colonial powers) and source countries (those countries that were the location of ancient civilizations, many of which are former

5 National ownership laws are domestic statutes that vest title to certain cultural property—typically antiquities and excavated or unexcavated archaeological objects—in the national government. Particularly since 1970, there has been an increasing recognition and enforcement of national ownership laws by other states, including the United States, the United Kingdom, and other states that are centers of the art and cultural property market.

6 U.S. v. McClain, 545 F.2d 988 (5th Cir. 1977); U.S. v. An Antique Platter of Gold, known as a Gold Phiale Mesomphalos c. 400 B.C., 184 F.3d 131 (2d Cir. 1999); U.S. v. Schultz, 333 F.3d 393 (2d Cir. 2003).

7 UNIDROIT Convention on Stolen or Illegally Exported Cultural Objects, June 24, 1995 (the "1995 UNIDROIT Convention"); Convention on the Protection of the Underwater Cultural Heritage, Nov. 2, 2001, 41 Int'l Legal Materials 40 (2002) (the "Underwater Cultural Property Convention"); Convention Concerning the Protection of World Cultural and Natural Heritage, Nov. 16, 1972, 1037 U.N.T.S. 151 (1972) (the "World Heritage Convention").

colonies, which are often rich in antiquities, archaeological, and ethnological objects).[8] In response to growing demands from source countries, in 1964 UNESCO appointed a committee of experts to prepare recommendations for a possible convention addressing trafficking in illicit cultural property. A drafting committee was convened in 1968, and a draft convention was circulated to member states. One of the chief points of contention was the desire of source countries to have the convention apply retroactively to objects that were removed prior to the convention entering into force, particularly cultural objects that were removed during colonial periods. Many of those objects are in important public and private collections of the market countries. The dispute involved substantially different conceptions of the relationship between ancient cultures, modern cultures, and modern political entities. Those differences persist and are exemplified by the continuing dispute over the Parthenon Sculptures, which I discuss in greater detail in Section H of this chapter. The ultimate text of the convention was a compromise between the draft text and a text proposed by the United States and was adopted at the UNESCO General Conference in Paris in October and November 1970.[9]

Importantly, the convention does not rely on an external or preexisting definition of "illicit import, export and transfer of ownership of cultural property." Rather, it defines such illicitness by reference to the mechanisms established by the convention itself. Article 3 states that "[t]he import, export or transfer of ownership of cultural property effected contrary to the provisions adopted under this Convention by the States Parties thereto, shall be illicit." In Article 11, the convention further declares the "export and transfer of ownership of cultural property under compulsion arising directly or indirectly from the occupation of a country by a foreign power [to be] regarded as illicit."

Article 4 of the 1970 UNESCO Convention identifies categories of cultural property that, for purposes of the convention, constitute "part of the cultural heritage of each State." The categories include not only an

---

[8] *See* PATRICK J. O'KEEFE, COMMENTARY ON THE UNESCO CONVENTION (2d ed. 2007).

[9] *See* Lyndel V. Prott, *Strength and Weaknesses of the 1970 Convention: An Evaluation 40 Years After Its Adoption*, UNESCO 2 (2011), *available at* http://www.unesco.org/new/fileadmin/MULTIMEDIA/FIELD/Brussels/pdf/strengths%20and%20weaknesses%20of%20the1970%20convention.pdf ("The United States became party to the Convention in 1983, but it took three separate drafts of legislation to implement the Convention in national law before Congress would pass it. Other major market states were even slower to ratify the Convention: France in 1997, Japan and the United Kingdom in 2002, Switzerland in 2003, Germany in 2007, and Belgium and the Netherlands in 2009.").

expansive vision of the relationship between cultural property and the modern country in which it is located, but also an acknowledgment of practices whereby cultural property has moved legitimately from the territory of one country to that of another (and acknowledges past practices such as partage, in which excavations undertaken by institutions in one country in the territory of another would, by agreement, divide the excavated objects between them). These categories are:

- Cultural property created by the individual or collective genius of nationals of the State concerned, and cultural property of importance to the State concerned created within the territory of the State by foreign nationals or stateless persons resident within such territory
- Cultural property found within the national territory
- Cultural property acquired by archaeological, ethnological, or natural science missions, with the consent of the competent authorities of the country of origin of such property
- Cultural property that has been the subject of a freely agreed exchange
- Cultural property received as a gift or purchased legally with the consent of competent authorities of the country of origin of such property

The specific mechanisms that the convention establishes to combat illicit import, export, and transfer of ownership of cultural property requires state parties to:

1. Introduce an export certificate required for the export of cultural property (Article 6)
2. "Prevent museums and similar institutions within their territories from acquiring cultural property originating in another State Party which has been illegally exported after entry into force of this Convention" (Article 7(a))
3. "Prohibit the import of cultural property stolen from a museum or a religious or secular public monument or similar institution in another State Party . . . after entry into force of this Convention for the States concerned, provided that such property is documented as appertaining to the inventory of that institution"
(Article 7(b)(i))

4. "At the request of the State Party of origin, to take appropriate steps to recover and return any such cultural property imported after the entry into force of this Convention in both States concerned, provided, however, that the requesting State shall pay just compensation to an innocent purchaser or to a person who has valid title to that property. Requests for recovery and return shall be made through diplomatic offices. The requesting Party shall furnish, at its expense, the documentation and other evidence necessary to establish its claim for recovery and return. The Parties shall impose no customs duties or other charges upon cultural property returned pursuant to this Article. All expenses incident to the return and delivery of the cultural property shall be borne by the requesting Party." (Article 7(b)(ii))
5. Impose penalties or administrative sanctions on persons exporting without an export certificate or acquiring cultural property stolen from a museum or similar institution (Article 8)

Countries whose cultural property is in jeopardy from pillage are authorized to seek assistance from other States Parties (Article 9).

C. The 1995 UNIDROIT Convention

As important and as influential as the 1970 UNESCO Convention has been, critics have identified a number of weaknesses. Chief among them is that the convention exclusively imposes obligations on states and does not directly apply to private law.[10] Prof. Francesco Francioni has noted that, in the 1970 UNESCO Convention:

> The obligation to prevent and suppress illicit traffic in cultural objects is limited to the hypotheses of theft, illicit export and illicit import and acquisition that involve as an active or passive party "museums and similar institutions. . . ." Thus this obligation does not extend to those situations of illicit export or import of cultural objects which involves

[10] For a more extensive discussion of the perceived weaknesses of the 1970 UNESCO Convention, see Lyndel V. Prott, *Strength and Weaknesses of the 1970 Convention: An Evaluation 40 Years After Its Adoption*, UNESCO 2 (2011), *available at* http://www.unesco.org/new/fileadmin/MULTIMEDIA/FIELD/Brussels/pdf/strengths%20and%20weaknesses%20of%20the1970%20convention.pdf.

> private parties. Another weakness of the [1970 UNESCO Convention] is the vagueness of its provision Art. 7(b)(ii) on compensation to the innocent purchaser or to persons who have valid title to the illegally transferred object. No criterion is indicated to establish what is a valid title, nor under what law its validity is to be determined.[11]

The effectiveness of the 1970 UNESCO Convention has also been hampered by many states attaching reservations to their ratifications of the convention, as well as by the manner in which a number of states (including the United States) have implemented the convention in their domestic law.

In response to these perceived weaknesses, the International Institute for the Unification of Private Law (UNIDROIT)[12] promulgated the UNIDROIT Convention on Stolen or Illegally Exported Cultural Objects, which was adopted in Rome on June 24, 1995.[13] The 1995 UNIDROIT Convention "applies to claims of an international character for: (a) the restitution of stolen cultural objects; (b) the return of cultural objects removed from the territory of a Contracting State contrary to its law regulating the export of cultural objects for the purpose of protecting its cultural heritage."[14]

Article 3(1) articulates the convention's principal purpose, mandating that "the possessor of a cultural object that has been stolen shall return it." The convention's remaining provisions detail how this is to be accomplished, beginning with its expended definition of "stolen," which explicitly acknowledges and incorporates countries' national ownership laws:

> A cultural object which has been unlawfully excavated or lawfully excavated but unlawfully retained shall be considered stolen, when consistent with the law of the State where the excavation took place.[15]

---

[11] Francesco Francioni, *Cultural Heritage*, in MAX PLANCK ENCYCLOPEDIA OF PUBLIC INTERNATIONAL LAW (2013).

[12] *See* http://www.unidroit.org/about-unidroit/overview.

[13] UNIDROIT Convention on Stolen or Illegally Exported Cultural Objects, June 24, 1995 (the "1995 UNIDROIT Convention"), *available at* http://www.unidroit.org/instruments/cultural-property/1995-convention.

[14] Article 1.

[15] Article 3(2).

The convention provides for limitation periods in which claims for the return of stolen cultural property must be made: (i) generally, a claim must be brought within 50 years of the date of the theft, and not more than 3 years after the claimant knows the location of the object and the identity of its possessor;[16] (ii) for objects that form part of an identified monument or archaeological site, or part of a public collection, claims are subject only to the limitation of having to be brought within not more than 3 years after the claimant knows the location of the object and the identity of its possessor;[17] and (iii) states may designate a longer limitation period or 75 years or longer, if consistent with such state's internal law.[18] The convention also provides for claims for the return of stolen indigenous cultural property. Article 3(8) states that:

> A claim for restitution of a sacred or communally important cultural object belonging to and used by a tribal or indigenous community in a Contracting State as part of that community's traditional or ritual use, shall be subject to the time limitation applicable to public collections.

The 1995 UNIDROIT Convention's provisions for the repatriation of indigenous cultural objects, however, are "less precise than those in NAGPRA [the Native American Graves Protection and Repatriation Act, discussed in Section F(2) in this chapter] (which sanctions the complete and unequivocal repatriation of Native American cultural and funerary objects to affiliated tribes)."[19] The 1995 UNIDROIT Convention specifically addresses several issues that are not covered by the 1970 UNESCO Convention. However, because the 1995 UNIDROIT Convention has been ratified by far fewer states than the 1970 UNESCO Convention (and has found little acceptance among the major market countries),[20] it has limited applicability for most art transactions.

---

16 Article 3(3).

17 Article 3(4).

18 Article 3(5).

19 MARILYN E. PHELAN, MUSEUM LAW: A GUIDE FOR OFFICERS, DIRECTORS, AND COUNSEL 400 (4th ed. 2014).

20 The 1995 UNIDROIT Convention entered into force on January 1, 1998. However, as of May 30, 2016, it had only 37 state parties, in contrast with the 131 state parties to the 1970 UNESCO Convention.

D. The Convention on Cultural Property Implementation Act

Under United States law, the 1970 UNESCO Convention is not self-executing. After a long delay involving three separate attempts at implementing legislation over the course of more than a decade, the United States enacted the Convention on Cultural Property Implementation Act, 19 U.S.C. 2601 *et seq.* (the CPIA)[21] in 1983. The CPIA implements two articles of the 1970 UNESCO Convention—Article 7(b)(i) and Article 9. It has been suggested that this limited approach to implementation was because the United States considered a number of provisions of the convention to already be adequately served by existing United States law.[22] However, it has also been suggested that this was because the art trade objected more strongly to the other provisions.[23] The CPIA defines "cultural property" with reference to Article 1 of the 1970 UNESCO Convention, incorporating all of the convention's categories.[24]

Article 7(b)(i) is implemented by Section 308 of the CPIA, under which "[n]o article of cultural property documented as appertaining to the inventory of a museum or religious or secular public monument or similar institution in any State Party which is stolen from such institution after the effective date of this title, or after the date of entry into force of the Convention for the State Party, whichever is later, may be imported into the United States."[25]

Article 9's provision for States Parties to give assistance to other States Parties whose cultural property is at risk is implemented by Section 303 of the CPIA, which authorizes the president to enter into bilateral agreements (also known as memoranda of understanding or MOUs) with other state parties to provide for United States assistance in the form of import restrictions on identified categories of cultural objects (as identified on a designated list).[26] However, the CPIA requires that requesting country must have undertaken its own measures to protect its cultural heritage,

---

[21] *See* http://eca.state.gov/files/bureau/97-446.pdf.

[22] *See* Patrick J. O'Keefe, Commentary on the UNESCO Convention (2d ed. 2007).

[23] *See* Patty Gerstenblith, Art, Cultural Heritage, and the Law: Cases and Materials 623 (2d ed. 2008).

[24] 19 U.S.C. § 2601(6) (stating "The term 'cultural property' includes articles described in article 1 (a) through (k) of the Convention whether or not any such article is specifically designated as such by any State Party for the purposes of such article.").

[25] 19 U.S.C. § 2607.

[26] 19 U.S.C. § 2602.

and the requested relief must be no more burdensome than necessary. In fact, each MOU has two sections—Article I sets out the United States agreement to prohibit importation of specified categories of objects, and Article II sets out a series of concrete actions that the United States and the requesting country will take to protect and preserve the identified cultural heritage, promote scholarship and scientific research, and provide for broader access to such cultural heritage to the American public (particularly through loans of objects to United States institutions).

Currently, the United States is party to 15 MOUs with Belize, Bolivia, Bulgaria, Cambodia, China, Colombia, Cyprus, El Salvador, Greece, Guatemala, Honduras, Italy, Mali, Nicaragua, and Peru. Additionally, the United States has taken emergency action to restrict importation of specific categories of cultural property from Iraq. A chart identifying current U.S. cultural property import restrictions under the CPIA is available here:[27]

Article 9 is also implemented by Section 304 of the CPIA, which authorizes the president to take emergency action with respect to the protection of at-risk international cultural property by imposing import restrictions. The CPIA created the Cultural Property Advisory Committee (CPAC), comprised of 11 members drawn from the archaeological/anthropological community, the art/cultural property trade, the museum community, and the general public. The CPAC reviews requests for assistance under the CPIA and advises as to the satisfaction of criteria established under the CPIA. The CPAC operates within the Department of State's Bureau of Educational and Cultural Affairs,[28] and so U.S. cultural property policy and the CPIA are aspects of United States cultural diplomacy.

Enforcement of import restrictions imposed under the CPIA is carried out by the Department of Homeland Security, through Immigration and Customs Enforcement (ICE) and Customs and Border Protection (CBP). Under the CPIA, the only enforcement actions available to the government are the seizure and forfeiture of the stolen or illicitly imported cultural property. No individual liability (criminal or otherwise) attaches with respect to such seizures and forfeitures, and the government does not need to establish that the importer had any knowledge of or intent to commit any wrongdoing.

---

27 *See* http://eca.state.gov/files/bureau/chart-of-import-restrictions.pdf.

28 *See* http://eca.state.gov/cultural-heritage-center/cultural-property-protection/process-and-purpose/cultural-property-advisory.

E. U.S. Cultural Property Policy and Enforcement

United States protection of international cultural property is not exclusively governed by the CPIA. For example, United States obligations under the Convention on International Trade in Endangered Species of Wild Fauna and Flora (CITES)[29] are enforced by the Department of the Interior, through the U.S. Fish and Wildlife Service.[30]

The protection of international cultural property touches on many different areas, and responsibility for various aspects of policy development and enforcement involves multiple departments and agencies. Currently, United States efforts at protecting and preserving international cultural property is spread across no fewer than seven federal agencies. This presents the risk of inconsistent, even contradictory, actions being taken. To better coordinate these efforts, the Protect and Preserve International Cultural Property Act (the "PPICPA") was enacted on May 9, 2016, as Public Law No. 114-151, 130 Stat. 369.[31] In the version of the PPICPA that was originally introduced, the act would have established a new position within the Department of State, a United States Coordinator for International Cultural Property Protection; however, this coordinator role was ultimately removed. In its final state, the PPICPA creates a Coordinating Committee on International Cultural Property Protection, and also directs the president to impose import restrictions on archaeological or ethnological material from Syria (akin to the emergency action taken concerning Iraqi cultural property).

In addition to the provisions of the CPIA and the PPICPA, the importation of cultural property into the United States may, in some circumstances, also violate United States law and result in seizure and forfeiture of the imported object and/or criminal liability for those involved in the importation (including those in possession of the illicitly imported objects). Cultural property importers have run afoul of United States law by, among other things, (i) making false statements of an object's value or country of origin (*see* 18 U.S.C. § 545); and (ii) importing cultural property that was stolen property, including objects illicitly excavated or removed from their country or origin in violation of a country's national ownership law (*see* 19 U.S.C. § 1595(c)), which may also violate the

[29] *See* http://www.cites.org/eng/disc/what.php.

[30] *See* http://www.fws.gov/international/cites/how-cites-works.html.

[31] H.R. 1493, *available at* https://www.congress.gov/bill/114th-congress/house-bill/1493.

National Stolen Property Act (18 U.S.C. §§ 2314 and 2315) and in certain circumstances even the Archaeological Resources Protection Act (16 U.S.C. § 470ee[c]).

F. Protection of U.S. Archaeological Heritage and Native American Cultural Heritage

United States domestic law regulates and protects certain forms of cultural property (principally, archaeological resources and Native American, Native Alaskan, and Hawaiian Native culture heritage) in ways that are important for parties to art transactions to have some familiarity with.

1. The Antiquities Act and the Archaeological Resources Protection Act

United States law regulates domestic antiquities and archaeological resources through two statutes: the Antiquities Act of 1906 (Antiquities Act)[32] and the Archaeological Resources Protection Act of 1979 (ARPA).[33]

a. The Antiquities Act

The Antiquities Act was the first United States law to address not only antiquities but historic preservation more generally, and it set the tone for subsequent United States national historic preservation policy. The statute is brief, having only four sections. Section 1 makes it unlawful to:

> appropriate, excavate, injure, or destroy any historic or prehistoric ruin or monument, or any object of antiquity, situated on lands owned or controlled by the Government of the United States, without the permission of the Secretary of the Department of the Government having jurisdiction over the lands on which said antiquities are situated.[34]

[32] 16 U.S.C. §§ 431–433, *available at* U.S. Department of the Interior, National Park Service, https://www.nps.gov/history/local-law/FHPL_AntiAct.pdf.

[33] 16 U.S.C. §§ 470aa–470mm; Public Law 96-95 and amendments, *available at* U.S. Department of the Interior, National Park Service, https://www.nps.gov/history/local-law/FHPL_ArchRsrcsProt.pdf.

[34] 16 U.S.C. § 433.

Violation of the act is a criminal offense, punishable by a fine in the maximum amount of $500, imprisonment for a term not longer than 90 days, or both.[35] Significantly, the Antiquities Act does not provide definitions of key terms such as "ruin," "monument," or "object of antiquity," which has been the source of judicial disagreement as to its applicability. In 1974, the United States Court of Appeals for the Ninth Circuit, in *U.S. v. Diaz*,[36] held the Antiquities Act to be unconstitutional because of this failure to define its terms. Other courts have declined to follow the *Diaz* decision, distinguishing between the facts of that case (in which the Native American objects that had been removed were of recent vintage) and cases involving more ancient objects, and the Antiquities Act remains in force.[37]

b. The Archaeological Resources Protection Act

The Archaeological Resources Protection Act ("ARPA") was enacted in 1979:

> to secure, for the present and future benefit of the American people, the protection of archaeological resources and sites which are on public lands and Indian lands, and to foster increased cooperation and exchange of information between governmental authorities, the professional archaeological community, and private individuals[38]

ARPA's key concept is that of the "archaeological resources," which the statute defines as:

> Any material remains of past human life or activities which are of archaeological interest, as determined under uniform regulations promulgated pursuant to this Act. Such regulations containing such determination shall include, but not be limited to: pottery, basketry, bottles, weapons, weapon projectiles, tools, structures or portions of structures, pit houses, rock paintings, rock carvings, intaglios, graves, human skeletal materials, or any portion or piece of any of the foregoing items.[39]

---

35 *Id.*

36 U.S. v. Diaz, 499 F.2d 113 (9th Cir. 1974).

37 *See, e.g.*, U.S. v. Smyer, 596 F.2d 939, 941 (10th Cir. 1979)(stating that "when measured by common understanding and practice, the challenged language conveys a sufficiently definite warning as to the proscribed conduct"); U.S. v. Corrow, 941 F.Supp. 1553 (D. N.M. 1996); Subaqueous Exploration & Archaeology, Ltd. v. Unidentified, Wrecked & Abandoned Vessel, 577 F.Supp. 597, 613 (D. Md. 1983)(stating "the Court declines to follow the Ninth Circuit's construction of the federal Antiquities Act as set forth in United States v. Diaz, 499 F.2d 113 (9th Cir. 1974)").

38 16 U.S.C. § 470AA(b).

39 16 U.S.C. § 470BB(1).

However, under ARPA, "no item shall be treated as an archaeological resource . . . unless such item is at least 100 years of age."[40] ARPA does not apply to either fossilized or nonfossilized paleontological objects unless those objects are found in an archaeological context.[41] Rather, paleontological objects are protected under the Paleontological Resources Preservation Act.[42]

ARPA vests ownership of archaeological resources located on federal lands and Indian lands in the federal government (subject to the specific exceptions with respect to Native American human remains and cultural items provided for under NAGPRA, discussed below) and prohibits the excavation or removal of any archaeological resource located on federal lands or Indian lands unless the party seeking to excavate or remove such resources first obtains a permit from the federal land manager responsible for the lands.[43] Significantly, ARPA also prohibits the trafficking in "archaeological resources the excavation or removal of which was wrongful under Federal law,"[44] as well as "trafficking in interstate or foreign commerce in archaeological resources the excavation, removal, sale, purchase, exchange, transportation or receipt of which was wrongful under State of local law."[45] Violations of these anti-trafficking provisions are criminal violations, punishable by a fine of up to $10,000 or imprisonment for up to one year or both.[46] However, if the "commercial or archaeological value" of the illicitly excavated or removed resource and the cost of restoration and repair of the recourse exceeds $500 (a low threshold that will likely be exceeded in most instances), the penalty may be a fine in the maximum amount of $20,000, imprisonment for a maximum term of 2 years, or both. For second and successive violations, penalties may be a

---

40 *Id.*

41 *Id.*

42 Paleontological Resources Preservation Act (the PRPA), 16 U.S.C. §§ 470aaa–470aaa-11, enacted March 30, 2009, *available at* U.S. Department of the Interior, National Park Service, http://nature.nps.gov/geology/nationalfossilday/prpa_text.cfm. The PRPA defines "paleontological resource" as "any fossilized remains, traces, or imprints of organisms, preserved in or on the earth's crust, that are of paleontological interest and that provide information about the history of life on earth, except that the term does not include -- (A) any materials associated with an archaeological resource (as defined in section 3(1) of the Archaeological Resources Protection Act of 1979 (16 U.S.C. 470bb(1)); or (B) any cultural item (as defined in section 2 of the Native American Graves Protection and Repatriation Act (25 U.S.C. 3001))."

43 16 U.S.C. § 470CC(b).

44 16 U.S.C. § 470EE(b).

45 16 U.S.C. § 470EE(c).

46 16 U.S.C. § 470EE(d).

fine in the maximum amount of $100,000, imprisonment for a term of up to 5 years, or both.

2. The Native American Graves Protection and Repatriation Act

The Native American Graves Protection and Repatriation Act of 1990[47] (NAGPRA) provides powerful but imperfect tools for the protection of Native American cultural heritage.

a. The Troubled History of Collecting Native American Cultural Heritage

NAGPRA was enacted fundamentally as human rights legislation, intended to address and provide some readdress for centuries of exploitation, displacement, and dispossession. Individual and institution collecting of Native American cultural items, including, as NAGPRA recognizes, human remains, associated funerary objects, unassociated funerary objects, sacred objects, and cultural patrimony, has a long, troubled history. Collecting efforts were frequently driven by racist and colonialist ideological or political projects.

The House Report submitted in connection with NAGPRA summarized this history as follows:

> Digging and removing the contents of Native American graves for reasons of profit or curiosity has been common practice. These activities were at their peak during the last century and the early part of this century.
>
> In 1868, the Surgeon General issued an order to all Army field officers to send him Indian skeletons. This was done so that studies could be performed to determine whether the Indian was inferior to the white man due to the size of the Indian's cranium. This action, along with an attitude that accepted the desecration of countless Native American burial sites, resulted in hundreds of thousands [of] Native American human remains and funerary objects being sold or housed in museums and educational institutions around the [country].

[47] Native American Graves Protection and Repatriation Act of 1990, 25 U.S.C. §§ 3001–3013.

> For many years, Indian tribes have attempted to have the remains and funerary objects of their ancestors returned to them. This effort has touched off an often heated debate on the rights of the Indian versus the importance to museums of the retention of their collections and the scientific value of the items.[48]

Thomas Jefferson was perhaps the first to document the excavation of a Native American burial mound. In 1788, Jefferson opened a burial mound near Monticello and of it wrote: "I conjectured that in this barrow might have been a thousand skeletons."[49] The ideological framework for these excavations and studies denied any affiliation between the earliest inhabitants of the Americas and modern Native Americans, who were believed to be degraded and inferior latecomers. As Patty Gerstenblith has written:

> The burial mounds and antiquities found on the American continent were not thought to be associated with the living Native Americans but rather the product of either a past civilization of the Old World or an extinct group of Indians who were clearly superior to the modern Indians.[50]

In the late 18th and early to mid-19th centuries, collecting of Native American culture focused primarily on human remains and burial objects. But "[i]n the post Civil War years, the study of [the] Indian shifted in focus. In archaeology, rather than a search for Indian racial origins, the emphasis now was on early human inhabitation in the Americas and on museum collecting."[51] Many of the most prominent collecting institutions—including the Smithsonian Institution (1846), the Peabody Museum (Harvard) (1856), the American Museum of Natural History (1869), and the Field Museum (1893)—were founded in this period, and with them the disciplines of anthology and archaeology.[52] In 1876, the Smithsonian's Bureau of American Ethnology sponsored the first large-scale collecting expedition to the pueblos of New Mexico and Arizona.

---

48 H.R. Rep. No. 101-877 (1990), reprinted in 1990 U.S.C.C.A.N. 4367, 4367–68.

49 THOMAS JEFFERSON, NOTES ON THE STATE OF VIRGINIA 92–96 (1964).

50 PATTY GERSTENBLITH, ART, CULTURAL HERITAGE, AND THE LAW 871 (3d ed. 2012).

51 ROBERT E. BEIDER, A BRIEF HISTORICAL SURVEY OF THE EXPROPRIATION OF AMERICAN INDIAN REMAINS 23 (1990), *available at* http://www.narf.org/nill/documents/NARF_bieder_remains.pdf.

52 For a discussion of evolving relations between museums and Native Americans, *see, e.g.*, AMY LONETREE, DECOLONIZING MUSEUMS: REPRESENTING NATIVE AMERICA IN NATIONAL AND TRIBAL MUSEUMS (2012).

It has been "commonplace for public agencies to treat Native American dead as archaeological resources, property, pathological material, data, specimens, or library books, but not as human beings."[53]

As Janet Berlo observed, "Our constructs of what comprises Indian art was largely molded by these institutions and their collecting policies."[54] The leading figures of the period, sought out the "oldest" objects, which they interpreted as being the "most authentic."

Jonathan King wrote:

> Most of the principal North American collections of Indian artifacts were created between 1860 and 1930, in large museums in eastern and central North America. It is inevitable, therefore, that most of the standards by which traditionalism in Indian art is judged depend upon these collections for purposes of definition and comparison. The late nineteenth and early twentieth centuries, however, saw enormous upheavals in Indian North America. . . . And ironically, this was the peak period of collecting. As a result, the most traumatic period in Native American history has provided the material basis for the definition of what is traditional and what is not. Basketry, bead costume, and carving from this time exist in such large quantities that they are used as a general, though unstated, yardstick by which the unconscious standards of traditionalism are set.[55]

b. NAGPRA

In 1979, Congress was presented with the report of a study mandated by the American Religious Freedom Act, which identified the frequently illegitimate means by which many Native American objects had been obtained. The report stated:

> Museum records show that some sacred objects were sold by their original Native owner or owners. In many instances, however, the chain of title does not lead to the original owners. Some religious property left the original ownership during military confrontations, was included in the spoils of war and eventually fell to the control of museums. Also in

[53] Jack F. Trope and Walter R. Echo-Hawk, *The Native American Graves Protection and Repatriation Act: Background and Legislative History*, 24 ARIZ. ST. L.J. 35, 43 (Spring 1992).
[54] *Id.*
[55] *Id.*

> times past, sacred objects were lost by Native owners as a result of less violent pressures exerted by federally-sponsored missionaries and Indian agents.
>
> Most sacred objects were stolen from their original owners. In other cases, religious property was converted and sold by Native people who did not have ownership or title to the sacred object.
>
> Today, in many parts of the country, it is common for 'pothunters' to enter Indian and public lands for the purpose of illegally expropriating sacred objects. Interstate trafficking in and exporting of such property flourishes, with some of these sacred objects eventually entering into the possession of museums.[56]

Soon thereafter, "a number of Northern Cheyenne leaders discovered that almost 18,500 human remains were warehoused in the Smithsonian Institution. This discovery served as a catalyst for a concerted national effort by Indian tribes and organizations to obtain legislation to repatriate human remains and cultural artifacts to Indian tribes and descendants of the deceased. Between 1986 and 1990, a number of bills were introduced in the 99th, 100th, and 101st Congresses to address this issue."[57] NAGPRA was enacted in November 1990.

NAGPRA is addressed to the rights of Native American lineal descendants, Indian tribes, and Native Hawaiian organizations concerning the treatment, repatriation, and disposition of specific classes of "cultural items," which are defined as follows:

- Human remains[58]
- Associated funerary objects ("objects that, as a part of the death rite or ceremony of a culture, are reasonably believed to have been placed with human remains either at the time of death or later, and both the human remains and associated objects are presently in the possession or control of a Federal agency or museum, except that other items exclusively made for burial purposes or to contain human remains shall be considered as associated funerary objects"[59])

---

[56] *Id.* at 44 (quoting Secretary of the Interior Fed. Agencies Task Force, Am. Indian Religious Freedom Act Rep. 77, Aug. 1979. The report to Congress was required by § 2 of the American Indian Religious Freedom Act. 42 U.S.C. § 1996.

[57] *Id.* at 54–55.

[58] 25 U.S.C. § 3001(3).

[59] 25 U.S.C. § 3001(3)(A).

- Unassociated funerary objects ("objects that, as a part of the death rite or ceremony of a culture, are reasonably believed to have been placed with individual human remains either at the time of death or later, where the remains are not in the possession or control of the Federal agency or museum and the objects can be identified by a preponderance of the evidence as related to specific individuals or families or to known human remains or, by a preponderance of the evidence, as having been removed from a specific burial site of an individual culturally affiliated with a particular Indian tribe")[60]
- Sacred objects ("specific ceremonial objects which are needed by traditional Native American religious leaders for the practice of traditional Native American religions by their present day adherents")[61]
- Cultural patrimony ("an object having ongoing historical, traditional, or cultural importance central to the Native American group or culture itself, rather than property owned by an individual Native American, and which, therefore, cannot be alienated, appropriated, or conveyed by any individual regardless of whether or not the individual is a member of the Indian tribe or Native Hawaiian organization and such object shall have been considered inalienable by such Native American group at the time the object was separated from such group")[62]

NAGPRA requires that federal agencies and museums receiving federal funds produce an inventory of their holdings of Native American human remains and funerary objects[63] and produce written summaries of other Native American cultural items.[64] The agencies and museums must consult with Indian tribes and Native Hawaiian organizations to attempt to reach agreements on the repatriation or other disposition of these remains and objects. Once lineal descent or cultural affiliation has been established, and in some cases the right of possession also has been demonstrated, lineal descendants, affiliated Indian Tribes, or affiliated Native Hawaiian organizations normally make the final determination about the disposition of cultural items. Disposition may take many forms from

[60] 25 U.S.C. § 3001(3)(B).
[61] 25 U.S.C. § 3001(3)(C).
[62] 25 U.S.C. § 3001(3)(D).
[63] 25 U.S.C. § 3003.
[64] 25 U.S.C. § 3004.

reburial to long-term curation, according to the wishes of the lineal descendent(s) or culturally affiliated Tribe(s).

The second major purpose of the statute is to provide greater protection for Native American burial sites and more careful control over the removal of Native American human remains, funerary objects, sacred objects, and items of cultural patrimony on federal and tribal lands. NAGPRA requires that Indian tribes or Native Hawaiian organizations be consulted whenever archeological investigations encounter, or are expected to encounter, Native American cultural items or when such items are unexpectedly discovered on federal or tribal lands (Section 3). Excavation or removal of any such items also must be done under procedures required by the Archaeological Resources Protection Act (Sec. 3 (c)(1)). This NAGPRA requirement is likely to encourage the in situ preservation of archaeological sites, or at least the portions of them that contain burials or other kinds of cultural items. In many situations, it will be advantageous for federal agencies and tribes undertaking land-modifying activities on their lands to undertake careful consultations with traditional users of the land and intensive archeological surveys to locate and then protect unmarked Native American graves, cemeteries, or other places where cultural items might be located.

Other provisions of NAGPRA include the following:

- NAGPRA stipulates that illegal trafficking in human remains and cultural items may result in criminal penalties (Section 4).
- NAGPRA authorizes the Secretary of the Interior to administer a grants program to assist museums and Indian tribes in complying with certain requirements of the statute (Section 10).
- NAGPRA requires the Secretary of the Interior to establish a review committee to provide advice and assistance in carrying out key provisions of the statute (Section 8).
- NAGPRA authorizes the Secretary of the Interior to penalize museums that fail to comply with the statute (Section 9).
- NAGPRA directs the Secretary to develop regulations in consultation with this review committee (Section 13).

"Cultural affiliation" is a key concept for implementing this statute; it is a cornerstone for repatriation requests and for asserting claims related to new discoveries on federal or tribal land. The statute defines cultural affiliation as a relationship of shared group identity which can be reasonably traced historically or prehistorically between a present day Indian tribe or Native Hawaiian organization and an identifiable earlier group (Sec. 2(2)).

c. Kennewick Man and the Definition of "Native American"

In 1996, several teens found a human skull and bones along the shore of the Columbia River outside Kennewick, Washington. Because the remains, subsequently referred to as "Kennewick Man," were discovered on federal land, they were sent to an anthropologist for analysis, consistent with the provisions of ARPA. Kennewick Man was excavated pursuant to a permit issued under ARPA.[65]

Because of physical characteristics—the shape of the skull and facial bones—scientists initially believed the remains were the remains of an early European settler. However, radiocarbon dating showed the remains to be approximately 9,000 years old.[66]

Five tribal groups from the area around the Columbia River opposed further scientific study of the remains and demanded, pursuant to NAGPRA, that the remains be turned over to the tribes for reburial. The U.S. Army Corps of Engineers, which controls the federal lands on which the remains were found, agreed with the tribes and seized the remains, intending to return them to the tribes for reburial.

A group of scientists requested that the U.S. Army Corps of Engineers postpone reinterment of Kennewick Man and allow qualified scientists to examine the remains, arguing:

> Human skeletons this old are extremely rare in the Western Hemisphere, and most found to date have consisted of very fragmented remains. Here, by contrast, almost 90% of this man's bones were recovered in relatively good condition, making "Kennewick Man" . . . one of the most complete early Holocene human skeletons ever recovered in the Western Hemisphere.[67]

---

[65] *See* Bonnichsen v. U.S., 217 F.Supp.2d 1116, 1166 (D. Ore. 2002).

[66] For a description of the initial analysis, see James C. Chatters, *Kennewick Man, available at* https://www.mnh.si.edu/arctic/html/kennewick_man.html.

[67] Bonnichsen v. U.S., 217 F.Supp.2d 1116, 1120–1121 (D. Ore. 2002).

The scientists received no response, and so filed suit in the United States District Court for the District of Oregon for, among other things, a finding that Kennewick Man was not "Native American" within the meaning of NAGPRA, and that therefore the repatriation requirements of NAGPRA did not apply. In 2002, the district court held in favor of the scientists:

> The physical features of the Kennewick Man appear to be dissimilar to all modern American Indians, including the Tribal Claimants. That does not preclude the possibility of a relationship between the two. However, absent a satisfactory explanation for those differences, it does make such a relationship less likely, and suggests that the Kennewick Man might have been part of a group that did not survive or whose remaining members were integrated into another group. . . . NAGPRA was intended to reunite tribes with remains or cultural items whose affiliation was known, or could be reasonably ascertained. At best, we can only speculate as to the possible group affiliation of the Kennewick Man, whether his group even survived for very long after his death, and whether that group is related to any of the Tribal Claimants.[68]

The U.S. Army Corps of Engineers and the tribal claimants appealed the decision, and in April 2004, the United States Court of Appeals for the Ninth Circuit issued its decision, affirming the district court's decision. The Ninth Circuit read the plain language of NAGPRA—and particularly its definition of "Native American"—to require that discovered human remains have a relationship to a presenting existing tribe.

The court noted that:

> NAGPRA vests "ownership or control" of newly discovered Native American human remains in the decedent's lineal descendants or, if lineal descendants cannot be ascertained, in a tribe "affiliated" with the remains. . . . NAGPRA mandates a two-part analysis. The first inquiry is whether human remains are Native American within the statute's meaning. If the remains *are not* Native American, then NAGPRA does not apply. However, if the remains are Native American, the NAGPRA applies, triggering the second inquiry of determining which persons or tribes are most closely affiliated with the remains.[69]

---

68 *Id.* at 1146–1147.

69 Bonnichsen v. U.S., 367 F.3d 864, 875 (9th Cir. 2004).

The court further observed that:

> NAGPRA defines human remains as "Native American" if the remains are "of, or relating to, a tribe, people, or culture that is indigenous to the United States." . . . The text of the relevant statutory clause is written in the present tense ("of, or relating to, a tribe, people, or culture *that is* indigenous"). Thus the statute unambiguously requires that human remains bear some relationship to a *presently existing* tribe, people, or culture to be considered Native American.[70]

The Ninth Circuit concluded:

> Because Kennewick Man's remains are so old and the information about his era so limited, the record does not permit the Secretary to conclude reasonably that Kennewick Man shares special and significant genetic or cultural features with presently existing indigenous tribes, people, or cultures. We thus hold that Kennewick Man's remains are not Native American human remains within the meaning of NAGPRA and that NAGPRA does not apply to them. Studies of the Kennewick Man's remains by Plaintiffs-scientists may proceed pursuant to ARPA.[71]

The court contrasted the definition of "Native American" with the definition of "Native Hawaiian," which is "any individual who is a descendant of the aboriginal people who, prior to 1778, occupied and exercised sovereignty in the area that now constitutes the State of Hawaii." The court reasoned that:

> The "United States" is a political entity that dates back to 1789. . . . This term supports that Congress's use of the present tense ("that is indigenous") referred to tribes, peoples, and cultures that exist in modern times, not to those that may have existed thousands of years ago but who do not exist now. By contrast, when Congress chose to harken back to earlier times, it described a geographic location ("the area that now constitutes the State of Hawaii") rather than a political entity ("the United States").[72]

---

[70] *Id.*
[71] *Id.* at 882.
[72] *Id.* at 878–879.

In 2007, Senators Byron L. Dorgan (D-N.D.) and John McCain (R-Ariz.) introduced the Native American Omnibus Technical Corrections Act of 2007,[73] which, among other things, would have revised NAGPRA's definition of "Native American." The revised definition would have read:

> "Native American" means of, or relating to, a tribe, people, or culture that is *or was* indigenous to *any geographic area that is now located within the boundaries of* the United States. (additions italicized)

The bill, however, was never enacted, and NAGPRA's original definition of "Native American" remains as it was.

However, nearly two decades after Kennewick Man's discovery, facts outstripped the evidence available to the Ninth Circuit. In June 2015, Danish geneticist Dr. Eske Willerslev and his colleagues at the University of Copenhagen published in the scientific journal *Nature* the results of their genetic sequencing of Kennewick Man's genome, concluding that the remains are more closely related to modern Native Americans than to any other living population.[74] More particularly, genetic testing shows that Kennewick Man is most closely related to the Colville Tribe, one of the original tribal claimants. The Kennewick Man results further support the Willersley team's 2014 study of the sole existing Clovis skeleton. The Clovis people were early inhabitants of the Americas, 13,000 years ago. They are known chiefly from their distinctive tools, which are found across the continental United States. The only skeleton to be discovered to date in association with Clovis Sites is a boy discovered at the Anzick Site in Montana in 1969, who is 12,600 years old. Willersley's study shows that Clovis people are also ancestors to contemporary Native Americans.[75] Willersley's study of the Anzick Clovis boy was undertaken in consultation with Native American tribes from the area around the Anzick Site, and, with the confirmation of affiliation that the study provides, the

---

[73] S. 2087, 110th Congress (2007–2008), *available at* https://www.congress.gov/bill/110th-congress/senate-bill/2087.

[74] Ewen Callaway, *Ancient American Genome Rekindle Legal Row*, NATURE (June 18, 2015), *available at* http://www.nature.com/news/ancient-american-genome-rekindles-legal-row-1.17797.

[75] *See, e.g.*, *America's Only Clovis Skeleton Had Its Genome Mapped* (Feb. 12, 2014), *available at* http://news.ku.dk/all_news/2014/02/americas-only-clovis-skeleton-had-its-genome-mapped; Richard Harris, *Ancient DNA Ties Native Americans from Two Continents to Clovis* (Feb. 13, 2014), *NPR, Morning Edition*, *available at* http://www.npr.org/2014/02/13/276021092/ancient-dna-ties-native-americans-from-two-continents-to-clovis.

decision was made to repatriate the Anzick Clovis boy to the tribes for reinterment.

At the present time, the future of Kennewick Man is uncertain. He remains in the custodial care of the Burke Museum in Seattle, where he has been since 1999, under a curatorial services agreement with the U.S. Army Corps of Engineers.[76]

d. The Whale House Artifacts and Express Nonalienation

Because NAGPRA does not reach Native American cultural items held by private individuals or entities, repatriation of such cultural items requires multiple methods of approach, both legal and nonlegal. Typically, successful repatriation of Native American cultural items from private parties requires a combination of the canny use of publicity with legal and moral arguments. Where applicable, it is important to establish common tribal ownership or the nonalienability of cultural items. If a cultural item cannot be alienated or requires the authorization of the tribe or tribal authorities before being alienated, then removal or sale of such items is wrongful and return justified. However, given the complex history of collecting and removal of Native American cultural items, establishing individual or tribal ownership is often difficult.

The removal and ultimate return of the Klukwan Whale House artifacts exemplifies this challenge. The artifacts, consisting of four intricately carved and ornamented house posts and a rain screen, were created around 1820 in the Alaskan Chilkat Indian Village of Klukwan. The Tlingit leader Xetsuwu resolved to build a new house (Whale House) to unify existing house groups of the Ganexteidi Clan. He commissioned the house posts, which represent the four groups that were brought together to form the new Whale House. Together with the rain screen, the house posts tell stories of the clan. The artifacts and the Whale House itself were created and dedicated in the traditional manner. The Ganexteidi hired another clan, the Eagles, to construct the original house. The Eagles were then repaid in a traditional "payback party," and the property was brought out in a potlatch and dedicated as clan property.[77]

The Whale House artifacts have long been identified as the finest examples of Native American art in Alaska, and collectors and museums

[76] *See* http://www.burkemuseum.org/kennewickman.

[77] Chilkat Indian Village, Ira v. Johnson, No. 90-01, *17–18 (Chilkat Tr. Ct., Nov. 3, 1993), *available at* http://www.ankn.uaf.edu/curriculum/tlingit/chilkatindianvillage/.

have sought to acquire them. The University of Pennsylvania Museum of Archaeology and Anthropology offered to purchase the artifacts in 1922, but the tribe refused to sell.[78] In the mid-1970s, the Arizona art dealer Michael Johnson twice attempted to acquire the artifacts. Tribal concern over those attempts resulted in the Chilkat Indian Village Council, the governing body of the Village under the Village's IRA-authorized constitution, enacting an ordinance prohibiting the removal of artifacts from Klukwan in 1976. That ordinance provided:

> No person shall enter on to the property of the Chilkat Indian Village for the purpose of buying, trading for, soliciting the purchase of, or otherwise seeking to arrange the removal of artifacts, clan crests, or other traditional Indian art work owned or held by members of the Chilkat Indian Village or kept within the boundaries of the real property owned by the Chilkat Indian Village, without first requesting and obtaining permission to do so from the Chilkat Indian Village Council.
>
> No traditional Indian artifacts, clan crests, or other Indian art works of any kind may be removed from the Chilkat Indian Village without the prior notification of and approval by the Chilkat Indian Village Council. Chilkat Indian Village Council Ordinance of May 12, 1976.[79]

As noted, "On April 22, 1984, several defendants removed the four posts and the rain screen from Klukwan and delivered them to defendant Michael Johnson, an Arizona art dealer. When the Village discovered that the artifacts had been removed, it notified authorities of the State of Alaska. The State began a criminal investigation, located the artifacts in a warehouse in Seattle, Washington, and took custody of the artifacts."[80] The Village filed suit against Johnson and several tribe members who had assisted him in the United States district court for the District of Oregon, seeking to enforce the ordinance. The district court held that enforcement of tribal law against tribe members did not give rise to federal jurisdiction, although enforcement against Johnson, a non-tribe-member, did. It noted that:

---

[78] *Id.* at 18.

[79] Chilkat Indian Village v. Johnson, 870 F.2d 1469, 1471 (9th Cir. 1989).

[80] *Id.*

> The court agrees with the plaintiff in that the power to pass the ordinance that is in dispute in this case was part of the retained, inherent power of the Chilkat Indian Village. In addition, it would appear that under its constitutional power, Chilkat Indian Village had the power to prevent the sale or disposition of any assets of the Village without the consent of the Council. The court further agrees that alleged acquisition by a non-Indian of the artifacts in question would constitute conduct that would have some direct effect on the welfare of the tribe. Slip op. at 13-14 (Oct. 9, 1990).[81]

The district court "submitted all issues pending in the case, including challenges to tribal jurisdiction as well as the merits of the tribe's claims that Johnson and his corporation violated the tribal ordinance" to the Chilkat Indian Village Tribal Court.[82] As a preliminary matter, the tribal court noted that "[t]he law applicable in this tribal court action is tribal law, which is comprised of both written and unwritten, custom law of the village."[83] After hearing testimony, the tribal court found that the Whale House artifacts were:

> "clan trust property," which great spiritual significance to the Ganexteidi Clan, which has primary custodial rights over them. . . . [P]roperty is confirmed as being clan trust property . . . [by] presenting it in a ceremony in which members of the opposite "tribe" (i.e., in this case members of clans of the Eagle moiety) are invited, which completes the confirmation of the clan trust status of property such as the Whale House artifacts, which . . . were subject to this process. . . . Under Tlingit law, such objects cannot be sold, unless for some reason (such as restitution for a crime) the entire clan decides to do so.[84]

Because the artifacts were clan trust property and could not be removed without authorization from the Chilkat Indian Village Council, the court held that the removal was illegal, and ordered that the artifacts be returned to Klukwan.

---

[81] Chilkat Indian Village, IRA v. Johnson, No. 90-01, *3 (Chilkat Tr. Ct., Nov. 3, 1993), *available at* http://www.ankn.uaf.edu/curriculum/tlingit/chilkatindianvillage.

[82] *Id.*

[83] *Id.* at *4.

[84] *Id.* at *7–13.

e. The Paris Hopi Auctions

In recent years, several Parisian auctions of Native American sacred objects[85] have highlighted the challenges for repatriation claims against private parties, particularly in cross-border contexts. The Paris auctions were by private parties, complicated by the cross-border aspect. NAGPRA could not apply. The tribal claimants sought to halt the auctions, or at least postpone them to allow time for a more complete investigation of the circumstances of the Katsinam's ownership. Their efforts were hampered by the auction house's refusal to disclose the name of the consignor and the presumption under French law that the owner of a good is acting in good faith absent evidence to the contrary. The tribal claimants brought international public opinion to bear and attempted to engage the United States and French governments to convince the auction house to negotiate with the tribes.

LeRoy N. Shinoitewa, Chairman, Hopi Tribe, wrote to the auction house, setting out the tribe's concerns and requesting postponement of the auction:

> These Katsinam, or friends, as the Hopi call them, represent the spirit of deceased ancestors, animals, natural features and events, and various deities. They are used by Hopis in connection with prayers and ceremonies in which Hopi religious leaders perform their trust obligation to protect the world. . . . At this stage in the Hopi investigation—which is nowhere near complete—potential buyers at your auction must be informed that the Hopi Tribe suspects that the items you are offering for sale are stolen religious patrimony and may not be purchased or transferred without violating United States, international and French norms. At a minimum potential purchasers need to understand that, in purchasing these objects, they run the risk of participating in illegality.[86]

The auction house refused the tribe's request, and the French *Conseil des ventes volontaires* denied the tribe's request for a temporary restraining order. The court held that it was not shown (1) that the Hopi tribal council authorized the lawsuit, (2) that any French law prohibited the sale of sacred objects when held by private persons, (3) that any U.S. law

---

85 See the Katsinam sale catalog, *available at* http://keridouglas.files.wordpress.com/2013/04/neretminet-12042013-bd.pdf.

86 Letter from LeRoy N. Shinoitewa, Chairman, Hopi Tribe to Gilles Neret-Minet, April 4, 2013.

prohibits the sale of Native American sacred objects when held by private persons, or (4) that the objects were obtained by illegal means.

The auctions proceeded. At auction, the Annenberg Foundation was the successful purchaser of certain objects and repatriated the objects to the tribes.[87] Subsequent Parisian auctions of Native American cultural items have also proceeded; however, several contested items that had been slated to be included in a May 2016 auction were removed following protests, including an Acoma shield that was believed to have been illegally acquired in the 1970s.[88] In a significant deviation from past experience with French auctions of Native American cultural property, on August 31, 2016, a judge of the United States District Court for the District of New Mexico issued a warrant for the in rem arrest of the Acoma shield.

In response to these auctions and the illicit trafficking in Native American cultural objects more generally, on March 2, 2016, Rep. Stevan Pearce (R-NM) introduced in the United States House of Representatives Congressional Resolution 122,[89] titled the Protection of the Right of Tribes to Stop the Export of Cultural and Traditional Patrimony Resolution (or the "PROTECT Patrimony Resolution"), which (1) condemns the theft, illegal possession or sale, transfer, and export of tribal cultural items, (2) calls upon the United States Departments of the Interior, State, Commerce, Homeland Security, and the Attorney General "to consult with tribes and traditional Native American religious leaders in addressing this important issue, to take affirmative action to stop these illegal practices, and to secure repatriation of tribal cultural items to tribes," (3) calls upon the Comptroller General to conduct a study of the scope of illegal trafficking in tribal cultural items and steps necessary to end such trafficking and to secure repatriation to tribes, (4) supports "the development of explicit restrictions on the export of tribal cultural items," and (5) encourages state and local governments to work cooperatively to deter illegal trafficking in tribal cultural items and in repatriating tribal cultural items. A corresponding Senate resolution was introduced by Sen. Tom

---

[87] *See Annenberg Foundation and Hopi Nation Announce Return of Sacred Artifacts to Native American Hopi Tribe* (December 2013), *available at* http://www.annenbergfoundation.org/node/51351.

[88] *See Andrew Westney, NM Judge Issues Warrant To Seize Tribal Shield, Law360 (Aug. 31, 2016); Allison Meier, US Judge Approves Warrant for Acoma Shield Listed for Sale by Paris Auction House, Hyperallergic (Sept. 7, 2016); see also* Allison Meier, *Smithsonian Hosts Emergency Meeting About Paris Auction of Indigenous Remains and Objects*, HYPERALLERGIC (May 24, 2016), *available at* http://hyperallergic.com/301031/smithsonian-hosts-emergency-meeting-about-paris-auction-of-indigenous-remains-and-objects.

[89] H.Con.Res 122–114th Congress (2015–2016), *available at* https://www.congress.gov/bill/114th-congress/house-concurrent-resolution/122/text.

Udall (D-NM) on July 14, 2016.[90] The House Resolution was referred to the House Subcommittee on Crime, Terrorism, Homeland Security, and Investigations, and the Senate Resolution was referred to the Senate Committee on Indian Affairs.

G. Illicit Excavation and Export and the Market

The tension between past trade, collector, and museum practices and international efforts to combat the illicit excavation and/or exportation of cultural property (particularly archaeological and ethnographic objects) reached a dramatic flashpoint in the late 1990s and early 2000s, in the aftermath of a raid on two Swiss warehouses used by the antiquities dealers Robert Hecht[91] and Giacomo Medici.[92] The raid and subsequent investigation produced photographs showing recently excavated antiquities (many still covered in earth) and documents tracing a network of illicit diggers, smugglers, middlemen, and dealers through which the objects were extracted from the countries of origin—in this case, chiefly Italy—and laundered into the mainstream antiquities trade. Ultimately, a number of pieces that had been handled by Hecht and Medici were in major private collections, as well as the collections of major United States and European museums.

As a result of the investigation, the Metropolitan Museum of Art returned a number of objects to Italy, including the *Euphronios Krater*,[93] which the museum had purchased from Hecht in 1972 for $1.2 million. Other museums similarly returned objects that were shown to have been looted. The J. Paul Getty Museum not only returned objects, but its curator of antiquities, Marion True,[94] was indicted by an Italian court and

---

[90] S.Con.Res. 49–114th Congress (2015–2016), *available at* https://www.congress.gov/bill/114th-congress/senate-concurrent-resolution/49/related-bills.

[91] Bruce Weber, *Robert Hecht, Antiquities Dealer, Dies at 92*, THE NEW YORK TIMES (Feb. 9, 2012), *available at* http://www.nytimes.com/2012/02/10/arts/design/robert-hecht-antiquities-dealer-dies-at-92.html?_r=0.

[92] *Antiquities Dealer's Conviction Stands*, LOS ANGELES TIMES (July 16, 2009), *available at* http://articles.latimes.com/2009/jul/16/entertainment/et-quick16.S2.

[93] Elisabetta Polovedo, *Ancient Vase Comes Home to a Hero's Welcome*, THE NEW YORK TIMES (Jan. 19, 2008), *available at* http://www.nytimes.com/2008/01/19/arts/design/19bowl.html.

[94] Hugh Eakin, *Marion True on Her Trial and Ordeal*, THE NEW YORKER (Oct. 14, 2010), *available at* http://www.newyorker.com/news/news-desk/marion-true-on-her-trial-and-ordeal; *see also* Elisabetta Povoledo, *Case Involving Former Curator Marion True Ends*, THE NEW YORK TIMES (Oct. 13, 2010), *available at* http://artsbeat.blogs.nytimes.com/2010/10/13/case-involving-former-curator-marion-true-ends; Thomas R. Kline, *The Fall and Rise of Marion True and the Getty Museum*, 13 IFAR J. 1, 54 (2012) (review of JASON FELCH & RALPH FRAMMOLINO, CHASING APHRODITE: THE HUNT FOR LOOTED ANTIQUITIES AT THE WORLD'S RICHEST MUSEUM (2011)); Hugh Eakin, *What Went Wrong at the Getty*, THE NEW YORK REVIEW OF BOOKS (June 23, 2011).

stood trial for "conspiracy [with Hecht] to traffic in tens of millions of dollars' worth of looted Greek vases, Etruscan bronzes, terracottas, and other objects."[95] Hecht died before the trial concluded, and the charges against True were eventually dismissed[96] after the applicable statute of limitations lapsed.

Following the Hecht-Medici matter, museums instituted more stringent collecting policies for antiquities, typically requiring evidence that any object the museum was to acquire had been outside of its country of origin (the country of its modern discovery or excavation) before entry into force of the 1970 UNESCO Convention.

H. Whose Culture? The Parthenon Debate

In the area of cultural property, it was common practice for millennia for invading or occupying powers to take as plunder or tribute the cultural treasures of the vanquished.[97] An international legal norm against these types of takings only began to emerge in the mid-19th century and even then it was the early 20th century before those norms crystalized into generally accepted (and enforceable) international legal rules (even so, it applied only to destruction or plunder of cultural property during periods of armed conflict, and said nothing of the protection of cultural property during peacetime). Inevitably, many public and private collections around the world contain objects that were removed—perhaps more than once—during this long age of plunder.[98]

As the late Prof. John Henry Merryman observed:

> Aggressive art imperialism became institutionalized under the Romans, beginning with the looting of cultural property by Roman forces in the

---

[95] Hugh Eakin, *Treasure Hunt: The Downfall of the Getty Curator Marion True*, THE NEW YORKER (Dec. 17, 2007), *available at* http://www.newyorker.com/magazine/2007/12/17/treasure-hunt-3.

[96] Hugh Eakin, *Marion True on Her Trial and Ordeal*, THE NEW YORKER (Oct. 14, 2010), *available at* http://www.newyorker.com/news/news-desk/marion-true-on-her-trial-and-ordeal.

[97] The late Prof. John Henry Merryman of Stanford Law School described such historical practices as "aggressive art imperialism" and "aggressive art acquisition." JOHN HENRY MERRYMAN, IMPERIALISM, ART AND RESTITUTION 4–5 (2006).

[98] For a discussion of the changing norms concerning the plunder of cultural property, see WAYNE SANDHOLTZ, PROHIBITING PLUNDER: HOW NORMS CHANGE (2007); CRAIG FORREST, INTERNATIONAL LAW AND THE PROTECTION OF CULTURAL HERITAGE (2010); COLIN RENFREW, LOOT, LEGITIMACY AND OWNERSHIP (2000); and THE ACQUISITION AND EXHIBITION OF CULTURAL ANTIQUITIES: PROFESSIONAL, LEGAL AND ETHICAL PERSPECTIVES (2007).

> sack of Veii, 'the richest and most powerful city of the Etruscan nation,' in 396 B.C. . . . The art was desired for itself but also for its role in political triumphalism: the practice of prominently displaying loot on the return to Rome in order to stimulate public admiration for the generals and their legions and public approval and support for the imperial enterprise. Many of these triumphal objects were displayed in the Roman Forum, which became the world's first great outdoor art museum.
>
> The same pattern was followed in the Eastern Empire.[99]

One of the earliest artworks documented to have been plundered is a victory stele of Naram-Sin of Akkadia,[100] which was erected in the city of Sippar to commemorate a victory in battle in ca. 2250 B.C.E. When the Elamites[101] conquered the area in ca. 1158 B.C.E., they carried off the stele as war booty, erecting it in their own city of Susa, in the territory of present-day Iran, and adding to it an inscription recording King Shutruk-Nahhunte I's victory.[102] In Jerusalem, the Temple of Solomon was looted and burned in 586 B.C.E., rebuilt a generation later, only to be sacked and destroyed by the Romans under the Emperor Titus in 70 C.E.[103] A panel on the Arch of Titus in the Roman Forum shows soldiers carrying off the treasures of the Second Temple.[104]

However, the removal of cultural property in this time was not simple destruction. The four horses that famously adorn the entrance to St. Mark's Basilica[105] may cast some light on how complex the issues surrounding cultural objects taken in this manner can be. The horses were taken from Constantinople as trophies during the Fourth Crusade in the 13th century. However, it is likely that they were already in Constantinople as loot, brought there by Constantine from any of three possible locations.[106] The horses were in turn taken from Venice by Napoleon and transported to Paris, along with many objects taken from areas his armies conquered. Venice is hardly alone in having incorporated plundered works

---

99 John Henry Merryman, *supra*, at 4–5.

100 *See* http://www.louvre.fr/en/oeuvre-notices/victory-stele-naram-sin.

101 *See* http://www.ancient.eu/elam.

102 Margaret M. Miles, Art as Plunder: The Ancient Origins of Debate About Cultural Property 16 (2008).

103 *Id.* at 18–19.

104 *See, e.g.*, Elisabetta Polovedo, *Technology Lost Color at Roman Forum*, The New York Times (June 24, 2012), *available at* http://www.nytimes.com/2012/06/25/arts/design/menorah-on-arch-of-titus-in-roman-forum-was-rich-yellow.html?_r=0.

105 *See* http://www.basilicasanmarco.it/basilica/scultura/?lang=en.

106 *See* http://penelope.uchicago.edu/~grout/encyclopaedia_romana/circusmaximus/sanmarco.html.

into the fabric of the city. In fact, many of the world's cities are bricolages of objects from disparate cultures and eras, ineluctably hybrid. Rome is dotted with obelisks, many of which were taken from Egypt by Emperor Augustus and others following the defeat of Mark Antony and Cleopatra. The obelisks were repurposed in the 16th century by Pope Sixtus V, marking Christian sites in the rebuilt city. Some of these objects that had been ancient trophies of war became materials in the creation of new works of art. Gian Lorenzo Bernini's remarkable Elephant and Obelisk, for instance, modeled on a design from Francesco Colonna's *Hypnerotomachia Poliphilli* (1499) and erected in 1667 in the Piazza della Minerva in front of the Church of S. Maria sopra Minerva,[107] incorporates a small obelisk that had originally been erected in Lower Egypt by the Pharaoh Apries into the sculpture.[108]

1. The Napoleonic Wars and the Beginnings of Change

> At the end of the Napoleonic wars, the victorious allies required that the horses (and much of the art that Napoleon had plundered for the *Musée Français*, which would become the *Musée du Louvre*[109]) be returned to the countries from which they were taken. Like the horses of San Marco, Napoleon's forces also removed to Paris, among much else, the Laocoön[110] and the Apollo Belvedere[111] from the Vatican, the Ghent Altarpiece from Saint Bavo Cathedral in Ghent, Belgium.[112]

The return of cultural objects at the end of the Napoleonic wars was a harbinger of the normative shift to come. The massive dislocation of cultural property/national treasure during the Napoleonic wars brought a renewed focus and emphasis in the peace treaty negotiations in Paris in 1815 on the return of such removed objects. Lord Castlereagh, the British foreign minister engaged in the treaty negotiations, emphasized that the treaty must require the "return of statues, pictures, and other works of art" since "the States in question, one after another, had been systematically pillaged

---

107 *See* https://en.wikipedia.org/wiki/Santa_Maria_sopra_Minerva.

108 *See, e.g.*, William S. Heckscher, *Bernini's Elephant and Obelisk*, 29 THE ART BULLETIN 155–82 (September 1, 1947), *available at* http://www.collegeart.org/pdf/BerniniPDF3r.pdf.

109 *See* http://www.louvre.fr/en.

110 *See* http://mv.vatican.va/3_EN/pages/x-Schede/MPCs/MPCs_Sala02_03.html.

111 *See* http://mv.vatican.va/3_EN/pages/x-Schede/MPCs/MPCs_Sala02_01.html.

112 *See* http://www.getty.edu/foundation/initiatives/current/panelpaintings/panel_paintings_ghent.html.

by the former Revolutionary Government of France, in spite of all principles of justice and customs of modern war."[113] The Treaty of Paris, however, *did not* establish a rule in favor of the return of all removed cultural property. There was a notable preference for the rights of European states. Those that had been taken, for instance, from Egypt were not included in the treaty's scope, and so for the most part they were not returned.

As Prof. Merryman noted, with respect to the looting of art by the Third Reich:

> The international law of war, which had not prohibited aggressive military art-looting campaigns like that of Napoleon in Italy in the late eighteenth century or the British Punitive Expedition in Benin in 1897,[114] had radically changed by the time of the Nazis' enterprise. Their seizure of works of art in occupied countries violated an international law prohibition on the confiscation of private property by aggressive occupying powers. This was, by 1939, a customary international law norm that had been formalized in Art 46 of the 1907 Hague Convention (Hague IV) on the Laws of War and in the Kellogg-Briand Pact of 1928, to both of which Germany was a party.[115]

2. The Debate over the Parthenon Sculptures

Among disputes over removed cultural objects, perhaps few are better known than that concerning what were formerly known as the Elgin Marbles, which even the British Museum now prefers to call the Parthenon sculptures.[116] It is important to note at the outset, however, that even though the Parthenon sculptures were removed during this long age of plunder, they were not actually plundered. They were removed with the apparent permission of the government that had ruled the territory for four centuries. The source of the conflict over the sculptures is twofold: (1) Ottoman rule of the territory of modern Greece was in its final decades, and the movement in favor of Greek independence was on the rise (Greece would attain independence in 1832); and (2) the Parthenon,

---

113 Wojciech W. Kowalski, Art Treasures and War 23 (1998).

114 Jonathan Jones, *Spoils of War*, The Guardian (Sept. 11, 2003), *available at* http://www.theguardian.com/culture/2003/sep/11/2.

115 John Henry Merryman (ed.), Imperialism, Art and Restitution 7–8 (2006).

116 *See* http://www.britishmuseum.org/about_us/news_and_press/statements/parthenon_sculptures.aspx.

which even at the time had long been recognized as one of the finest examples of classical architecture and sculpture, became an important symbol of Greek independence and nationalism.

It is timely to consider the Parthenon sculptures as one example of how the past is sometimes not even past. The 200th anniversary of the British Museum's acquisition of the sculptures from Lord Elgin was commemorated in 2016. The sculptures comprise roughly 50 percent of the surviving sculptures from the temple, with the other half held by the Acropolis Museum in Athens.[117] Additionally, fragments from the Parthenon are held by several other museums, including the Musée du Louvre[118] and the Vatican Museums.[119] Some fragments have been returned to Greece, including those given by the University of Heidelberg[120] and a museum in Palermo, Sicily[121] (the Greek government then loaned this fragment back to Palermo).[122] The Vatican Museums loaned one of its fragments to the Acropolis Museum.[123]

The Parthenon[124] was constructed between 447 and 432 B.C.E. and is regarded as the exemplar of classical art and architecture at the height of Periclean Athens.[125] It was designed and built by the architects Ictinus and Callicrates under the supervision of the sculptor Phidias, and it originally served as a temple to Athena and as a symbol of Athenian civic life. Part of the temple was destroyed by fire in 195 B.C.E., with more destructive fires occurring with the invasion of the Germanic Heralic tribe in A.D. 267 and the Visigoth sack of Athens under Alaric in 396 C.E. In the 5th century C.E. it was transformed into a Greek Orthodox cathedral (Theotokos Atheniotica), then a Roman Catholic cathedral (Notre Dame d'Athenes) under the Franks in 1204; in 1458, under Ottoman rule, it was again transformed into a mosque. In 1687, the Parthenon was being used as a military center. During the bombardment of Athens by Venetian

117 *See* http://www.theacropolismuseum.gr/en/content/gallery-slopes-acropolis.

118 *See* http://www.louvre.fr/en/oeuvre-notices/tenth-metope-south-facade-parthenon.

119 *See* http://mv.vatican.va/3_EN/pages/x-Schede/MGPs/MGPs_Sala01_01.html.

120 *See* http://www.uni-heidelberg.de/press/news/news06/2601par_e.html. For more information about the Parthenon and its history, *see* Joan Breton Connelly, The Parthenon Enigma: A New Understanding of the West's Most Iconic Building and the People Who Made It (2014); James H.S. McGregor, Athens (2014); and Thomas R. Martin, Ancient Greece: From Prehistoric to Hellenistic Times (2013).

121 *See* http://www.telegraph.co.uk/news/worldnews/europe/greece/3074735/Italy-returns-Elgin-Marbles-fragment-to-Greece.html. For more information about Pericles and Periclean Athens, see Vincent Azoulay, Pericles of Athens (2014).

122 *See* http://news.bbc.co.uk/2/hi/europe/8620640.stm.

123 *See* http://news.bbc.co.uk/2/hi/europe/7717269.stm.

124 *See* http://www.britannica.com/topic/Parthenon.

125 *See* http://www.britannica.com/biography/Pericles-Athenian-statesman.

forces, a powder magazine located in the Parthenon suffered a hit, and the resulting explosion destroyed a large part of the structure. At the time of Lord Elgin's ambassadorship, the Parthenon was still being used by the Ottoman army, and was referred to as the "citadel."

Thomas Bruce, the seventh Earl of Elgin and the Eleventh Earl of Kincardine, was appointed British ambassador to the Sublime Porte (the Ottoman central government in Constantinople) in 1799. Lord Elgin engaged the painter Giovanni Lusieri[126] to supervise a team of artisans and workmen to travel to Athens to make drawings and plaster casts of Greek sculptures and architectural fragments.[127] Although Lord Elgin obtained a document from the Ottoman government (referred to as the "First Firman") giving his team access to the Parthenon, the access given was unsatisfactory. Lord Elgin's chaplain, the Rev. Philip Hunt, obtained a second document of permission. This document (referred to as the "Second Firman"),[128] which survives only in an Italian translation, directed local officials to allow Lord Elgin's team to (1) go in and out of the "citadel," (2) erect scaffolding, (3) make casts of sculptures and architectural features, (4) take measurements, (5) undertake necessary excavations "in search of inscriptions," and (6) take away any pieces of stone with inscriptions or figures ("*qualche pezzi di pietra con inscritzioni, e figure*").[129] Lord Elgin, Hunt, and others at the time describe these documents as "*firmans*," which were Ottoman legal documents issued directly by the

---

126 *See* http://www.getty.edu/art/collection/artists/819/giovanni-battista-lusieri-italian-about-1755-1821.

127 For more information about Lord Elgin's removal of the Parthenon sculptures, see WILLIAM ST. CLAIR, LORD ELGIN & THE MARBLES: THE CONTROVERSIAL HISTORY OF THE PARTHENON SCULPTURES (2003).

128 The British Museum acquired the Italian translation of the Second Firman as part of the Philip Hunt archive in 2005. In 2009, Dyfri Williams, of the museum's Greek and Roman Department, published an extensive and important analysis of the Second Firman and its historical context, *Lord Elgin's Firman,* JOURNAL OF THE HISTORY OF COLLECTIONS 1–28 (2009). Images of the pages of the Second Firman from the Hunt Archive may be viewed on the British Museum website, *available at* http://www.britishmuseum.org/research/collection_online/collection_object_details/collection_image_gallery.aspx?partid=1&assetid=259656001&objectid=3008350.

129 The relevant language (in the English translation that was appended to the *House of Commons Select Committee on the Earl of Elgin's Collection of Sculptured Marbles & C., Report*, 25 March 1816) reads: "It is our desire that on the arrival of this Letter you use your diligence to act conformably to the instances of the said Ambassador, as long as the said five Artists dwelling at Athens shall be employed in going in and out of the said citadel of Athens,...; or in fixing scaffolding around the ancient Temple of the Idols, or in modelling with chalk or gypsum the said ornaments and visible figures thereon; or in measuring the fragments and vestiges of other ruined edifices; or in excavating, when they find it necessary, the foundations, in search of inscriptions among the rubbish; that they be not molested by the said Disdar (or commandant of the citadel) nor by any other persons, nor even by you (to whom this letter is addressed;) and that no one meddle with their scaffolding or implements, nor hinder them from taking away any pieces of stone with inscriptions or figures."

Sultan. As we will see, some scholars have challenged that designation and the claim of legal authority associated with it.

For some, Lord Elgin's removal of the sculptures from Athens was controversial. Lord Byron, a proponent of Greek nationalism and independence, loudly protested the removals, pillorying Lord Elgin in "The Curse of Minerva" (1811):

> For Elgin's fame the grateful Pallas pleads,
> Below, his name—above, behold his deeds!
> Be ever hailed with equal honor here
> The Gothic monarch and the Pictish peer:
> arms gave the first his right, the last had none,
> But basely stole what less barbarians won.

More accessible in London than they had previously been in Ottoman-ruled Athens, the sculptures inspired many, including Keats, whose viewing of the sculptures on display at the British Museum in 1817 inspired both "On Seeing the Elgin Marbles" and "Ode on a Grecian Urn."[130] The acquisition and display of the sculptures were part of a broader European fascination with classical art and culture that had begun in the mid-18th century, and which had a wide influence on European art and design.[131]

Following Greek independence, the successive restorations of the Acropolis were undertaken, removing later additions and changes in favor of a restoration of the site to the ruins of its Periclean state. Greece has insisted that the monuments of ancient Greece, including the removed Parthenon sculptures, are national cultural patrimony that is the exclusive property of the Greek nation.[132] However, Greece did not make a

---

[130] *See* http://www.poetryfoundation.org/poem/173742#about.

[131] *See, e.g.*, Sara J. Oshinsky, *European Revivalism*, in HEILBRUNN TIMELINE OF ART HISTORY, The Metropolitan Museum of Art (Oct. 2006), *available at* http://www.metmuseum.org/toah/hd/eurv/hd_eurv.htm.

[132] In 2002, Greece enacted Law 3028/2002, "On the Protection of Antiquities and Cultural Heritage in General," which provides for the protection of cultural property located within Greek territory (including its territorial waters), and provides that cultural property of national significance is *res extra commercium*, and cannot be transferred to individuals or institutions. Greece has enacted a series of laws protecting its cultural heritage, and particularly its ancient objects, beginning with pronouncements even before Greek's war of independence was concluded. Greek Law 2646/1899 established "an exclusive right of ownership of the state over all antiquities, movable and immovable, to be found anywhere in Greece, even on private law." Daphne Voudouri, *Greek Legislation Concerning the International Movement of Antiquities and Its Ideological and Political Dimensions*, in D. Damaskos and D. Plantzos (eds), A SINGULAR ANTIQUITY. ARCHAEOLOGY AND HELLENIC IDENTITY IN TWENTIETH-CENTURY GREECE (3rd Supp.), 125–139 (2008).

formal demand for the return of the Parthenon sculptures until 1982, which the British Museum declined.

3. The Legal Claims

Although Greece recently considered its options for bringing suit to compel the return of the Parthenon sculptures to Athens, it ultimately decided against taking legal action, concentrating instead on cultural diplomacy.[133] Considering the nature of such a claim with respect to the Parthenon sculptures and the obstacles it would face promotes a more general understanding of the legal issues involved more generally in claims for the return of cultural property that was removed during this period. For the Parthenon sculptures, the main substantive issues are (1) whether Lord Elgin had the permission of the Ottoman government to remove the sculptures from the Parthenon and to ship them to England, and (2) whether any international law exists that would require the sculptures to be turned over. The main procedural issues are (1) in what court could a case be brought (this involves both what court[s] would have jurisdiction to hear such a claim as well as whether a judgment entered by the court could actually be enforced), and (2) whether suit is barred by statutes of limitations or other technical barriers.

4. Elgin's Permission to Remove the Sculptures

Central to the discussion of whether Lord Elgin had permission to remove the sculptures is the status of the Second Firman. The original Ottoman document, which would have been issued in Turkish, has not survived. What does survive is an Italian translation of that document that was made by Antonio Dane for Rev. Hunt. Commentators have objected to the description of this document as a *firman*, since is does not bear the distinctive attributes of a *firman*. It was not issued by the Sultan and does not bear the Sultan's seal. Both V. Demetriades[134] and

---

133 Liz Alderman, *Greece Rules Out Suing British Museum Over Elgin Marbles*, THE NEW YORK TIMES (May 14, 2015), *available at* http://www.nytimes.com/2015/05/15/world/europe/greece-british-museum-elgin-marbles.html.

134 V. Demetriades in *Cultural Property: Return and Illicit Trade*, Seventh Report of House of Commons, Culture, Media and Sport Committee (London 2000), Appendix 12, Annex A, *available at* http://www.greece.org/parthenon/marbles/illegal.htm.

David Rudenstine[135] have argued that the Second Firman is a *mektub* rather than a *firman*, and they have challenged the authority of any Ottoman official other than the Sultan to give permission to remove the sculptures.[136] Dyfri Williams, Research Keeper in the British Museum's Department of Greek and Roman Antiquities,[137] acknowledges that the Second Firman is not a Sultan-issued *firman*, and has pointed out instead that the document was issued by Seijid Abdullah, who served as Kaimakam, the next-highest Ottoman official, answerable directly to the Sultan.[138] Rudenstine suggested that the Second Firman may have been a draft letter prepared at Hunt's bequest as a proposal for the permission Elgin sought. But Williams rejects this theory, stating that "not only does the document explicitly state that it is a translation of a letter, not a proposal, but also draft documents were naturally presented to the Porte in Ottoman Turkish, not in Italian."[139]

Williams pointed out that "[t]he word *firman* . . . was clearly used within the Ottoman court and by foreign diplomats and travellers for a wide variety of documents, including travel permits, employment appointments and important imperial instructions, whether authorized by the Sultan or a member of his court."[140] From a review of the Elgin and Hunt papers, he identifies several documents of permission that were issued in connection with Lord Elgin's collecting of antiquities during his tenure as ambassador. When Lord Elgin acquired the Sigeion inscription,[141] permission for the removal was given by the Capitan Pasha (Hussein, admiral of the Ottoman navy), and was then "reinforced by a *buyuruldi* from Hadim Oglou, the governor of the Dardanelles, and an imperial

135 David Rudenstine, *A Tale of Three Documents: Lord Elgin and the Missing, Historic 1801 Ottoman Document*, 22 Cardozo Law Review 1853 (2001), *available at* http://www.tomminogue.com/media/blogs/tom/A%20Tale%20of%20Three%20Documents.pdf; *Lord Elgin and the Ottomans: The Question of Permission*, 23 Cardozo Law Review 452 (2003); *Did Elgin Cheat at Marbles?*, The Nation (May 29, 2000), *available at* http://www.cardozo.yu.edu/life/summer2000/elgin.

136 Demetriades argues that three types of Ottoman legal documents were in use at the time: (i) a *firman* (an imperial document issued by the Sultan himself, which the Letter by the Museum's own admission is not), (ii) a *buyuruldi* (a lower level document with more limited authority), and (iii) a *mektub* (a letter carrying a far more limited ability to convey permission).

137 *See* http://web.archive.org/web/20090107132102/www.britishmuseum.org/the_museum/departments/staff/greece_and_rome/dyfri_j_r_williams.aspx.

138 Dyfri Williams, *Lord Elgin's Firman*, Journal of the History of Collections 1 (2009).

139 *Id.* at 8.

140 *Id.*

141 *See* http://www.britishmuseum.org/research/collection_online/collection_object_details.aspx?objectId=459473&partId=1.

firman from Constantinople that apparently declared the marbles to have been given by the Sultan to Lord Elgin."[142]

Even if the author of the Second Firman had the necessary authority to permit Lord Elgin's removals, commentators comparing the language of that permission with the actual removals that were undertaken have generally agreed that what was removed and the manner in which it was removed exceeded what is described in the Second Firman.[143] In his testimony before Parliament, Rev. Hunt was asked whether the Second Firman gave Lord Elgin the necessary permission:

> **Q:** Do you imagine that the *fermaun* gave a direct permission to remove figures and pieces of sculpture from the walls of temples, or that that must have been a matter of private arrangement with the local authorities of Athens?
>
> **Hunt:** That was the interpretation which the Vaivode of Athens was induced to allow it to bear.
>
> **Q:** In consequence of what was the Vaivode induced to give it this interpretation?
>
> **Hunt:** With respect to the first metope, it was to gratify what he conceived to be the favourable wishes of the Turkish Government towards Lord Elgin, and which induced him rather to extend than contract the precise permissions of the *fermaun*.[144]

---

142 *Id.* at 8–9. Williams identifies a further example of documents of permission given in connection with Lord Elgin's collecting: "A second example, dating from the summer of 1801, concerned the securing of pieces of porphyry from various locations in Constantinople, including the lid of the so-called sarcophagus of Constantine that was in the courtyard of the Osmaniye Mosque, although *firmans* seem not to have been issued, but rather letters and annotated memoranda exchanged between the Reis Effendi and the Sultan."

143 *See, e.g.*, John Henry Merryman, *Thinking About the Elgin Marbles*, 83 MICH. L. REV. 1881, 1899 (Aug. 1985) ("The document appears to contemplate measuring, drawing, and making casts as the principal activity of Elgin's artists and workmen. The reference to 'taking away any pieces of stone' seems incidental, intended to apply to objects found while excavating. That was certainly the interpretation privately placed on the *firman* by several of the Elgin party, including Lady Elgin."); and JEANNETTE GREENFIELD, THE RETURN OF CULTURAL TREASURES 81 (3rd ed.) ("Even if the terms of the *firman* as translated are accurate, it is clear that Elgin exceeded them. He acted in a breach of the conditions allowing him to remove items from the Parthenon site, and what he did remove was not included within the descriptions contained in the *firman*.").

144 Rev. Philip Hunt testimony, *House of Commons Select Committee on the Earl of Elgin's Collection of Sculptured Marbles & C., Report*, 25 March 1816.

For Prof. Merryman, although the removals exceeded the Second Firman's permission, nevertheless subsequent documents from and actions of the Ottoman authorities ratified Lord Elgin's actions. Merryman noted:

> It is the law everywhere that an act in excess of the authority originally granted can be ratified, expressly or by implication from conduct indicating acquiescence. There is evidence that the Ottomans twice ratified what Elgin had done. For one thing, it appears that Elgin caused the Sultan to issue additional *firmans* addressed to the Voivode and Disdar of Athens, in which the Sultan generally sanctioned what these local officials had done for Elgin and his party. For another, a large shipment of Marbles was held up in Piraeus (the port of Athens) because the Voivode, under pressure from the French, refused to give his permission for their embarkation. Eventually the Ottoman government gave written orders to the Athenian authorities to permit the shipment, and the Marbles were allowed to leave for England. Together these two events make a strong case for ratification of the removal, even if it exceeded the authority given in the original *firman*. If the removal was so ratified, then as a matter of international law the removal was legal, and Elgin was able to transfer title in the Marbles to the British Museum.[145]

Williams expanded on Merryman's theme of ratification, providing further documentary detail, but the idea of ratification has not quelled challenges to the legality and propriety of Lord Elgin's actions.[146]

5. Procedural Issues and International Law

It is often said that the primary obstacle a claim for the return of the Parthenon sculptures would encounter is the running of the statute of limitations. Statutes of limitations are certainly the most obvious initial procedural challenge to such ancient claims, but they apply variously in different jurisdictions (for instance, when the statute of limitations begins to run and whether they can be tolled under certain

---

[145] John Henry Merryman, *Thinking About the Elgin Marbles*, 83 MICH. L. REV. 1881, 1889 (Aug. 1985).

[146] For a discussion of the arguments made in favor of the turnover of the Parthenon sculptures to Greece, *see* CHRISTOPHER HITCHENS, THE PARTHENON MARBLES: THE CASE FOR REUNIFICATION (1997). For a brief debate of the question of turnover of the sculptures, see the debate sponsored by Intelligence Squared, *Send Them Back: The Parthenon Marbles Should Be Returned to Athens* (June 11, 2012), *available at* http://www.intelligencesquared.com/events/parthenon-marbles.

circumstances). More importantly, statutes of limitations are creatures of domestic law, with limited application in international law. Jeanette Greenfield has noted that "international law does recognize a bar of claims by lapse of time, although this argument is more likely to succeed where there is estoppel through acquiescence."[147] Limitations periods would be applicable and would need to be addressed through arguments for tolling in both the United Kingdom and the United States. Laches would also present a challenge because Greece has known where the sculptures are held for two centuries without instituting legal action. No limitations period would bar litigation in the Greek court, but any judgment entered would likely be regarded and politically motivated and recognition and enforcement of such a judgment would be difficult. Although no limitations period would bar the bringing of an action before the International Court of Justice (ICJ), the ICJ statute allows parties to limit the court's jurisdiction to restrict retroactive effect. Greece included no temporal restriction in its declaration of ICJ jurisdiction, but the United Kingdom has restricted its agreement to the court's jurisdiction to disputes arising after January 1, 1984. No limitations period applies directly in an action brought before the European Court of Human Rights, but the claimant would need to first exhaust domestic remedies, in which domestic limitations periods would apply.

Apart from the procedural challenges to bringing such an action, the most significant obstacle to a legal claim for the return of the Parthenon sculptures is whether Lord Elgin's removal of the sculptures violated international law applicable at the time or their return is mandated by modern international law. As I have described earlier in this chapter, although a number of commentators have challenged Ottoman power to allow the removal of the sculptures, the Ottoman Empire was the recognized government of the territory, with the power to dispose of objects within its territory. No customary international law norm existed in the early 19th century prohibiting the plunder of cultural objects during times of war, much less the removal of cultural objects with the apparent consent or acquiescence of the recognized government.[148] When we look to

---

147 JEANNETTE GREENFIELD, THE RETURN OF CULTURAL TREASURES (3rd ed.), 82.

148 *Id.* (stating that "There was no body of international law governing removal or protection at that time.").

modern international legal norms, we see that the Hague Convention[149] and similar international instruments protecting cultural property during armed conflict do not directly apply to either the original removal of the sculptures or their current retention, since the removals were not undertaken in connection with armed conflict. The Napoleonic wars are certainly in the background, and Ottoman solicitude toward Lord Elgin was strongly colored by the desire to maintain Britain as an ally against Napoleon, but the sculptures were not removed pursuant to an armed conflict. Similarly, neither the 1970 UNESCO Convention[150] (which has no retroactive effect) nor the 1995 UNIDROIT Convention[151] (to which the United Kingdom is not a party) applies.

For an action to legally compel the return of the Parthenon sculptures to succeed, what would be required is the articulation of a new rule of customary international law that certain types of cultural property that are central to a nation or a people are the perpetual and exclusive property of that nation or people as a whole and can never be alienated. The argument in favor of such a rule would rely on existing international conventions such as the Hague Convention, the 1970 UNESCO Convention, and the 1995 UNIDROIT Convention, as well as the European Convention on Human Rights[152] and the 1993 EU Directive on the Return of Cultural Objects,[153] and would argue that these conventions and instruments evidence a trend toward the protection of cultural property *in situ* in the nations and cultures of their creation. The argument would be that with respect to certain types of cultural property central to the life and identity of a culture or a people, the right

---

[149] Convention for the Protection of Cultural Property in the Event of Armed Conflict, 249 UNTS 240, *available at* http://portal.unesco.org/en/ev.php-URL_ID=13637&URL_DO=DO_TOPIC&URL_SECTION=201.html; *see also* Protocol to the Convention for the Protection of Cultural Property in the Event of Armed conflict 1954, *available at* http://portal.unesco.org/en/ev.php-URL_ID=15391&URL_DO=DO_TOPIC&URL_SECTION=201.html; and Second Protocol to the Hague Convention of 1954 for the Protection of Cultural Property in the Event of Armed Conflict, 1999, 2253 UNTS 172, *available at* http://portal.unesco.org/en/ev.php-URL_ID=15207&URL_DO=DO_TOPIC&URL_SECTION=201.html.

[150] Convention on the Means of Prohibiting and Preventing the Illicit Import, Export and Transfer of Ownership of Cultural Property ("UNESCO Convention"), signed Nov. 14, 1970, entered into force Apr. 24, 1972, 96 Stat. 2329, 823 U.N.T.S. 231, *available at* http://portal.unesco.org/en/ev.php-URL_ID=13039&URL_DO=DO_TOPIC&URL_SECTION=201.html.

[151] UNIDROIT (International Institute for the Unification of Private Law) Convention on Stolen or Illegally Exported Cultural Objects (Rome, June 24, 1995)("UNIDROIT Convention"), registered with the U.N. Mar. 31, 2007, No. 43718, *available at* http://www.unidroit.org/instruments/cultural-property/1995-convention.

[152] *See* http://www.echr.coe.int/pages/home.aspx?p=basictexts.

[153] *See* http://eur-lex.europa.eu/legal-content/EN/TXT/?uri=URISERV%3Al11017b.

to retain, have access to, and preserve such cultural property for posterity is a human right.

It has long seemed that if any resolution were to be reached, whether permanent or provisional, and if the matter is not to be intractable, the discussion would need to move away from questions or title, ownership, and recrimination. Absolute positions, as well as national and political emotions, would need to be set aside. Flexibility would be essential, and a negotiated resolution, or series of resolutions, would need to be mutually beneficial. Although it arose in a very different context (antiquities looted in modern times), the accord entered into between the Metropolitan Museum of Art and Italy in 2006, which arose out of the Giacomo Medici affair described earlier, illustrates one of the ways that disputes over removed cultural property may be resolved.[154]

However, on July 11, 2016, Mr. Mark Williams presented a bill in the House of Commons, the Parthenon Sculptures (Return to Greece) Act 2016,[155] that, if enacted, would transfer ownership and possession of the Parthenon Sculptures to the Hellenic Republic, and amend Sections 5 and 9 of the British Museum Act 1963 to allow that transfer.

I. Destruction of Cultural Property

The destruction of sculptures and other objects in the Mosul Museum,[156] as well as the ancient cities and archaeological sites of Nimrud,[157]

154 Elisabetta Polovedo, *Italy and U.S. Sign Antiquities Accord,* THE NEW YORK TIMES (Feb. 22, 2006), *available at* http://www.nytimes.com/2006/02/22/arts/design/22anti.html?pagewanted-all.

155 The Parthenon Sculptures (Return to Greece) Act 2016, *available at* http://www.publications.parliament.uk/pa/bills/cbill/2016-2017/0048/17048.pdf.

156 UNESCO Director-General, Irina Bokova, condemned the destruction, noting that "the attack was in direct violation to the most recent Security Council resolution 2199 that condemns the destruction of cultural heritage and adopts legally-binding measures to counter illicit trafficking of antiquities and cultural objects from Iraq and Syria." *Iraq: UNESCO Outraged over Terrorist Attack against Mosul Museum,* UN NEWS CENTRE (Feb. 26, 2015), *available at* http://www.un.org/apps/news/story.asp?NewsID=50190#.VQdHyk1OXcu. To view a video of the destruction at the museum, see Ben Wedeman and Dana Ford, *Video Shows ISIS Militants Destroying Antiquities in Iraq,* CNN (Feb. 27, 2015), *available at* http://edition.cnn.com/2015/02/26/middleeast/isis-antiquities-vandalism/. *See also* Kareen Shaheen, *Isis fighters destroy ancient artefacts at Mosul museum,* THE GUARDIAN (Feb. 26, 2015), *available at* http://www.theguardian.com/world/2015/feb/26/isis-fighters-destroy-ancient-artefacts-mosul-museum-iraq.

157 *See* Anne Barnard, *ISIS Attacks Nimrud, a Major Archaeological Site in Iraq,* THE NEW YORK TIMES (Mar. 5, 2015), *available at* http://www.nytimes.com/2015/03/06/world/middleeast/isis-attacks-iraqi-archaeological-site-at-nimrud.html.

Hatra,[158] Dur Sharrukin, [159] the 14th-century mosque that housed the Tomb of Jonah,[160] and many sites within the ancient city of Palmyra, a 2,000 year old World Heritage Site,[161] has been widely condemned.[162] Many have identified the motivation behind the destruction as an ideology-driven iconoclasm. Art historian Simon Schama, placing these actions in the context of many other historical iconoclasms, observed that:

> [t]he obliterators . . . act from the same instinct of cultural panic that the supreme works of the past will lead people astray from blind, absolute obedience. Neither beauty nor history have the least interest for them because they live in and force others to inhabit a universe of timeless subjection. The mere notion that the achievements of humanity might rise to the level of sublimity is itself a sacrilegious affront. In a way this is a backhanded compliment to the power of images. And yet

---

158 *See, e.g.*, Lucy Wescott, *Why ISIS Is Plundering the Ancient World,* NEWSWEEK (Mar. 13, 2015), *available at* http://www.newsweek.com/why-isis-plundering-ancient-world-313695; Borzou Daragahi, *Artefacts under Attack,* THE FINANCIAL TIMES (Mar. 13, 2015), *available at* http://www.ft.com/cms/s/2/5f5e1bec-c80e-11e4-8fe2-00144feab7de.html#slide0.

159 *See* Kareem Shaheen, *Isis Ransacking of Ancient Assyrian City Confirmed by Iraq's Head of Antiquities,* THE GUARDIAN (Mar. 12, 2015), *available at* http://www.theguardian.com/world/2015/mar/12/isis-ransack-ancient-assyrian-city-confirmed-iraq-head-of-antiquities-dur-sharrukin ("[Dur-Sharrukin's] city walls were razed, and some elements of the temples, but we don't know the exact extent [of the damage]," Iraq's director of antiquities, Qais Rasheed, told Reuters. "Looting took place, and then the razing."); Anne Barnard, *Race in Iraq and Syria to Record and Shield Art Falling to ISIS,* THE NEW YORK TIMES, Mar. 8, 2015, *available at* http://www.nytimes.com/2015/03/09/world/middleeast/race-in-iraq-and-syria-to-record-and-shield-art-falling-to-isis.html ("In just a few days last week, [ISIS] destroyed parts of two of northern Iraq's most prized ancient cities, Nimrud and Hatra. On Sunday, residents said militants destroyed parts of Dur Sharrukin, a 2,800-year-old Assyrian site near the village of Khorsabad.").

160 *See* Mark Movesian, *Why Did ISIS Destroy the Tomb of Jonah?* FIRST THINGS (July 28, 2014), *available at* http://www.firstthings.com/blogs/firstthoughts/2014/07/why-did-isis-destroy-the-tomb-of-jonah#print; *see also Video Shows Islamic State Blowing Up Iraq's Tomb of Jonah,* NPR (July 25, 2014), *available at* http://www.npr.org/blogs/thetwo-way/2014/07/25/335192229/video-shows-islamic-state-blowing-up-iraqs-tomb-of-jonah.

161 Kereem Shaheen, *ISIS Destroys Palmyra Shrines in Syria* (June 23, 2015), THE GUARDIAN, *available at* http://www.theguardian.com/world/2015/jun/23/isis-destroys-palmyra-shrines-in-syria.

162 UNESCO Director-General, Irina Bokova ("The destruction of Hatra marks a turning point in the appalling strategy of cultural cleansing under way in Iraq.") (*Islamic State 'Demolishes' Ancient Hatra Site in Iraq,* BBC (Mar. 7, 2015), *available at* http://www.bbc.com/news/world-middle-east-31779484); Thomas P. Campbell, Director of the Metropolitan Museum of Art ("It's the erasure of human identity, and nothing less than cultural cleansing.") (Kia Makarechi, *At Persian New Year Gala, Met Museum C.E.O. Condemns ISIS's "Sickening" Destruction of Antiquities,* VANITY FAIR (Mar. 13, 2015), *available at* http://www.vanityfair.com/culture/2015/03/noruz-at-the-met-gala-2015). *See also* Graham Bowley and Robert Mackey, *Destruction of Antiquities by ISIS Militants Is Denounced,* THE NEW YORK TIMES (Feb. 27, 2015), *available at* http://www.nytimes.com/2015/02/28/world/middleeast/destruction-of-antiquities-by-militants-is-denounced.html?_r=0; Sturt Manning, *Why ISIS Destroys Antiquities,* CNN (Mar. 9, 2015), *available at* http://www.cnn.com/2015/03/06/opinions/manning-isis-antiquities/; Zack Beauchamp, *ISIS's War on History: 11 Cultural Treasures Lost Forever to the Group and Its Predecessors* (Mar. 11, 2015), *available at* http://www.vox.com/2015/3/11/8184207/islamist-monuments.

> when this puerile and fearful instinct leads to irreversible acts of annihilation, it is not only their own immediate culture that is the victim but the entirety of humanity, which loses a piece of its memory as surely as if a slice of our collective brain had been removed by a mad lobotomist.[163]

The Taliban's demolition of the Bamiyan Buddhas in March 2001[164] exemplifies this "cultural cleansing," but it also shows how changeable iconoclasts' views can be. In 1999, shortly after the Taliban assumed power in Afghanistan, the Taliban Minister of Culture "spoke about the respect due to pre-Islamic antiquities and also mentioned the risk of retaliation against mosques in Buddhist countries. . . . He made clear that, though there were no Buddhist believers in Afghanistan, 'Bamiyan would not be destroyed but, on the contrary, protected.'"[165] However, on February 26, 2001, Taliban leader Mullah Muhammad Omar "issued a decree ordering the elimination of all non-Islamic statues and sanctuaries in Afghanistan."[166] Within weeks, the Buddhas had been destroyed.

Similarly, in 2012, the Al-Qaeda-related Islamic group Ansar Dine engaged in widespread ideologically driven destruction of mosques, monuments, and manuscripts in Timbuktu, Mali.[167] "Timbuktu's ancient mosques and monuments," observers noted, "built of mud and limestone bricks, [had] endured centuries [until Ansar Dine] swept across Mali's north. . . . Intolerant of the city's mystical Sufi traditions, they banned music, and took hoes, pickaxes and bulldozers to the shrines where saints were buried, and which they considered idolatrous. Sixteen mausoleums were destroyed, including two that sat alongside the vast 14th-century Djingareyber mosque." [168] In the case of the monuments of Timbuktu, the destruction of the buildings was itself not enough. Complete elimination—including making it impossible for the monuments to

---

163 Simon Schama, *Artefacts under Attack*, THE FINANCIAL TIMES (Mar. 13, 2015), *available at* http://www.ft.com/cms/s/2/5f5e1bec-c80e-11e4-8fe2-00144feab7de.html#slide0.

164 A video of the destruction is *available at* https://www.youtube.com/watch?v=xYYBlPWYb7Y.

165 Pierre Centlivres, *The Death of the Bamiyan Buddhas* (Dec. 2009), *available at* http://www.mei.edu/content/death-buddhas-bamiyan#edn3.

166 *Id.*

167 Federico Lenzerini, *The Role of International and Mixed Criminal Courts in the Enforcement of International Norms Concerning the Protection of Cultural Heritage*, in Francesco Francioni and James Gordley eds., ENFORCING INTERNATIONAL CULTURAL HERITAGE 60 (2013).

168 William Wallis, *Artefacts under Attack*, THE FINANCIAL TIMES (Mar. 13, 2015), *available at* http://www.ft.com/cms/s/2/5f5e1bec-c80e-11e4-8fe2-00144feab7de.html#slide0.

be rebuilt with the same materials—was the goal. After the monuments were destroyed, Ansar Dine "carried the clay obtained from the monuments outside the city . . . to prevent them from being rebuilt with the same clay in the future."[169]

Iconoclasm and "cultural cleansing" do not appear to be the sole motivation for the contemporary destruction of ancient sites. While ISIS declares that "ancient art [is] idolatry that must be destroyed," reports indicate that the destruction of that ancient art is part of a looting scheme that monetizes that ancient art to fund ISIS's activities. "[T]he archaeological devastation is not about ideology," David Kohn has reported, "but income. . . . [ISIS] often brings in contractors who use bulldozers to dig up sites as efficiently as possible."[170] Louise Shelley, writing in *Foreign Affairs*, described the sources of ISIS's funding, including the sale of oil, but also "the sale of counterfeit cigarettes, pharmaceuticals, cell phones, antiquities, and foreign passports."[171]

United Nations Secretary General Ban Ki-moon condemned the destruction, designating the actions as war crimes and issuing a statement calling on the international community "to swiftly put a stop to such heinous terrorist activity and to counter the illicit traffic in cultural artefacts."[172] UNESCO Director-General Irina Bokova likewise issued a statement after the destruction of Nimrud, stating that she had "alerted the president of the Security Council as well as the Prosecutor of the International Criminal Court" concerning the unlawfulness of the destruction under international law.[173]

International law protects cultural heritage from destruction and plunder during armed conflict (both international and internal) through a variety of instruments. Many of these instruments impose obligations on countries, not individuals, setting out the rules of war.[174] These instruments include Convention (IV) Respecting the Laws and Customs of War

---

169 Lenzerini *supra*, at 61.

170 David Kohn, *ISIS's Looting Campaign*, The New Yorker (Oct. 14, 2014), *available at* http://www.newyorker.com/tech/elements/isis-looting-campaign-iraq-syria.

171 Louise Shelley, *Blood Money: How ISIS Makes Bank*, Foreign Affairs (Mar. 2015).

172 Kareem Shaheen, *Isis Attacks on Ancient Sites Erasing History of Humanity, Says Iraq*, The Guardian (Mar. 9, 2015), *available at* http://www.theguardian.com/world/2015/mar/09/iraq-condemns-isis-destruction-ancient-sites.

173 *UNESCO: ISIS Antiquities Destruction in Iraq a "War Crime,"* Arutz Sheva (Mar. 6, 2015), *available at* http://www.israelnationalnews.com/News/News.aspx/192238#.VQOo90I9VkM.

174 Lenzerini *supra*, at 41–42.

on Land of 1907,[175] the 1954 Hague Convention for the Protection of Cultural Property in the Event of Armed Conflict (which imposes not only obligations to safeguard cultural heritage during international/cross-border conflicts, but also, importantly, during internal conflicts), [176] the two 1977 Protocols to the Geneva Conventions on Humanitarian Law of 1949,[177] the Second Protocol to the Hague Convention,[178] and the 2003 UNESCO Declaration on the Intentional Destruction of Cultural Heritage.[179] Individual criminal liability for the destruction of cultural heritage was slower to develop, but is embodied in the statutes of the International Criminal Tribunal for the Former Yugoslavia and the International Criminal Court (ICC), which, like the 1954 Hague Convention,

---

175 Convention (IV) Respecting the Laws and Customs of War on Land and Its Annex: Regulations Concerning the Laws and Customs of War on Land, The Hague, 18 Oct. 1907, *available at* http://www.icrc.org/ihl.nsf (The Regulations annexed to the Convention state: "In sieges and bombardments all necessary steps must be taken to spare, as far as possible, buildings dedicated to religion, art, science, or charitable purposes, historic monuments, hospitals, and places where the sick and wounded are collected, provided they are not being used at the time for military purposes. It is the duty of the besieged to indicate the presence of such buildings or places by distinctive and visible signs, which shall be notified to the enemy beforehand.").

176 Convention for the Protection of Cultural Property in the Event of Armed Conflict, 249 UNTS 240, *available at* http://portal.unesco.org/en/ev.php-URL_ID=13637&URL_DO=DO_TOPIC&URL_SECTION=201.html (Article (4)(1) states: "The High Contracting Parties undertake to respect cultural property situated within their own territory as well as within the territory of other High Contracting Parties by refraining from any use of the property and its immediate surroundings or of the appliances in use for its protection for purposes which are likely to expose it to destruction or damage in the event of armed conflict; and by refraining from any act of hostility, directed against such property." Article 19(1) imposes a corresponding obligation to safeguard cultural heritage in internal (not international or cross-border) conflicts: "In the event of an armed conflict not of an international character occurring within the territory of one of the High Contracting Parties, each party to the conflict shall be bound to apply, as, a minimum, the provisions of the present Convention which relate to respect for cultural property.").

177 Protocol Additional to the Geneva Conventions of 12 August 1949, and Relating to the Protection of Victims of International Armed Conflicts (Protocol I), 1125 UNTS 5 (Article 53 provides: "Without prejudice to the provisions of the Hague Convention for the Protection of Cultural Property in the Event of Armed Conflict of 14 May 1954, and of other relevant international instruments, it is prohibited: (a) to commit any acts of hostility directed against the historic monuments, works of art or places of worship which constitute the cultural or spiritual heritage of peoples; (b) to use such objects in support of the military effort; (c) to make such objects the object of reprisals."); and Protocol Additional to the Geneva Conventions of 12 August 1949, and Relating to the Protection of Victims of Non-International Armed Conflicts (Protocol II), 1125 UNTS 609 (Article 16 provides: "it is prohibited to commit any acts of hostility directed against historic monuments, works of art or places of worship which constitute the cultural or spiritual heritage of peoples, and to use them in support of the military effort.").

178 Second Protocol to the Hague Convention of 1954 for the Protection of Cultural Property in the Event of Armed Conflict, 1999, 2253 UNTS 172.

179 *See* http://portal.unesco.org/en/ev.php-URL_ID=17718&URL_DO=DO_TOPIC&URL_SECTION=2-1.html (Article VII, in proclaiming the principle of individual criminal responsibility for acts of destruction of cultural heritage, affirms: "States should take all appropriate measures, in accordance with international law, to establish jurisdiction over, and provide effective criminal sanctions against, those persons who commit, or order to be committed, acts of intentional destruction of cultural heritage of great importance for humanity, whether or not it is inscribed on a list maintained by UNESCO or another international organization.").

imposes criminal liability not only for actions taken during international conflicts, but also during internal conflicts.[180]

In the case of individual criminal responsibility for ISIS militants for the destruction in Mosul, Nimrud, and elsewhere, an initial obstacle lies in neither Iraq nor Syria being party to the Rome Statute. However, while the ICC's jurisdiction is limited, states may accept the court's jurisdiction for a particular case. Even in the absence of such state acceptance, the ICC has jurisdiction in cases in which the Security Council refers the matter to the prosecutor. Either option, however, faces steep political obstacles.

These barriers to ICC jurisdiction do not apply to Ansar Dine's actions in Mali. On July 13, 2012, the Government of Mali referred the case of Ahmad Al Faqi Al Mahdi to the ICC. Faqi, a leader of Ansar Dine, was accused of ordering the destruction of numerous Sufi shrines and saints' tombs, as well as a 15th century mosque in Timbuktu. The Prosecutor opened an investigation and, on September 18, 2015, issued a warrant for Faqi's arrest. Faqi was charged with the commission of a war crime, pursuant to articles 25(3)(a)(perpetration and coperpetration), 25(3)(b)(soliciting, inducing), 25(3)(c)(aiding, abetting or otherwise assisting), and 25(3)(d)(contributing in any other way), for intentionally directing attacks on the sites.[181] It was a landmark case, the first where an individual was charged with the war crime of destruction of cultural heritage. At the trial, which was held on August 22-24, 2016, Faqi entered a plea of guilty.

Challenges to enforcement do not reduce the importance of establishing and maintaining the international legal norms that have developed in this area. Resolutions and declarations by the United Nations and the international community's condemnation of these acts of destruction carry significance in themselves, even though they do not halt the acts themselves. It is also important to recognize that treaty-based legal

---

[180] UN General Assembly, Rome Statute of the International Criminal Court (last amended 2010), 17 July 1998, ISBN No. 92-9227-227-6, *available at* http://www.refworld.org/docid/3ae6b3a84.html (Article 8(2)(b)(IX) provides that the term 'war crimes' includes "Intentionally directing attacks against buildings dedicated to religion, education, art, science or charitable purposes, historic monuments, hospitals and places where the sick and wounded are collected, provided they are not military objectives." Article 8(2)(e)(IV) imposes a corresponding liability during internal conflicts, stating that war crimes includes, in conflicts not of an international character, "Intentionally directing attacks against buildings dedicated to religion, education, art, science or charitable purposes, historic monuments, hospitals and places where the sick and wounded are collected, provided they are not military objectives.").

[181] The Prosecutor v. Ahmad Al Faqi Al Mahdi, ICC-01/12-01/15, case information *available at* https://www.icc-cpi.int/mali; *see also* Adam Klasfeld, *War-Crime Plea for Leveled Timbuktu Shrines*, Courthouse News Service, Aug. 22, 2016, *available at* http://www.courthousenews.com/2016/08/22/war-crime-plea-for-leveledtimbuktu-shrines.htm.

protections for cultural heritage not only have deep roots in the norms of customary international law,[182] but also contribute to the articulation and development of those customary international law norms, which have an independent legal validity in international law.

182 Francesco Francioni and Federico Lenzerini, *The Destruction of the Buddhas of Bamiyan and International Law,* 14 EJIL 619, 634 (2003).

CHAPTER 4

The Art Trade

A. A Globalizing Marketplace

The trade in art is global.[1] For decades, it has had two great centers—New York and London. However, the liberalization of many emerging economies and changing patterns of global wealth distribution and concentration have had a profound effect on the global art trade.[2] Its expansion in emerging markets has been uneven, with some countries' trade policies being more open

---

1 TEFAF ART MARKET REPORT 2014, 26 (2014) (stating, "Apart from its rapidly increasing size, the art market has undergone an intense period of globalization since the turn of the century. The distribution of sales has changed fundamentally over the last ten years, with significant changes in the size and distribution of world wealth, leading to the emergence of new markets and buyers. New collectors from Asia, Latin America, the Middle East and elsewhere have increased global buying in the traditional art hubs of London and New York, while also helping to support some thriving local markets. China has been the most dominant of all these newer markets, both as an important buyer of art globally, and as one of the largest markets in the world for domestic sales."). But see Melanie Gerlis, *Is the Global Art Market a Myth? The Academic Olav Venthuis Argues that the Business of Art Isn't as International as It Seems*, THE ART NEWSPAPER (April 25, 2014), *available at* http://www.theartnewspaper.com/articles/Is-the-global-art-market-a-myth/32400 (stating Velthuis "has found that the majority of businesses are organized 'extremely locally', despite aspiring to the borderless ideals of international artists who command global demand—which he said has been 'vastly exaggerated.'").

2 *See* DELOITTE ART & FINANCE REPORT 2013, 19 (2nd ed. 2013) ("The marketplace has undergone radical change. While the art market was previously dominated by buyers and artists from the U.S. and Europe, the last 10-15 years have seen the emergence of new art markets across the world, bringing collectors, artists and art professionals together in a truly global market place. The advent of art fairs, biennials, auctions, new online ventures and the rapid expansion in galleries and museums have led the market to more than double in size since 2002.").

than others.[3] Despite such unevenness, the trend in the global cultural property trade is clear, and an expanded geography of art dealers, galleries, auction houses, and sales is the reality of the cultural property trade.

However, New York and London themselves reach a global customer base, serving as *entrepôts*, where favorable trade and tax regimes facilitate the concentration of high-quality goods whose sales are transacted in those cities, although their ultimate sellers and buyers may be located elsewhere.

The United States is the global leader in art sale transactions, by value (43 percent), followed by the United Kingdom (21 percent) and China (19 percent).[4] However, a review of import and export figures shows more clearly the cross-border nature of a great number of art sale transactions. In 2014, United States cultural property imports were valued at $9.184 billion, and exports were valued at $10.193 billion.[5] The vast majority of art imports into the United States were from the countries of the European Union, with 71 percent of imports coming from the top five sources in Europe (France, the United Kingdom, Germany, Italy, and Spain). Four percent of art imports into the United States were from China. Twenty-nine percent of exports of art from the United States were to the United Kingdom, with 22 percent to Switzerland. Fourteen percent of United States art exports were made to China.[6]

---

[3] *See* TEFAF ART MARKET REPORT 2013, 78-81 (2013) ("Over the last decade, emerging art markets such as China and Brazil have opened their economies significantly. Nonetheless, while there have been significant moves to liberalize trade, there are some major trade regulations and policies that persist and have hindered the internationalization of these markets. Brazil . . . maintained a highly protectionist approach to trade as part of import-substituting policies that lasted for half a century. These were reduced significantly in the late 1980s and through the 1990s, but little progress has been made since then. China . . . also operated high import tariffs at the start of the 1990s, although certain specifically designated economic zones, such as Hong Kong, had already enjoyed a more liberal regime since the late 1970s. Import tariffs on general trade were more than halved in the early 1990s and then reduced further with China's accession to the WTO in 2011. The Middle East, on the other hand, has a relatively free trading regime, particularly through the UAE, although trade remains relatively low and is heavily dominated by imports. Despite the rapid growth in domestic sales in some emerging markets, there is still a very significant difference in the value of the trade carried out in the traditional market hubs and in the new large market centres. It is interesting therefore to analyze the different patterns of trade over the last decade in these contrasting markets.")

[4] TEFAF ART MARKET REPORT 2016, 15 (2016) (the quoted percentages are based upon 2015 sales reports).

[5] *Id.* at 60.

[6] *Id.* at 63.

B. Types of Art Transactions

Art sales often occur in a more informal, courtly and less business-like context than many other types of sales. To a greater degree than is true in most commercial transactions, the parties to art transactions have historically tended to rely on reputations and personal relationships. Art sales may also be less fully or formally documented than other kinds of commercial sales. This practice is changing, as lenders and other commercial parties demand greater documentation and transparency. Regulatory mandates are also driving a trend toward more complete documentation of art transactions, including export and reimportation permits, bills of sale, appraisals, and authentication, and tax documentation.

In the art trade, roles can be fluid and may frequently overlap.[7] Although a sale transaction may be as straightforward as a single seller selling a work to a single buyer, such a direct line is far from the norm. Rather, sales are more likely to be intermediated, not uncommonly through several levels, as one dealer or group of co-owning dealers buy, sell, or consign art objects to still other levels of dealers,[8] galleries, or auction houses. Even the relationship between collector and dealer may be lacking in sharp edges, as dealers also collect or hold works for their own use and collectors, in turn, engage in sales.[9]

In broad terms, art sales can be divided into public auction sales and dealer sales (what are often called private sales or private treaty sales).

---

[7] *See* Patty Gerstenblith, Art, Cultural Heritage, and the Law 299 (3d ed. 2012) ("The art market consists of a primary and secondary market. In the primary market, which is a relatively small part of the market, the buyer buys directly from the artist. The larger segment is the secondary market, in which art works are resold. Buyers and sellers in the secondary market, and frequently artists as well, generally transact through intermediaries rather than directly with one another. The most typical intermediaries in the art world are dealers and auction houses. Traditionally, dealers were viewed as sellers who owned the art works and sold on their own account, while auction houses did not own the works and sold on behalf of the owner, usually through a public sale. Today, however, this traditional distinction no longer pertains. Dealers often sell works on consignment on behalf of the owner who may be the artist, a collector, or another dealer who holds works in inventory, while auction houses often engage in private sales of works and may own the works they sell or have a partial ownership or other financial interest in the work.").

[8] *See* Alexandra Darraby, Art, Artifact, Architecture and Museum Law § 2:12 (17th ed. 2014) (noting that "Dealers, and gallerists who fit the genre, have been described variously as those who trade art with the intent to profit by buying and selling, and those acting as consignors and consignees. Dealers, unlike mercantile gallery owners, may or may not have exhibition spaces open to the public.").

[9] *See id.* at § 2:1 (observing that a trade in cultural property "is a mercantile purchase, sale, exchange or transfer ordinarily made by professional traders that include dealers, gallery owners, auctioneers, gallerists, consultants, and, on occasion, collectors. This cadre of dealers, galleries, and auctioneers is supplemented by numerous persons and entities engaged in art dealing, sometimes on a part-time or intermittent basis.").

In 2015, auction sales made up approximately 47 percent of global art sales, [10] with dealer sales (including dealer, gallery, and private sales) making up 53 percent.[11] However, such dealer sales "varied widely between countries. In the larger mature markets, the share was generally over 55%, while in China it remained at close to 30%."[12] Online sales of art in 2015 "were estimated conservatively to have reached $4.7 billion, or around 7% of global art and antiques sales by value."[13]

While the category of "private collector" includes individuals (i.e., consumers) who purchase works for their own use or enjoyment, it also includes purchases made by corporations for corporate collections and by art funds or other investment or financing vehicles.[14] As the *AAM Guide to Provenance Research* noted,

> At times, the line between collector and dealer can be a blurry one. Collectors often change the emphasis of their collections, dispersing their juvenilia in order to concentrate on newly discovered passions. Other collectors 'trade up' earlier purchases when better examples become available. And, of course, most dealers maintain private collections that are not generally for sale.[15]

---

10 TEFAF ART MARKET REPORT 2016, 27 (2016).

11 *Id.* at 39.

12 *Id.*

13 *Id.* at 45.

14 DELOITTE ART & FINANCE REPORT 2013, 14 (2nd ed. 2013) ("[T[he global art investment fund market reached a conservative estimate of US $1.62 billion in 2012, up from US $960 million in 2011, driven by growth in art investment funds and trusts in China."); TEFAF ART MARKET REPORT 2014, 201–203 (2014)("In 2013, the estimated value of corporate collections in China reached RMB 45 billion (€5.6 billion). . . . Art funds in China have increased rapidly in size over the last five years. It is estimated that there were over 70 art funds when the market peaked in 2011, with total funds under management of approximately €1.5 billion, but in 2012 their valuations declined by over 70%. . . . Trust funds have been the main format used by art funds. . . . These funds tend to be built around two models: as a financing vehicle or as an investment vehicle. . . . Besides trusts, many art funds in China have been built around private equity or limited partnership structures.").

15 NANCY H. YEIDE, KONSTANTIN AKINSHA & AMY L. Walsh, THE AAM GUIDE TO PROVENANCE RESEARCH, 2 (2001).

CHAPTER 5

Questions of Authenticity

A. Overview: Authentication and Attribution

Authenticity is art's defining feature, and the terms *authenticity* and *authentication* mean that an object is genuine. For art transactions, authenticity is important because of its link to an object's cultural and monetary value. Parties to these transactions need to understand that authentication and appraisal are separate processes, with distinct areas of expertise.

Attribution is commonly confused with authenticity, but it is distinct. Attribution is the process of evaluating a work and "attributing" it to a particular artist or school (say, a painting by Rembrandt or Van Gogh). An object may be *authentic*, but nevertheless wrongly attributed (a genuine 17th-century painting, but *not* by Rembrandt).

Art authentication and attribution can be difficult, costly, time-consuming, and even uncertain processes. They typically combine three elements, in varying proportions: provenance, connoisseurship, and materials analysis:

- **Provenance** is the history an object's ownership from its creation to the present day. For recent works, the chain of ownership may be clear. However, for many older objects, documentation may be spotty. Gaps in an object's provenance raise doubts about the object's authenticity and attribution, but they may also raise doubts as to an owner's good title to the object. I will discuss provenance in greater detail in Chapter 9.
- **Connoisseurship** is the informed opinion of experts.

- **Materials analysis** applies scientific methods to evaluate an object's constituent materials. While materials analysis can provide important information, it cannot alone conclusively establish an object's authenticity, and is even less likely to be able to confirm an attribution.

1. Risks for Authenticators

Over the last decade, art authentication experts have increasingly left the field, declining to give opinions on works for fear of expensive litigation. The lawsuits brought against them have not only been for negligence or malpractice, but for statements of professional opinion. They may also have liability when stating that a work of art is not authentic and this causes a loss to the owner or someone else with an interest in the work. When an expert states that a work is not authentic, a dissatisfied owner has a number of different legal theories from which to choose as a basis for a claim. Typical bases in recent cases have included defamation, libel, slander, unfair business practices, unfair competition, and disparagement. The core distinction in many of these doctrines is whether the speaker gave an opinion or made a statement of fact.

It is not unusual for the authentication of the work of contemporary artists to be placed in the hands of a specific group of experts—often the artist's friends, family, or gallerists. In some forms, the practice derives from the European *droit moral*, where the right to authenticate works lies exclusively with the artist, who has an absolute right to declare a work inauthentic. In France, for instance, where the right is perpetual, the right to authenticate works passes through the artist's estate to either family or close friends. U.S. practice tends to be concentrated more in artists' foundations, which often work with scholars to establish and confirm the artist's authentic oeuvre.

In recent years, many of these artists' foundation authentication boards—such as the Pollock-Krasner Foundation, Inc.[1] and the Andy Warhol Art Authentication Board, Inc.[2]—have been the subject of litigation when they refused to authenticate works and include them in the

---

[1] *See* Patricia Cohen, *A Real Pollock? On This, Art and Science Collide*, New York Times (Nov. 24, 2013), *available at* http://www.nytimes.com/2013/11/25/arts/design/a-real-pollock-on-this-art-and-science-collide.html?pagewanted=all&_r=0; The Pollock-Krasner Foundation, Inc., website, FAQ, *available at* http://www.pkf.org/faqs.html (stating that "The Foundation does not authenticate works of art.").

[2] *See* The Andy Warhol Foundation for the Visual Arts website, *available at* http://www.warholfoundation.org/legacy/authentication_procedure.html.

artists' *catalogue raisonné*.[3] As a result, they have ceased authenticating works. For the work of many artists in the United States, finding any expert willing to risk providing an opinion on authenticity has become next to impossible.[4]

In a United Kingdom case that garnered considerable press attention, the former owner of a painting, *The Cardsharps*, filed suit against Sotheby's for having identified the work as a copy of a Caravaggio painting when he sold the work through the auction house in 2006. The sale price was £42,000.[5] The purchaser later had the painting authenticated by certain experts as an original Caravaggio, which is valued at £10 million. The seller alleged that Sotheby's "did not consult enough experts or sufficiently test the painting before the sale."[6]

On January 16, 2015, the High Court of Justice, Chancery Division, issued its decision, finding in favor of Sotheby's and dismissing the case.[7] The decision in worth reading in its entirety for the length and depth of the court's discussion of the legal standard of skill and diligence required of a major auction house in its authentication efforts and for the court's extended discussion of the differing views of both internal and external consultants on the case. A link to the full decision is provided in the footnote citation to the case.

2. Proposed Protections for Authenticators

In an attempt to provide art authenticators with some measure of protection, on June 15, 2015, the New York Senate approved a bill entitled "An Act To Amend the Arts and Cultural Affairs Law, In Relation to Opinions Concerning Authenticity, Attribution and Authorship of Works of Fine

---

3 *See, e.g.*, Eileen Kinsella, *A Matter of Opinion*, ARTNEWS (Feb. 28, 2012), *available at* http://www.artnews.com/2012/02/28/a-matter-of-opinion; Jennifer Maloney, *The Deep Freeze in Art Authentication*, THE WALL STREET JOURNAL (April 24, 2014), *available at* http://online.wsj.com/articles/SB10001424052702304279904579518093886991908.

4 *See* Danielle Rahm, *Warhols, Pollocks, Fakes: Why Art Authenticators Are Running for the Hills*, FORBES (June 18, 2013), *available at* http://www.forbes.com/sites/daniellerahm/2013/06/18/warhols-pollocks-fakes-why-art-authenticators-are-running-for-the-hills.

5 *See* Jane Peel, *Sotheby's Sued Over "Misattributed" Caravaggio Claim*, BBC (Oct. 27, 2014), *available at* http://www.bbc.com/news/entertainment-arts-29791571.

6 *See* Paul Peachey, *Caravaggio in Court: Sotheby's Sued Over Misattribution of Painting Later Valued at £10m*, THE INDEPENDENT (Oct. 26, 2014), *available at* http://www.independent.co.uk/arts-entertainment/art/news/caravaggio-in-court-sothebys-sued-over-misattribution-of-painting-later-valued-at-10m-so-the-man-who-sold-it-for-42000-is-not-happy-9819798.html.

7 Thwaytes v. Sotheby's, (2015) EWHC 36 (ch), *available at* http://www.bailii.org/ew/cases/EWHC/Ch/2015/36.html.

Art," S. 1229-A-2015.[8] The bill would amend New York's Art and Cultural Affairs Law to (i) add a definition of "Authenticator," (ii) heighten the pleading standards for plaintiffs bringing actions against authenticators, (iii) preclude a prevailing plaintiff from receiving legal costs in suits against authenticators, and (iv) authorize courts to grant prevailing authenticator legal costs, upon a finding of good and just cause.

The bill would define "Authenticator" as "a person or entity recognized in the visual arts community as having expertise regarding the artist, work of fine art, or visual art multiple with respect to whom such person or entity renders an opinion as to the authenticity, attribution or authorship of a work of fine art or visual art multiple, or a person or entity recognized in the visual arts or scientific community as having expertise in uncovering facts that serve as a direct basis, in whole or in part, for an opinion as to the authenticity, attribution or authorship of a work of fine art or visual art multiple." This definition of "Authenticator" includes "authors of *catalogues raissonné* or other scholarly texts in which an opinion as to the authenticity, attribution or authorship of a work of fine art or visual arts multiple is expressed or implied." But the definition expressly excludes "a person or entity that has a financial interest in the work of fine art or visual art multiple for which such opinion is rendered" other than compensation for an authenticator's services in providing the opinion.

A previous version of the bill not only required plaintiffs to "specify with particularity in the complaint facts sufficient to support each element of the claim or claims asserted," but also imposed a higher pleading standard on plaintiffs in such suits.[9] The earlier bill required that the plaintiff "prove the elements of such claim or claims by clear and convincing evidence." Similarly, the earlier bill included a stronger legal fees provision in favor of prevailing authenticators, stating that "the authenticator shall be entitled to recover his, her or its reasonable attorneys' fees, costs and expenses if and to the extent that the authenticator prevails in such action."

While fee-shifting provisions may cause a plaintiff with a weak case to reconsider filing suit, prevailing after years of costly litigation and being given an award of legal costs does the authenticator little good if the

[8] *See* http://open.nysenate.gov/legislation/bill/S1229A-2015.

[9] *See* http://assembly.state.ny.us/leg/?default_fld=&bn=S06794&term=2013&Summary=Y&Actions=Y&Text=Y.

award proves uncollectable. However, that is always a risk with any judgment. The more important provision in the proposed bill (which was stronger in the earlier bill) is the requirement that a plaintiff meet a more stringent pleading requirement at the outset of the case. The earlier bill's pleading standard would have helped weed out weak or frivolous suits at an early stage, avoiding both angst and cost.

While New York is an important art center, the risk faced by authenticators is a global risk. There are some signs of a growing recognition of the problem and a desire for change.

B. Fakes and Forgeries

> We need to examine the anxieties that forgeries elicit in us now. We need to compare the shock of getting duped to the cultivated angst evoked by legitimate art, and we need to recognize what the art establishment will never acknowledge: No authentic modern masterpiece is as provocative as a great forgery. Forgers are the foremost artists of our age.[10]

In the press and in popular culture, art theft and art forgery tend to be linked and are often glamorized to a greater or lesser extent.[11] The reality, however, is usually more mundane, if not outright seedy (although efforts at recovery often have admirable, even heroic, overtones).[12]

In recent years, there have been several highly publicized instances of forgery, including the sales of fake works by modern masters such as Mark Rothko and Jackson Pollock that brought down Knoedler & Company, and the extraordinarily successful fakes of the German painter Wolfgang

---

10 Jonathon Keats, Forged: Why Fakes are the Great Art of Our Age 4 (2013).

11 Consider, for example, "How to Steal a Million" (Audrey Hepburn, Peter O'Toole) (1966); "F is for Fake" (Orson Wells, 1973); "The Thomas Crown Affair" (Steve McQueen, Faye Dunaway, 1968; and also Pierce Brosnan, Rene Russo, 1999); "Entrapment" (Sean Connery, Catherine Zeta-Jones, 1999); and more recently "The Monuments Men" (George Clooney, Matt Damon, 2014), and "The Grand Budapest Hotel" (Ralph Fiennes, F. Murray Abraham, Tilda Swinton, 2014).

12 *See, e.g.*, Randy Kennedy, *Art Theft's Less Than Glamorous Reality*, New York Times (Feb. 17, 2008), *available at* http://www.nytimes.com/2008/02/17/world/europe/17iht-art.1.10109814.html?_r=0. For a pragmatic and realistic look at art theft, *see FBI Art Theft Program*, *available at* http://www.fbi.gov/news/videos/fbi-art-theft-program.

Beltracchi,[13] who after his fraud was disclosed, became the subject of many press articles, newscasts, and even a documentary, "Beltracchi: The Art of Forgery" (2014).

Unlike art thieves, art forgers and art fakers sometimes go on to a secondary career as fake artists in their own right, enjoying a kind of glamorous notoriety, as Beltracchi has done.[14] However, Beltracchi is not alone in this. John Myatt now sells his "legitimate fakes."[15] Others have included Elmyr de Hory[16]; Eric Hebborn, whose posthumous reputation as a master forger resulted in a recent auction of a number of his drawings in the style of old masters[17]; and Mark Landis, who, somewhat uniquely, donated his faked works to museums.[18] Perhaps the most famous forger was Han van Meegeren, who forged Vermeers, one of which was sold to Hermann Goering.[19] Fakes and forgeries are even not infrequently the subject of exhibitions highlighting the forger's own art.[20] Some commentators have even suggested that fakes may be "the great art of our age."[21]

The aura of the master forger, though, means little to the buyer who finds himself or herself the proud owner of something considerably less than what was expected. When a work fails to conform to expectations

---

[13] Knoedler & Company, a well-regarded New York art gallery, closed its doors in 2011 amid allegations that it had been selling fake artworks for decades. *See* Patricia Cohen, *A Gallery That Helped Create the American Art World Closes Shop After 165 Years*, NEW YORK TIMES (Nov. 30, 2011), *available at* http://www.nytimes.com/2011/12/01/arts/design/knoedler-art-gallery-in-nyc-closes-after-165-years.html; similarly, in 2010, German authorities arrested Wolfgang Beltracchi, who until that time had enjoyed a decades-long career creating fake works by well-known and highly salable 20th-century artists. Joshua Hammer, *The Greatest Fake-Art Scam in History?*, VANITY FAIR (Oct. 10, 2012), *available at* http://www.vanityfair.com/culture/2012/10/wolfgang-beltracchi-helene-art-scam.

[14] *See* http://www.beltracchi-art.com (in German).

[15] *See* http://www.johnmyatt.com. *See also* LANEY SALISBURY, PROVENANCE: HOW A CON MAN AND A FORGER REWROTE THE HISTORY OF MODERN ART (2010).

[16] *See* http://www.elmyr.net.

[17] *See* Amanda Williams, *MailOnline* (Oct. 14, 2014), *available at* http://www.dailymail.co.uk/news/article-2792288/secret-work-master-forger-sketches-artist-duped-dealers-galleries-decades-auctioned.html.

[18] *See* http://marklandisoriginal.com; *see also* Alec Wilkinson, *The Giveaway*, THE NEW YORKER (Aug. 26, 2013), *available at* http://www.newyorker.com/magazine/2013/08/26/the-giveaway. Landis, like Beltracchi, was the subject of a recent documentary, "Art & Craft" (2014).

[19] *See, e.g.*, Peter Schjedahl, *Dutch Master: The Art Forger Who Became a National Hero,* THE NEW YORKER (Oct. 27, 2008), *available at* http://www.newyorker.com/magazine/2008/10/27/dutch-master; EDWARD DOLNICK, THE FORGER'S SPELL: A TRUE STORY OF VERMEER, NAZIS, AND THE GREATEST ART HOAX OF THE TWENTIETH CENTURY (2008); JONATHAN LOPEZ, THE MAN WHO MADE VERMEERS: UNVARNISHING THE LEGEND OF MASTER FORGER HANS VAN MEEGEREN (2009).

[20] *See Intent to Deceive: Fakes and Forgeries in the Art World*, *available at* http://www.intenttodeceive.org.

[21] *See* JONATHON KEATS, FORGED at 4; *see also* Jonathon Keats, *In Praise of the Fake*, THE NEW STATESMAN (May 3, 2013), *available at* http://www.newstatesman.com/art-and-design/2013/05/praise-fake.

(and a seller's representations), the buyer normally will demand that the seller rescind the sale, take back the forged work, and return the purchase price. For the seller, the incentive to quietly unwind the sale is a face-saving move—where the notoriety of a lawsuit carries significant reputational risk, as well as cost, angst, and uncertainty.

However, if an amicable rescission of the sale is not feasible, the disgruntled buyer will likely bring an action against the ultimate seller of the work, the art merchant (dealer, gallery, or auction house), or both. The basis of such a claim is typically a mixture of tort law and contract law—fraud, misrepresentation, or breach of warranty. While the elements the buyer will need to show are different for each of these causes of action, a common additional consideration for all of them is timing—(1) what statute of limitations will apply, after which the action cannot be brought, (2) when that limitations period will begin to run (whether at the time the event occurred, when the buyer should have known about it, or when the buyer actually discovered it), and (3) whether a court will apply the equitable doctrine of laches to bar the buyer's claim (laches is essentially the position that the buyer has waited too long to bring the claim, and that as a result of that delay, the seller suffers damage or prejudice, which usually has to be in the form of evidence or witnesses no longer being available). The details of each of these three timing elements will vary, depending on where the action is brought and which state's (or country's) law applies.

To bring a claim for fraud, the buyer must establish that (1) a representation of a material fact was made, (2) the representation was untrue, (3) the party making the representation knew it was untrue, (4) the party made the representation intending to deceive the buyer and in order to induce the buyer to act on the representation, (5) the buyer justifiably relied on the representation, and (6) by relying on it, the buyer suffered harm (i.e., damages). A claim for misrepresentation similarly will require the buyer to show that (1) the party making the statement was aware that the buyer would use the information for a particular purpose, (2) the relationship of the parties required that the information be provided with care, and (3) the buyer justifiably relied on the information. The factual needs for making successful claims of fraud and misrepresentation can be challenging.

Claims based on breaches of warranties are closer to breaches of a contractual relationship between the parties. Therefore, depending on the documentation involved in the sale, it is possible that certain warranties may have been waived or curtailed. Close attention to all documentation is critical. In U.S. art transactions, warranties will typically be governed by the Uniform Commercial Code (the UCC, enacted in each individual state with some modifications). The UCC warranties applicable to art transactions are (1) express warranties,[22] (2) implied warranties of merchantability,[23] and (3) implied warranties of fitness for a particular purpose.[24] For certain types of cross-border art sales (usually those between art dealers or galleries), the Convention on the International Sale of Goods (CISG) may apply instead. The UCC warranties find their CISG analogues in the presumptions set out in CISG article 35(2), concerning what qualifies as conforming goods. More extended discussions of warranties under the CISG and the UCC, as well as the differences between them, are included in Chapter 8 (which discusses the CISG) and Chapter 9 (which discusses the UCC).

For art sales, the warranty that is the subject of most litigation is the express warranty. The express warranty can come into existence through (1) the seller's affirmation of a fact or promise,[25] (2) the seller's description of the artwork,[26] or (3) the seller's statements of opinion about the artwork.[27] The key elements for an express warranty are what are called the "core description" of the artwork (i.e., artist, period, date, etc.)[28] and any statements the seller makes that become "part of the basis of the bargain."[29] If the artwork fails to conform to the seller's affirmations or promises, the warranty is breached, regardless of the seller's good-faith or malicious intentions in making the false statement. Unlike in fraud or misrepresentation, with warranties, the seller does not need to intend to deceive the buyer.

Disputes concerning implied warranties occur less frequently in art sales, but they do sometimes arise; when they do, they almost always involve implied warranties of merchantability (that an object is saleable) or implied warranties of fitness for a particular purpose (which

---

22 UCC § 2-313 (a promise or description of the goods that becomes the basis of the bargain creates an express warranty).

23 UCC § 2-314 (a warranty that goods are merchantable is implied in the sale of goods by a merchant with respect to goods of that kind).

24 UCC § 2-315 (a buyer's reliance on a seller's particular skill or judgment to select or furnish suitable goods for a particular purpose will give rise to an implied warranty).

25 *See, e.g.*, Tunick v. Kornfeld, 838 F.Supp. 848 (S.D.N.Y. 1993) (finding a breach of a seller's express warranty where a Picasso print was authentic, but the signature was forged).

26 *See, e.g.*, Weber v. Peck, Case No. 97 Civ. 7625(JSM), 1999 WL 493383 (S.D.N.Y. July 8, 1999) (finding a breach of a seller's express warranty where a bill of sale described a painting's provenance, which was later impossible to confirm).

27 *See, e.g.*, Levin v. Gallery 63 Antiques Corp., No. 04 CV 1504 KMK, 2006 WL 2802008 (S.D.N.Y. Sept. 28, 2006)(denying a seller's summary judgment motion where the seller stated that sculptures were by and signed by artists, but were shown to be multiples produced in the artists' ateliers).

28 UCC § 2-313, cmt. 1, 4.

29 UCC § 2-313, cmt. 8.

will depend upon the statements made by seller to buyer and also by buyer to seller—if a seller knows that a buyer has specific requirements, and is relying on the seller's expertise to meet those requirements, an implied warranty of fitness for that particular purpose may exist).

As in many kinds of transactions, art sales require caution, due diligence (research and confirmation into the seller as well as the work and the work's provenance), and a skepticism to serve as a counterbalance to the collector's natural impulse, which usually is passion and enthusiasm. Much of the art trade still operates more loosely and informally than typical business transactions, and buyers may hesitate to ask questions for fear of losing out on an opportunity or seeming to be out of step. Nevertheless, *caveat emptor* remains wise counsel.

C. The Processes of Authentication: Knoedler & Company

In 2011, the 165-year-old Knoedler & Company ("Knoedler"), one of Manhattan's most venerable galleries, abruptly closed its doors amid accusations that the gallery had been selling fakes for more than a decade. Ten lawsuits have been filed against the gallery and its former director, Ann Freedman,[30] six of which have ended in settlements. Four suits remain pending. These cases have involved works purporting to be by Robert Motherwell,[31] Jackson Pollock,[32] Clyfford Still,[33] Willem de Kooning,[34]

---

30 James Panero, *"I Am the Central Victim": Art Dealer Ann Freedman on Selling $63 Million in Fake Paintings*, New York Magazine (Aug. 27, 2013), *available at* http://nymag.com/daily/intelligencer/2013/08.

31 Patricia Cohen, *Motherwell Painting Declared a Forgery*, The New York Times (Oct. 11, 2011), *available at* http://www.nytimes.com/2011/10/12/arts/design/motherwell-painting-declared-a-forgery.html?scp=1&sq=knoedler%20Dedalus&st=cse.

32 Patricia Cohen, *Settlement Agreement Ends Lawsuit Over Disputed Pollock*, The New York Times (Oct. 5, 2012), *available at* http://artsbeat.blogs.nytimes.com/2012/10/05/settlement-agreement-ends-lawsuit-over-disputed-pollock; Patricia Cohen, *Hearings Shed Light on Pollock Dispute*, The New York Times (Dec. 16, 2011), *available at* http://www.nytimes.com/2011/12/17/arts/design/hearings-shed-light-on-dispute-over-authenticity-of-pollocks.html; Laura Gilbert, *Knoedler Gallery and Former Director Quietly Settle Three Claims over Fake Paintings*, The Art Newspaper (Aug. 11, 2015), *available at* http://theartnewspaper.com/news/news/knoedler-gallery-and-former-director-settle-three-claims-over-fake-paintings.

33 Laura Gilbert, *Knoedler Gallery and Former Director Quietly Settle Three Claims Over Fake Paintings*, The Art Newspaper (August 11, 2015), *available at* http://theartnewspaper.com/news/news/knoedler-gallery-and-former-director-settle-three-claims-over-fake-paintings.

34 Laura Gilbert, *Knoedler Gallery Settles Lawsuit Over Fake Willem de Kooning*, The Art Newspaper (Dec. 3, 2015), *available at* http://theartnewspaper.com/news/knoedler-gallery-settles-lawsuit-over-fake-willem-de-kooning/.

and Mark Rothko.[35] The most recent of these to settle is the suit brought by collectors Domenico and Eleanore De Sole (the "De Soles") against Knoedler and Freedman, which produced two weeks of closely watched testimony before the parties reached separate agreements on February 7, 2016 (with respect to Freedman),[36] and February 10, 2016 (with respect to the gallery).[37]

Since the De Sole case settled, it did not elicit a refined judicial statement on the due diligence required of a sophisticated collector when purchasing a work of art or, conversely, the due diligence required of a leading gallery when investigating a work's provenance and authenticity, as some commentators had hoped. However, the trial is important because it opened a window onto how an artwork's provenance is investigated, how a work is authenticated, and how an attribution is established. It is a case study in interpretation, misinterpretation, and misdirection. This case offers lessons not only in due diligence, but also in the importance of maintaining a self-protective skepticism in the highly relationship-based environment of art transactions. The question this case asks, for the collector, the gallerist, and the authenticator, is "On what information can and should a person rely?"[38]

1. The De Sole Rothko

In late 2004, the De Soles purchased a painting from Knoedler, a red-and-black canvas identified as *Untitled, 1956* by the American Abstract Expressionist artist, Mark Rothko. In connection with the sale, Freedman provided the De Soles with a letter stating that the gallery "warrants the authenticity and good title of the painting, *Untitled, 1956*, and confirms its 'remarkably good condition.'" The De Soles were told that the painting

---

[35] Patricia Cohen, *Knoedler Gallery Again Accused of Fraud in New Lawsuit*, The New York Times (Jan. 30, 2013), *available at* http://artsbeat.blogs.nytimes.com/2013/01/30/knoedler-gallery-again-accused-of-fraud-in-new-lawsuit/?_r=0; Laura Gilbert, *Knoedler Gallery and Former Director Quietly Settle Three Claims Over Fake Paintings*, The Art Newspaper (Aug. 11, 2015), *available at* http://theartnewspaper.com/news/news/knoedler-gallery-and-former-director-settle-three-claims-over-fake-paintings/.

[36] Colin Moynihan, *Knoedler Gallery Director Settles Lawsuit Over Fake Rothko*, The New York Times (Feb. 7, 2016), *available at* http://www.nytimes.com/2016/02/08/arts/design/knoedler-gallery-director-settles-lawsuit-over-fake-rothko.html?_r=0.

[37] Colin Moynihan, *Knoedler Gallery and Collectors Settle Case Over Fake Rothko*, The New York Times (Feb. 10, 2016), *available at* http://www.nytimes.com/2016/02/11/arts/design/knoedler-gallery-and-collectors-settle-case-over-fake-rothko.html.

[38] I have previously written about the legal position of buyers and sellers with respect to art fakes and forgeries at http://www.gtlaw-culturalassets.com/2014/11/authenticity-fakes-and-forgeries.

had been viewed by many scholars and specialists, including Christopher Rothko, the artist's son, that the authors of the Rothko *catalogue raissoné* intended to include it in a forthcoming supplement, and that the gallery had been approached concerning a loan request for the painting for an exhibition at Basel's *Fondation Beyeler*.

However, the painting's provenance (that is, the history of its ownership from the time of its creation to the present day) was problematic. It was new to the market, never having been exhibited, and was previously unknown to scholars. No record of it existed. The De Soles were told that the painting came from the collection of a couple (now deceased) who had lived in Switzerland and Mexico, and who had acquired it along with many other works directly from the artists, with the assistance of art dealer David Herbert[39] (who died in 1995). The couple's son had inherited the painting, along with other works in his parents' collection. Since he desired anonymity, the gallery could not disclose his identity or the identities of his parents.

Seven years after they acquired the painting, Eleanore De Sole happened to read an article about a lawsuit between Knoedler and another collector over the sale of a Jackson Pollock painting that turned out to be fake. One fact in particular caught her attention. The Pollock had originally been purchased directly from the artist himself with the assistance of David Herbert.

2. A Mysterious Provenance

When Ann Freedman was introduced to the Long Island art dealer Glafira Rosales in the mid-1990s, Rosales spoke to Freedman of a client with a collection of Abstract Expressionist paintings. The paintings, she said, had been acquired by a wealthy businessman (whom Rosales would identify only as "Mr. X") who lived in Mexico and Switzerland. The collector had acquired the paintings in the 1940s and 1950s directly from the artists in studio sales. The paintings had been in storage for decades and were unknown to the art world. None had ever been exhibited. When the collector and his wife passed away, their son and daughter had inherited the works, Rosales told Freedman that the owner (the son) was a very private person, and would not permit his name or the names of his parents to be

[39] *See* http://www.aaa.si.edu/collections/david-herbert-papers-6259.

disclosed. In response to inquiries, Freedman was told that no records of the paintings' purchase had been retained—no bills of sale, no correspondence.

3. Expert Disagreements

The authenticity of a work of art is established through a combination of three distinct types of expert opinion—(1) provenance (the documented history of the work from its creation to the present); (2) connoisseurship (the analysis of an artist's style, subject, and typical manner of working—often by scholars, the artist's friends and family or estate representatives, and formal authentication boards); and (3) scientific analysis of the object itself (to determine if its materials are consistent with those available to and used by the artist). As in many areas, art experts frequently disagree with each other's conclusions. This was certainly true of the paintings from Mr. X's collection.

A perfect provenance would document a work from the moment it was created or left the artist's studio down to the present day. It would include any bills of sale, correspondence, art transport documents, conservation documents, as well as the work's exhibition history, catalogs, and scholarly publications. For a painting to arrive on the market out of the blue, without a documented provenance, is a tremendous problem. Knoedler engaged art historian Stephen Polcari, the author of *Abstract Expressionism and the Modern Experience*, to review the paintings, and to research and assess their provenance and historical significance. Polcari initially believed that the paintings had been acquired through the painter Alfonso Ossorio,[40] a colleague and close friend of many of the artists. But when that provenance was disproven by a report issued by the International Foundation for Art Research (IFAR),[41] which cast doubt on the authenticity of a Knoedler-Rosales Pollock, he and Knoedler revised that provenance, replacing Ossorio with David Herbert. Polcari considered the paintings to be of "obvious quality and achievement." In his April 2012 deposition (more than a year before Rosales admitted that all of the paintings were fakes), he stated, "I was convinced of the works' authenticity because of the quality of the artists achievement, and the variety, depth,

---

40 *See* http://www.ossoriofoundation.org.

41 *See* http://ifar.org/home.php.

and breadth of the works. I never for a moment doubted that the Silver Pollock or the De Sole Rothko were by their respective artists."[42]

Even where a work's provenance is better documented, experts may nevertheless disagree based on either connoisseurship or materials analysis. A cache of 32 unsigned paintings purported to be by Jackson Pollock were discovered in 2003 in an East Hampton storage locker that had belonged to artist Mercedes Matter and filmmaker Herbert Matter, who had been friends of Pollock and his wife, Lee Krasner. After his parents' deaths, the Matters' son discovered the paintings wrapped in brown paper on which was written "Pollock (1946–49), Tudor City (1940–49), 32 Jackson Pollock experimental works (gift + purchase)." Leading scholars of Pollock's work, reviewing the group of paintings, disagreed sharply on whether they were in fact by Pollock.[43] Ellen Landau believed them to be by Pollock, but Eugene Victor Thaw said that they were not.[44] Both Landau and Thaw are former members of the Pollock-Krasner Foundation authentication board (which disbanded in 1996),[45] and Thaw is an author of the Pollock *catalogue raisonné.*

Materials analysis of the Matters' paintings tipped the balance of opinion. They were subjected to several types of scientific analysis, which cast serious doubt on claims that the paintings were Pollock's. Analysis of the pigments used in the paintings revealed that the paintings included pigments that were not available until considerably after Pollock's death in 1956. A study conducted by the Harvard University Art Museums concluded that "a pigment in one of the paintings wasn't introduced as artists' paint until 1996, and a pigment on a second work has been available

---

42 DECLARATION OF STEPHEN POLCARI (April 27, 2012), at 3.

43 Randy Kennedy, *Is This a Real Jackson Pollack?* THE NEW YORK TIMES (May 29, 2005), *available at* http://www.nytimes.com/2005/05/29/arts/design/is-this-a-real-jackson-pollock.html.

44 Kelly Devine Thomas, *The Newfound Pollocks: Real or Fake?* ARTNEWS (July 1, 2005), *available at* http://www.artnews.com/2005/07/01/the-newfound-pollocks-real-or-fake.

45 Because of the threat of litigation, many scholars and authentication boards have ceased giving opinions on the authenticity of works of art. Jack Flam, president of the Daedalus Foundation, and co-author of the Robert Motherwell *catalogue raisonné*: "In the US, unfortunately, the relationship between scholarship and the market is asymmetrical. Anyone can say with impunity that a painting is an authentic work, based solely on personal opinion. Even if they are wrong, their saying so is not necessarily actionable in court. But if a scholar who specializes in that artist's work says the painting is not authentic, the threat of a lawsuit arises—even though the scholar's opinion is right and is being offered gratis and in the public interest." Jack Flam, *Break the Silence Over Fakes*, THE ART NEWSPAPER (April 12, 2012), *available at* http://old.theartnewspaper.com/articles/Break%20the%20silence%20over%20fakes/26124. I have previously written about this, and attempted to craft legislation to provide authenticators with some measure of protection from suit, at http://www.gtlaw-culturalassets.com/2015/06/new-york-senate-passes-bill-to-protect-art-authenticators and at http://www.gtlaw-culturalassets.com/2014/11/authenticity-and-attribution.

only since 1971."[46] Additional testing identified a specific pigment that was used in 10 of the Matter paintings (Red 254, which is also known as "Ferrari Red"), which was only patented in 1980.[47] The paintings were also subjected to fractal analysis to determine whether they contained repeating patterns researchers believed to have been found in authentic Pollock paintings.[48] This analysis failed to find patterns in the Matter paintings consistent with those in works by Pollock.

With the Knoedler/Rosales paintings, which came with no documented provenance, experts disagreed over the paintings' authenticity, with some voicing doubt from the start. Among the first paintings Rosales brought to Knoedler were several purportedly by Richard Diebenkorn. Freedman showed the paintings to a number of Diebenkorn experts, including members of the Diebenkorn family. Based upon a combination of provenance and connoisseurship, the Diebenkorn experts expressed strong skepticism about the works and also pointed out that it would have been highly unlikely that any genuine work by Diebenkorn in that period would have left the artist's studio with no record of it existing.[49] But other experts, examining the style of the paintings, praised their quality and how finely they fit into the artist's known oeuvres. When IFAR issued its report calling into question the authenticity of the Greenish Pollock, Polcari rejected IFAR's conclusions. "I do not believe," Polcari stated in his deposition testimony, "that an IFAR opinion on authenticity is inherently definitive, and I do not regard IFAR as the authority on modern art. . . . I have reviewed the IFAR report and I do not find it convincing. IFAR never asked for my opinion on the authenticity of the Greenish Pollock." [50]

Notably, Polcari and Knoedler did accept IFAR's conclusion that the paintings could not have been acquired through Ossorio. Although

---

[46] Geoff Edgers, *Harvard Study Casts More Doubt on Disputed Pollock Paintings*, THE BOSTON GLOBE (Jan. 30, 2007), *available at* http://www.boston.com/ae/theater_arts/articles/2007/01/30/harvard_study_casts_more_doubt_on_disputed_pollock_paintings/?page=full.

[47] M. Rae Nelson, *Authentic or Not? Chemistry Solves the Mystery*, CHEMMATTERS (April 2011), *available at* https://www.acs.org/content/dam/acsorg/education/resources/highschool/chemmatters/videos/chemmatters-april2011-authentic-or-not.pdf.

[48] *See, e.g.*, J.R. Minkel, *Pollock or Not? Can Fractals Spot a Fake Masterpiece?* SCIENTIFIC AMERICAN (Oct. 31, 2007), *available at* http://www.scientificamerican.com/article/can-fractals-spot-genuine; *see also* Michael Schreyach, *"I Am Nature": Science and Jackson Pollock*, APOLLO (July 2007), *available at* http://digitalcommons.trinity.edu/cgi/viewcontent.cgi?article=1003&context=art_faculty.

[49] Eileen Kinsella, *Richard Diebenkorn's Daughter Challenges Ann Freedman's Story at Knoedler Forgery Trial*, ARTNET NEWS (Jan. 27, 2016), *available at* https://news.artnet.com/market/gretchen-diebenkorn-knoedler-forgery-trial-414617.

[50] *Declaration of Stephen Polcari* (April 27, 2012), at 5.

Knoedler and Polcari replaced Ossorio with David Herbert, that surmise, which was presented to potential buyers as a fact, lacked any documentary support. Provenance researchers engaged by the gallery to research the relevant archives were unable to find any such connection. One of the experts listed in the Knoedler authentication letter for the De Sole Rothko, art historian Jack Flam, testified that he was surprised to find himself so included. While Flam is an expert in the work of Robert Motherwell, he stated that he is not an expert in the work of Mark Rothko.[51]

Scientific analysis of the De Sole Rothko also played an important role, and simultaneously highlighted how the seemingly objective, implacable factuality of scientific analysis can itself be the subject of expert disagreement. The De Soles engaged a materials analysis and consulting firm to examine the Rothko. The resulting report identified a number of elements of the canvas inconsistent with Rothko's known materials and techniques, including the presence of (1) "crossbar marks" (marks on the canvas where it "presses against the edge of a crossbar . . . [which] can cause primer and paint to crack, primer and paint to build up along the edge, or both"),[52] (2) white opaque primer layers, (3) a polyvinyl acetate based ground, and (4) an acrylic polymer emulsion "which did not appear in Rothko's paintings until the mid 1960s, nearly a decade after the date on the back of *Untitled, 1956*."[53] The report concluded that "materials and techniques used to create the Painting are inconsistent and irreconcilable with the claim that *Untitled* was painted by Mark Rothko . . . in 1956 or any other date."[54]

Polcari rejected the report's conclusions, persisting in his assessment that the painting was a "work of obvious quality and achievement." He pointed out that some artists in the 1950s were given access to paints that were not yet commercially available. "[T]he fact that the De Sole Rothko may contain paints that Rothko decided not to use in other works in the mid-1950s, or used sparingly," Polcari said, "is unremarkable."[55] However, except for raising a broad caution, Polcari failed to explain why the particular materials identified in the report should be regarded as consis-

---

51 Brian Boucher, *Art Historian Jack Flam Bristles on the Stand at Knoedler Fraud Trial*, ARTNET NEWS (Feb. 3, 2016), *available at* https://news.artnet.com/art-world/knoedler-fraud-trial-jack-flam-martha-parrish-419594.

52 *Report of Orion Analytical, LLC [Orion Project No. 1745]*, Feb. 6, 2012.

53 *Id.*

54 *Id.*

55 *Declaration of Stephen Polcari* (April 27, 2012), at 9.

tent with the artist's practice in this period. Materials analysts examined sixteen of the Knoedler/Rosales paintings and identified the same materials (including the puzzling primers and grounds—"what you would find if you went to Home Depot for primer"). Of the sixteen paintings examined, fourteen "used historically inaccurate materials, six had suspicious signatures, five showed signs of deliberate aging, and nine had been created on top of old paintings."[56]

4. The Forger's Art

In a case involving the sale of a fake or forged work of art, typically the first order of business is for the plaintiff to establish that the work is, in fact, not authentic, with each side marshaling its experts. In the case of the De Sole Rothko, this step was unnecessary. Before the trial commenced, Rosales entered a plea, admitting guilt, in a criminal action brought by the U.S. government. In a statement read into the record at the time of her plea, Rosales admitted that "I agreed with others to sell works of art claimed to be created by various expressionist artists, including Mark Rothko, Jackson Pollock, and Robert Motherwell, and to make false representations as to the authenticity and provenance of those works. . . . All of the works I sold to [Knoedler Gallery] . . . were, in fact, fakes."[57] Rosales's accomplices—her boyfriend, art dealer Jose Carlos Bergantiños Diaz, his brother, Jesus Angel Bergantiños Diaz, and the actual forger, Pei Shen Qian[58]—were also indicted.[59] All three men fled the United States—the Diaz brothers to Spain and Qian to China.[60]

---

[56] Cait Munro, *Conservator Found Rothko Painting in Knoedler Trial to Be a "Deliberate Fake,"* ArtNet News (Feb. 4, 2016), *available at* https://news.artnet.com/art-world/former-librarian-hot-seat-knoedler-fraud-trial-420161?utm_campaign=artnetnews&utm_source=020516daily&utm_medium=email.

[57] Plea, Sept. 16, 2013, U.S. v. Rosales, 13-CR-518(KPF).

[58] *Accused Master Forger Tracked Down in Shanghai*, ABC News Nightline (July 15, 2014), *available at* http://abcnews.go.com/Blotter/accused-master-art-forger-tracked-shanghai/story?id=24558288.

[59] U.S. v. Jose Carlos Bergantinos Diaz, Jesus Angel Bergantinos Diaz, and Pei Shen Qian, Sealed Indictment, 14 Crim. 217, Mar. 31, 2014, *available at* http://www.justice.gov/sites/default/files/usao-sdny/legacy/2015/03/25/Bergantinos%20Diaz%20%26%20Qian%20Indictment.pdf.

[60] Javier Pes, *Brother of Spanish Dealer in Alleged Forgery Ring Could Be Extradicted to US*, The Art Newspaper (Feb. 16, 2016), *available at* http://theartnewspaper.com/news/news/brother-of-spanish-dealer-could-be-extradited-to-us/.

There are two distinct roles in every forgery scheme—the artist and the con man. Some forgers, like Han Van Meegeren,[61] Elmyr de Hory,[62] Eric Hebborn,[63] Ken Perenyi,[64] and Wolfgang Beltracchi,[65] combine both in a single person. They are impresarios of fraud. But this is not always the case. John Myatt was a successful forger, but his role in the scheme was chiefly artistic. It was his accomplice, John Drewe, who conceived of the con and was its principal author.[66] Drewe commissioned paintings from Myatt, but it was Drewe who forged the elaborate provenance documents for the works and orchestrated their sales. Similarly, Ely Sakhai, a New York dealer, orchestrated the scam. He purchased original (albeit second-tier) works that had genuine certificates of authenticity. Sakhai then hired artists to copy them in a workshop above his gallery. Like Drewe, Sakhai handled the provenance (switching the genuine certificates of authenticity

---

61 Van Meegeren was a Dutch forger of the works of Johannes Vermeer, who gained notoriety in the aftermath of WWII when he was accused of selling national patrimony (a painting by Vermeer) to Nazi official Hermann Goring. Van Meegeren's defense was that the painting was a forgery that he had himself produced, and that Goring had been duped. To prove his claim, officials required Van Meegeren to paint a Vermeer on the spot, which he did. Ironically, the forger was acclaimed a national hero in the press. For more information, see Peter Schjeldahl, *Dutch Master,* THE NEW YORKER (Oct. 27, 2008), *available at* http://www.newyorker.com/magazine/2008/10/27/dutch-master; JONATHAN LOPEZ, THE MAN WHO MADE VERMEERS: UNVARNISHING THE LEGEND OF MASTER FORGER HAN VAN MEEGEREN (2009); AND EDWARD DOLNICK, THE FORGER'S SPELL: A TRUE STORY OF VERMEER, NAZIS, AND THE GREATEST ART HOAX OF THE TWENTIETH CENTURY (2009).

62 De Hory was an extravagant personality best known for his forgeries of Picasso and Matisse. He was the subject of a biography FAKE! THE STORY OF ELMYR DE HORY, THE GREATEST ART FORGER OF OUR TIME (1969) by Clifford Irving (who was himself later revealed as a literary forger for producing a fraudulent Howard Hughes biography) and of the Orson Welles documentary "F for Fake" (1973)(see Roger Ebert review of the film, Oct. 13, 1977, *available at* http://www.rogerebert.com/reviews/f-for-fake). *See also* MARK FORGY, THE FORGER'S APPRENTICE: LIFE WITH THE WORLD'S MOST NOTORIOUS ARTIST (2012).

63 Hebborn was an accomplished artist and graduate of the Royal Academy. His specialization was producing works in the style of Old Masters. He produced several best-selling memoirs, including DRAWN TO TROUBLE: CONFESSIONS OF A MASTER FORGER (1993) and THE ART FORGER'S HANDBOOK (1996). *See also* the documentary: "Eric Hebborn: Portrait of a Master Forger," *available at* https://www.youtube.com/watch?v=8jKbbajb5pE.

64 Perenyi produced numerous forgeries in the style of 19th-century American painters Martin Jonson Heade, J.E. Buttersworth, and Charles Bird King. He produced a memoir, CAVEAT EMPTOR: THE SECRET LIFE OF AN AMERICAN ART FORGER (2013).

65 Wolfgang Beltracchi produced fakes in the styles of Kees Van Dongen, Max Ernst, Max Pechstein, and Heinrich Campendonk. He and his wife, Helène, produced an elaborate false provenance for the works, claiming they were part of a collection built by Heléne's grandparents. They staged what appeared to be old photos of Helène in period costume, posing as her grandmother, with Beltracchi's fakes hanging on the walls behind her. For more information, see Joshua Hammer, *The Greatest Fake-Art Scam in History?*, VANITY FAIR (Oct. 10, 2012), *available at* http://www.vanityfair.com/culture/2012/10/wolfgang-beltracchi-helene-art-scam; the documentary *Beltracchi: The Art of Forgery* (2014), http://www.imdb.com/title/tt3212568/; and a profile on *60 Minutes* (Feb. 24, 2014), *available at* https://www.youtube.com/watch?v=8TZppXXsLUw.

66 For more information on the Myatt/Drewe forgeries, see LANEY SALISBURY AND ALY SUJO, PROVENANCE: HOW A CON MAN AND A FORGER RE-WROTE THE HISTORY OF MODERN ART (2010).

to the forgeries) and made the sales.[67] Drewe and Myatt's scheme collapsed when Drewe's estranged girlfriend turned him in. Sakhai, on the other hand, was caught when both Christie's and Sotheby's happened to offer exactly the same Gauguin still life for sale (one the original, the other a Sakhai forgery).

Money is usually a compelling motive for forgers. An outlier in this was Mark Landis,[68] who instead donated his fakes to museums and universities across the country. But an important motivation for most forgers is also the dual satisfaction of (1) seeing their work acknowledged as equal to that of renowned artists and (2) revealing art world experts as dupes and frauds. Many forgers begin as technically accomplished artists who, like many artists, find success elusive. They wish to prove themselves superior to the experts.

The artist who actually produced the Knoedler/Rosales fakes was Pei Shen Qian, who made a name for himself as an abstract artist in China but then struggled for any recognition after he immigrated to New York. Jose Carlos Bergantiños Diaz, no stranger to fraudulent art dealing, discovered Qian selling his paintings on the street and commissioned him to produce paintings in the style of other artists. [69] Although in interviews Qian has claimed that he did not know his paintings were being represented as originals, the facts laid out in the indictment suggest otherwise. Qian was initially paid a few hundred dollars per painting, but after he spotted one of his paintings offered at an art show for a substantially higher price, he demanded more money, and Bergantiños Diaz and Rosales thereafter paid Qian several thousand dollars per painting. Bergantiños Diaz, like Drewe and Sakhai, conceived and organized the scheme. Qian used materials that were meant to give his paintings the appearance of age, employing old canvases, old paint, and Masonite panels taken from antique furniture that Bergantiños Diaz provided to him. In Qian's studio, the FBI discovered books on Abstract Expressionist artists and

---

67 Clive Thompson, *How to Make a Fake*, NEW YORK MAGAZINE (June 19, 2012), *available at* http://nymag.com/nymetro/arts/features/9179/; *see also* Julia Preston, *Art Gallery Owner Pleads Guilty in Forgery Found by Coincidence*, THE NEW YORK TIMES (Dec. 14, 2004), *available at* http://www.nytimes.com/2004/12/14/nyregion/art-gallery-owner-pleads-guilty-in-forgery-found-by-coincidence.html.

68 Landis is the subject of the documentary *Art and Craft* (2014), and also of a profile by Alec Wilkinson, *The Giveaway*, THE NEW YORKER (Aug. 26, 2013), *available at* http://www.newyorker.com/magazine/2013/08/26/the-giveaway.

69 U.S. v. Jose Carlos Bergantinos Diaz, Jesus Angel Bergantinos Diaz, and Pei Shen Qian, Sealed Indictment, 14 Crim. 217, Mar. 31, 2014, *available at* http://www.justice.gov/sites/default/files/usao-sdny/legacy/2015/03/25/Bergantinos%20Diaz%20%26%20Qian%20Indictment.pdf.

their techniques, auction catalogues, art materials, and even "an envelope of old nails marked 'Mark Rothko.'"[70]

5. Object Lessons

There are many victims in the fall of Knoedler & Company, and many victimizers. Yet reading through the voluminous testimony the De Sole case produced with the clarity that only hindsight can provide, some lessons can be taken. The lessons are not new, but it is helpful to be reminded of them.

- Although some forgers replicate existing works, the more common practice is to create new works in the style of an artist and to present it as a new discovery. Previously unknown works by marketable artists are the forger's stock in trade.
- Provenance matters. Provenance can be faked. It can be misrepresented and overrepresented. However, a lack of provenance documented from multiple sources is the reddest of red flags. Provisional research or unverified provenance claims should be presented with qualifiers, not as established facts.
- The authentication of a work by style or manner alone is vulnerable to error.
- Experts frequently disagree. This is because determining the authenticity of any object is a highly contextual, highly contingent process, drawing on a broad host of facts and educated guesses.
- While scientific analysis of the materials and techniques of an object must be interpreted like other forms of expert opinion, the presence of materials or techniques that would not have been available or employed by the artist or at a particular period is compelling evidence that must be considered and evaluated.
- The *catalogue raisonné* of an artist's work is an important tool. However, while the *catalogue raisonné* is being researched and written, its findings are provisional. A statement that a work is being considered for inclusion in a *catalogue raisonné* (or a supplement) should not be

[70] *Id.*

understood to be a statement concerning that work's authenticity. Even after a *catalogue raisonne's* publication, if information emerges calling a work into question, the work may be designated as problematic.[71]

- While personal relationships and reputations are paramount in the art world, reliance on reputation alone is never wise. A healthy self-protective skepticism is no less necessary in art transactions than in any other type of business transaction.

6. An Artist's Own Attribution

While disputes over authentication and attribution generally arise posthumously and involve parties other than the artist, this is not always the case. Occasionally disagreements arise between living artists and collectors when the artist disavows a work (under the rights of attribution and integrity, discussed in Chapter 2) when a work has been damaged or altered (including being restored in a manner the artist deems unauthorized or inappropriate). Controversy has arisen in connection with Cady Noland's disavowal (or apparent disavowal) of several works.[72] But Noland is hardly alone, and disavowals by other artists have also made news, including Lucian Freud, Pablo Picasso, Frank Stella, and Gerhard Richter.[73]

A unique case, however, arose when a former officer at a Canadian juvenile corrections facility and a Chicago gallery sued artist Peter Doig for denying that a painting the corrections officer had purchased in the 1970s from a teen inmate of the facility (the painting was signed

[71] See, for example, the deposition testimony of Ruth Fine, formerly of the National Gallery of Art's Mark Rothko *catalogue raisonné* project: "I would see the *catalogue raisonné* as being the documentation of all known works by Rothko at the time of its publication, and I don't think I would describe it as all known authentic works by Rothko, I would describe it as all known works by Rothko." For more information about the Rothko *catalogue raisonné* see National Gallery of Art, press release (Mark Rothko *Catalogue Raisonné*), Mar. 15, 2002 (updated Feb. 4, 2008), *available at* http://www.nga.gov/content/ngaweb/press/2002/rothko-works-on-paper.html.

[72] *See, e.g.*, Martha Buskirk, *Marc Jancou, Cady Noland, and the Case of the Authorless Artwork*, Hyperallergic (Dec. 9, 2013), *available at* http://hyperallergic.com/97416/marc-jancou-cady-noland-and-the-case-of-anauthorless-artwork/; Laura Gilbert, *Did Cady Noland Disavow Another Work?*, The Art Newspaper (June 25, 2015), *available at* http://theartnewspaper.com/news/news/did-cady-noland-disavow-another-work/.

[73] *See* Hazel Rowland, *When Artists Deny, Disavow or Reject Their Work*, Apollo (Sept. 5, 2016), *available at* http://www.apollo-magazine.com/when-artists-deny-disavow-or-reject-their-work/; Daniel Grant, *Artistic* Paternity: When *and How Artists Can Disavow Their Work*, The Observer (July 28, 2016), *available at* http://observer.com/2016/07/artistic-paternity-when-and-how-artists-can-disavow-their-work/.

"Pete Doige"). Doig denied that the work was his, and when the gallery consigned the painting with an auction house for sale, Doig, through counsel, contacted the auction house, insisting that the painting not be sold as his work. The corrections officer and the gallery sued Doig for interference with contractual relations and demanded that he acknowledge the painting as his work. What emerged in discovery in the case was that an amateur artist named Pete Doige, who died in 2012, was an inmate at the Thunder Bay, Ontario, juvenile correctional facility in the 1970s. Had the painting, which the officer purchased from Doige for $100, actually been a work by Doig, its present value was estimated at $8 million. Following a week-long bench trial, the judge issued his decision orally, finding for Doig and stating that Doig "absolutely did not paint the disputed work."[74]

[74] Fletcher v. Doig, Case No. 13 C 3270 (N.D. Ill.). *See* Dan Duray, *Chicago Judge Rules Peter Doig "Absolutely Did Not Paint" Disputed Work*, The Art Newspaper (Aug. 23, 2016), *available at* http://theartnewspaper.com/news/judge-rules-peter-doig-absolutely-did-notpaint-disputed-work/

CHAPTER 6

Questions of Title

A. Good Title

In typical transactions involving personal or real property, parties know at least the preliminary questions they need to ask and the steps they need to take to ensure that the transaction will be valid. They examine lien searches, needing to know if other parties have security interests in or liens on the property, if there are outstanding judgments that could attach to the property, or other claims that may potentially impair the exchange of rights in the property. In the case of real property, they undertake a search of the land records, verifying the metes and bounds of the property, the existence of any easements or rights of way, and any issues involving adjacent properties. They look at the various deeds to the property, making certain that they understand what the property is, who owns it, who has rights in connection with it, and that it is otherwise free of problems and issues. In acquiring real property, they obtain title insurance, which guaranties that there are no issues at the time of acquisition (or insures over them). They also obtain various forms of insurance on both personal and real property, to hedge the risk of damage or loss.

Art is no different in this respect: taking precautions to minimize risk is essential. However, when it comes to art and cultural property transactions, people are frequently reluctant to require the same level of disclosure and transparency that is considered commonplace, even mandatory, in transactions involving other kinds of property. This reluctance is changing, as the art trade itself changes, and as art and cultural property are ever more involved in other kinds of business transactions. But parties to these transactions are not always aware that there are issues that are unique to art, issues that can easily create problems for the unwary.

B. Provenance

As discussed in Chapter 5, provenance is the history of an object,[1] not simply the history of where it originated, but also the history of where it has been—ideally, continuously from the beginning down to the present. Such completeness is rare. Provenance can be an important element in the authentication or attribution of art, but it also plays an important role in tracing and establishing title to it.[2]

Provenience is an allied concept, but one with a specific meaning and function. Provenience refers to an archaeological or excavated object's documented find spot. This is the place where the object was discovered in modern times. Having a "known provenience or find spot adds to an object's authenticity and consequently increases its market value."[3] For archaeological objects, provenience is part of the object's provenance.

An object's provenance can be established through evidence from the object itself (stretchers, backing/relining), dealer marks, transport labels, customs stamps, exhibition stickers, curatorial records, conservation files, donor files, dealer records, sales catalogs, exhibition catalogs, and of course bills of sale, wills, gift agreements, and other documents. A complete record for older objects is hard to come by. The importance currently placed on provenance (or even authenticity, for that matter) has not always been the case. It is a fairly recent concern, which has been given far greater urgency in the last few decades.

> In the last quarter of the twentieth century . . . lightning struck what had seemed a quiet, essentially antiquarian pursuit. Revelations about systematic and extensive Naziera looting and forced sales ignited heated discourse around disputed claims of ownership; these claims posed real-life ethical dilemmas and held legal consequences for prominent stakeholders. . . . In parallel with this development, the international archaeological community forcefully articulated a position against the looting and illegal importation of antiquities from

[1] NANCY H. YEIDE, KONSTANTIN AKINSHA & AMY L. WALSH, THE AAM GUIDE TO PROVENANCE RESEARCH, 1 (2001). *See also Provenance & Due Diligence: Proceedings of Workshop/Conference: April 29, 2000*, 3 IFAR JOURNAL (2000).

[2] *Id.*

[3] Julie Hollowell, *St. Lawrence Island's Legal Market in Archaeological Hoods*, *in* Neil Brodie et al., eds., ARCHAEOLOGY, CULTURAL HERITAGE, AND THE ANTIQUITIES TRADE 120–121 (2006).

sites around the world. New legislation, a heated discourse, and claims for restitution prompted a surge of provenance research targeting traffic in such artifacts. Ethnographic collections likewise came under scrutiny, and questions of what constituted legitimate ownership were hotly debated.[4]

C. Stolen Art

1. Overview

We instinctually understand why the original owner would want the stolen object returned. Popular culture is sometimes ambivalent, though, regarding the theft of art as both glamorous and, to some extent, unserious. Art is a luxury good. The art heist is a familiar film trope, generally lighthearted, such as in *Gambit* (Michael Caine and Shirley MacLaine, 1966,[5] remade in 2012,[6] with Colin Firth, Cameron Diaz, and Alan Rickman), *Topkapi*[7] (Maximilian Schell, Melina Mercouri, Peter Ustinov, Robert Morley, and George Segal, 1964), *How to Steal a Million*[8] (Peter O'Toole and Audrey Hepburn, 1966), and *The Thomas Crown Affair* (Steve McQueen and Faye Dunaway, 1968,[9] remade in 1999,[10] with Pierce Brosnan and Rene Russo). However, it is sometimes considerably harsher, as in *Headhunters*[11] (Aksel Hennie, Synnove Macody Lund, and Nikolaj Coster-Waldau 2011) and *Trance*[12] (James McAvoy, Rosario Dawson, and Vincent Cassel, 2013). In its light-hearted variation, the art heist is perpetrated by a dashing, raffish thief (often a playboy, engaged in a dual life). After plot complications and reversals, the thief, on the verge of his

---

4 GAIL FEIGENBAUM & INGE REIST, PROVENANCE: AN ALTERNATE HISTORY OF ART 2 (2012).

5 *Gambit* (1966) (Internet Movie Database) http://www.imdb.com/title/tt0060445/?ref_=fn_al_tt_3.

6 *Gambit* (2012) (Internet Movie Database) http://www.imdb.com/title/tt0404978/?ref_=tt_rec_tt.

7 *Topkapi* (1964) (Internet Movie Database) http://www.imdb.com/title/tt0058672/?ref_=nv_sr_1.

8 *How to Steal a Million* (1966) (Internet Movie Database) http://www.imdb.com/title/tt0060522/?ref_=nv_sr_1.

9 *The Thomas Crown Affair* (1968) (Internet Movie Database) http://www.imdb.com/title/tt0063688/?ref_=nv_sr_2.

10 *The Thomas Crown Affair* (1999) (Internet Movie Database) http://www.imdb.com/title/tt0155267/?ref_=tt_rec_tti.

11 *Headhunters* (2011) (Internet Movie Database) http://www.imdb.com/title/tt1614989/.

12 *Trance* (2013) (Internet Movie Database) http://www.imdb.com/title/tt1924429/?ref_=fn_al_tt_1.

(or her) identity being revealed, outwits the lumbering authorities and escapes with the artwork, and usually his (or her) romantic interest.

Off-screen, art theft is less dashing, less romantic, and often involves (at some level) formal criminal networks. Among the highest-profile thefts from museums are (1) the brief theft of the *Mona Lisa* from the Louvre in 1911, taken by museum handyman Vincenzo Peruggia, who attempted to return the painting to Italy (the irony being that the painting had never been unlawfully removed from Italy);[13] (2) the 1990 theft of thirteen works (including paintings by Rembrandt, Vermeer, Degas, and Manet) from Boston's Isabella Stewart Gardner Museum,[14] which remains unsolved and the works unrecovered, although the FBI has identified persons of interest in the case, all of whom have ties to organized crime;[15] (3) the 2002 theft of two paintings from Amsterdam's Van Gogh Museum,[16] in which thieves entered the museum through the roof; the thieves were later arrested and convicted of the theft, but the paintings have not been recovered;[17] and (4) the 2012 theft of seven paintings (including works by Freud, Gauguin, Matisse, Monet, and Picasso) from Rotterdam's Kunsthal Museum,[18] taken by a group of Romanian thieves, and allegedly incinerated by the mother of one of the thieves to destroy evidence after the group had been arrested.[19]

Museums are not the exclusive targets of art theft. Art is perhaps even more frequently taken from private collections and other types of historic and cultural institutions. A few recent examples highlight how most art thefts are not the glamorous, highly planned affairs of film, but tend to be crimes of opportunity, often by those who simply happen (for

---

13 Sheena McKenzie, *Mona Lisa: The Theft that Created a Legend,* CNN (Nov. 19, 2013), *available at* http://www.cnn.com/2013/11/18/world/europe/mona-lisa-the-theft/.

14 Isabella Stewart Gardner Museum website, *available at* http://www.gardnermuseum.org/resources/theft; *see also* the FBI Art Crime Division's dedicated webpage on the Gardner theft, *available at* http://www.fbi.gov/news/stories/2013/march/reward-offered-for-return-of-stolen-gardner-museum-artwork/reward-offered-for-return-of-stolen-gardner-museum-artwork.

15 *FBI Has Confirmed Sightings of Gardner Artwork,* The Boston Globe (May 22, 2014), *available at* http://www.bostonglobe.com/news/nation/2014/05/22/fbi-has-confirmed-sightings-gardner-artwork-agent-says/ganlgCOOl6dSB66AOYsEcK/story.html.

16 *Two Van Gogh Paintings Stolen,* BBC News (Dec. 7, 2002), *available at* http://news.bbc.co.uk/2/hi/europe/2552877.stm.

17 FBI website, *available at* http://www.fbi.gov/about-us/investigate/vc_majorthefts/arttheft/van-gogh.

18 *Picasso, Matisse, Monet and More: Spectacular Art Heist Stuns Rotterdam Museum,* Der Spiegel Online (Oct. 16, 2012), *available at* http://www.spiegel.de/international/zeitgeist/thieves-steal-works-by-matisse-picasso-and-more-in-rotterdam-art-heist-a-861647.html.

19 *Rotterdam Art Heist: Stolen Masterpieces Likely Incinerated,* Der Spiegel Online (July 18, 2013), *available at* http://www.spiegel.de/international/europe/stolen-rotterdam-picasso-and-monet-paintings-destroyed-a-911775.html.

different purposes) to have access to the objects. In 2009, twelve paintings, including works by Marc Chagall, Chaim Soutine, Arshile Gorky, and Diego Rivera, were stolen from a residence in southern California. Nine of the paintings, reportedly valued at $12 million, were later recovered.[20] In 2011, a 12th-century illuminated musical manuscript, the Codex Calixtinus, was discovered missing from the Cathedral of Santiago de Compostela.[21] The manuscript had been taken by a former electrician, who had been engaged in an ongoing series of thefts from the cathedral, having taken, in addition to the manuscript, more than €2.4 million in cash. The thief was recently convicted and sentenced to a 10-year prison term.[22] Still another workman (another electrician, even) with opportunistic access to artworks has also made news recently, although the theft occurred decades ago. An electrician who worked for Pablo Picasso at his house in Mougins, France, and the electrician's wife, are currently on trial for stealing 271 artworks from the Picasso house, which the couple then stored in their garage for 37 years.[23] The Picasso works are valued at between €60 and €80 million.

Whether taken from museums or from private collections, when stolen objects are sold, they are moved through progressively higher-level intermediaries, cleansing them of information about the original owner and the circumstances of the theft. [24] With the passage of time, the stolen object is sold (possibly several times), and the current owner may have innocently purchased the object, with no inkling that its history is tainted. This situation is sometimes spoken of as involving "two innocents"—the

---

20 Michael Martinez, *Police Get Break in "Greatest". Art Heist in Recent L.A. History, Valued at $12 Million*, CNN (Dec. 20, 2014), *available at* http://www.cnn.com/2014/12/19/justice/los-angeles-art-heist-paintings-recovered/.

21 Belen Palanco, *Trial of Medieval Manuscript Theft to Begin Next Week*, THE ART NEWSPAPER (Jan. 1, 2015), *available at* http://www.theartnewspaper.com/articles/Trial-of-Medieval-manuscript-theft-due-to-start-next-week/36816 (fire wall).

22 Lorena Munoz-Alonso, *Spanish Electrician Who Stole Priceless Manuscript and €2.4 Million from Santiago Cathedral Gets 10 Years,*" ARTNET NEWS (Feb. 19, 2015), *available at* http://news.artnet.com/in-brief/spanish-electrician-who-stole-priceless-manuscript-and-eur24-million-from-santiago-cathedral-gets-10-years-260703?utm_campaign=artnetnews&utm_source=021915daily&utm_medium=email.

23 Lorena Munoz-Alonso, *Prosecutor Asks for Five-Year Suspended Prison Sentence for Picasso's Electrician Pierre Le Guennec*, ARTNET NEWS (Feb. 17, 2015), *available at* http://news.artnet.com/in-brief/prosecutor-asks-for-five-year-suspended-prison-sentence-for-picassos-electrician-pierre-le-guennec-256595.

24 Interpol, *Frequently Asked Questions*, *available at* http://www.interpol.int/Crime-areas/Works-of-art/Frequently-asked-questions.

original owner from whom the object was taken and the good faith purchaser with no knowledge of the theft.[25]

2. The Original Owner's Claim

To recover stolen artwork (rather than to recover money damages), the original owner brings an action in replevin for its return.[26] As a legal principle, a work of art (or any movable property) that is stolen remains stolen, no matter how many hands the artwork has passed through since the theft occurred. This principle is part of the common law, derived from the Roman law principle that was expressed as *nemo dat quod non habet* (one cannot give what one does not have) (sometimes abbreviated as "*nemo dat*"). This principle has been codified in state law at UCC § 2-403(1),[27] which states that:

> a purchaser of goods acquires all title which his transferor had or had power to transfer except that a purchaser of a limited interest acquires rights only to the extent of the interest purchased. A person with voidable title has power to transfer a good title to a good faith purchaser for value. When goods have been delivered under a transaction of purchase the purchaser has such power even though (a) the transferor was deceived as to the identity of the purchaser, or (b) the delivery was in exchange for a check which is later dishonored, or (c) it was agreed that the transaction was to be a "cash sale", or (d) the delivery was procured through fraud punishable as larcenous under the criminal law.

In English law and in European civil law, there are certain exceptions to this principle of *nemo dat,* such as in the medieval legal concept of the *market ouvert*, which permitted a purchaser to acquire good title to stolen

---

[25] *See* Menzel v. List, 267 N.Y.S.2d 804, 809 (Sup. Ct. 1966) ("The resolution of these problems is made the more difficult in view of the fact that one of two innocent parties must bear the loss."), *modified,* 279 N.Y.S.2d 608 (App. Div. 1967) (per curiam), *modification rev'd,* 246 N.E.2d 742 (N.Y. 1969). *See also* Ashton Hawkins, Richard A. Rothman, and David B. Goldstein, *A Tale of Two Innocents: Creating an Equitable Balance Between the Rights of Former Owners and Good Faith Purchasers of Stolen Art,* 64 FORDHAM L. REV. 49 (1995), *available at* http://ir.lawnet.fordham.edu/flr/vol64/iss1/3.

[26] *See, e.g.,* O'Keeffe v. Snyder, 416 A.2d 862 (N.J. 1980); Menzel v. List, 246 N.E.2d 742 (N.Y. 1969); Solomon R. Guggenheim Foundation v. Lubell, 569 N.E.2d 426 (N.Y. 1991), *available at* http://www.leagle.com/decision/199138877NY2d311_1361.xml/GUGGENHEIM%20FOUND.%20v.%20LUBELL *See also* Andrea E. Hayworth, *Stolen Artwork: Deciding Ownership Is No Pretty Picture,* 43 DUKE L.J. 337 (1993–1994).

[27] UCC § 2-403(a), *available at* https://www.law.cornell.edu/ucc/2/2-403.

property, provided that the sale was transacted in a public market during daylight.[28]

Under U.S. law, as UCC § 2-403(1) indicates, a transferor lacking good title can nevertheless pass good title to a good faith purchaser either (i) if the transferor has voidable title to the property (where the transferor has obtained the property by purchase from the original owner, even if that acquisition was made by fraud or deception),[29] or (ii) if the owner entrusted the property to the transferor and the transferor is a merchant who deals in goods of that kind.[30]

3. Statutes of Limitation

An original owner's right to bring a claim for the return of stolen artwork can be cut off by the application of an applicable statute of limitation. In the United States, most statutes of limitation applicable to actions to recover stolen art are set out in state law, and are of relatively short duration—typically between one and six years. These short limitation periods are intended to encourage claimants to promptly and diligently prosecute their claims. In addition to the length of the limitation period, state law also determines the critical issue of when the cause of action accrues (and when the statute of limitations begins to run). A state's approach to when a cause of action accrues for the recovery of stolen art will fall into one of three categories: (1) accruing when the claimant makes demand upon the current possessor of the artwork, and the current possessor refuses to return the work (known as the "demand and refusal" rule);[31] (2) accruing upon the owner's discovery of facts which form the basis of a cause of action, or should have discovered such facts by the exercise of

---

28 *See* PATTY GERSTENBLITH, ART, CULTURAL HERITAGE, AND THE LAW: CASES AND MATERIALS 428 (3rd ed. 2012).

29 *See id.* at 429.

30 *See e.g.*, Porter v. Wertz, 416 N.Y.S.2d 254 (N.Y. 1979).

31 This is the rule applicable in New York. *See* Kunstsammlungen zu Weimar v. Elicofon, 678 F.2d 1150 (2d Cir. 1982)(articulating the New York rule, and stating that "[u]nder New York law an innocent purchaser of stolen goods becomes a wrongdoer only after refusing the owner's demand for their return. Until the refusal the purchaser is considered to be in lawful possession."). *See also* Solomon R. Guggenheim Foundation v. Lubell, 569 N.E.2d 426 (N.Y. 1991), *available at* http://www.leagle.com/decision/199138877NY2d311_1361.xml/GUGGENHEIM%20 FOUND.%20v.%20LUBELL (stating that "[o]ur case law already recognizes that the true owner, having discovered the location of its lost property, cannot unreasonably delay making demand upon the person in possession of that property. Here, however, where the demand and refusal is a substantive and not a procedural element of the cause of action . . . it would not be prudent to extend that case law and impose the additional duty of diligence before the true owner has reason to know where its missing chattel is to be found.").

reasonable diligence and intelligence (the "constructive discovery" rule);[32] and (3) accruing upon the owner's actual discovery of (i) the theft, (ii) the identity of the thief, or (iii) the identity of the person in possession of the stolen property (the "actual discovery" rule).[33] The actual discovery rule, which has long been a feature of California law, has been modified in significant ways, both by statute[34] and by judicial decision. This change has occurred in connection with political and litigation efforts in support of claims for the return of art confiscated by the Nazis during the Second World War. These developments will be discussed in greater detail in Section D below in the context of a broader discussion of Nazi-looted art.

Although courts have tightened the availability of statute of limitations defenses in stolen art cases, current possessors of stolen (or allegedly stolen) art are increasingly making use of the equitable defense of laches, which operates very similarly to statutes of limitations in cutting off an original owner's right to bring suit for the recovery of an object if (i) the original owner has unreasonably delayed bringing suit, and (ii) that delay has resulted in prejudice to the current owner (chiefly, resulting in lack of evidence or witnesses).[35]

---

[32] The discovery rule is applicable in most states, but New Jersey applies a modified discovery rule, requiring the exercise of diligence on the part of the owner. *See e.g.,* Lopez v. Swyer, 62 N.J. 267 (N.J. 1973); O'Keeffe v. Snyder, 416 A.2d 862 (N.J. 1980)(stating that under New Jersey law "[t]he discovery rule provides that, in an appropriate case, a cause of action will not accrue until the injured party discovers, *or by exercise of reasonable diligence and intelligence should have discovered,* facts which form the basis of a cause of action." (italics added]). The O'Keeffe court also questioned whether the doctrine of adverse possession would or should apply to movable property.

[33] The actual discovery rule is applied in California, and is established by statute. *See* Cal. Code Civ. P. § 338; Naftzger v. American Numismatic Society, 49 Cal. Rptr.2d 784 (Cal. Ct. App. 1996) (stating that even prior to enactment of the California actual discovery rule statute, "the cause of action accrued when the owner discovered the identity of the person in possession of the stolen property, without regard to the owner's diligence or lack thereof in ferreting out that information.").

[34] In 2002, the California legislature enacted the Holocaust Art Recovery Statute of Limitations, which provided for the limitation period for the recovery of Holocaust-looted art until December 31, 2010. That provision was held to be unconstitutional as infringing the federal government's exclusive foreign affairs power. *See* von Saher v. Norton Simon Museum of Art at Pasadena, 592 F.3d 954 (9th Cir. 2010). In 2010, in response to the von Saher decision, the California legislature amended the statute of limitations to provide for a six-year limitation period and reemphasized the actual discovery rule.

[35] *See, e.g., In re* Peters, 821 N.Y.S.2d 61 (N.Y. 2006); Vinberg v. Bissonnette, 548 F.3d 50 (1st Cir. 2008) (stating, with respect to the second prong of the laches analysis, that "[t]ypically, the kind of prejudice that will support a laches defense arises out of a loss of evidence, the unavailability of important witnesses, the conveyance of the property in dispute for a fair market value to a bona fide purchaser, or the expenditure of resources in reliance upon the status quo ante.").

D. Nazi-Looted Art: The Developing Law

Some of the most important developments in the restitution of cultural objects and other assets confiscated in the period surrounding World War II have occurred only within the last decade or so. Some restitution was done, of course, at the conclusion of the war. The cultural objects that the Allied forces recovered were returned to the countries from whose citizens or museums they had been taken (in a process known as "external restitution"), for those countries to then return to their owners ("internal restitution"). However, those actions were complicated by the loss of people, records, communities, and communal memory. They were also complicated, prevented, or delayed by the resistance of governments and legal systems to adequately address the question of restitution, as well as a variety of political complications, not least of which was the Cold War, which locked people, cultural objects, and information behind the Iron Curtain. It took a combination of the end of Communism (with the unlocking of museums and archives in the former Soviet territories), the publication of pioneering studies of Nazi-era looting, and the persistent efforts of organizations like the Claims Conference[36] and the World Jewish Congress[37] to raise public awareness of the continuing problem of restitution. The statements of principles, statements of ethics, settlements, and court decisions have produced (and continue to produce) a profound change in the art trade and museum practice with respect to the understanding and treatment of confiscated and duress sale cultural objects. These efforts have produced an ongoing reassessment of the question of restitution, whose effects will be felt in many other restitution contexts as well.[38]

---

36 *See* The Conference on Jewish Material Claims Against Germany website, *available at* http://www.claimscon.org/about/.

37 *See* World Jewish Congress website, *available at* http://www.worldjewishcongress.org/en.

38 For example, with potentially more open relations between the U.S. and Cuba, some have proposed that we will see a wave of restitution claims arising from Cuba's confiscation of cultural property. *See, e.g.*, Alistair Bell, *Despite détente, search for art looted in Cuba could take years*, REUTERS (Jan. 7, 2015), *available at* http://in.reuters.com/article/2015/01/07/cuba-usa-art-idINKBN0K-G0EH20150107; Celestine Bohlen, *Reclaiming Art Caught in the Cuban Revolution; In Cases Reminiscent of Looted Nazi Art, Émigrés Trace Fate of their Collections*, THE NEW YORK TIMES (June 6, 2002), *available at* http://www.nytimes.com/2002/06/06/arts/reclaiming-art-caught-cuban-revolution-cases-reminiscent-looted-nazi-art-emigres.html; Patrick Symmes and Stephen Lewis, Cuba's Rising Art Scene, CONDE NAST TRAVELER, May 20, 2014, *available at* http://www.cntraveler.com/stories/2014-05-20/discovering-cuban-culture. While the Act of State Doctrine could apply to bar restitution claims by Cuban citizens whose property was seized by the Cuban government, no such bar would apply to claims by non-Cuban citizens.

In the 12 years between the Nazi Party's rise to power in 1933 and the end of the war in 1945, the Third Reich's policies and actions (as well as the policies and actions of others) wrought devastation and disruption on a massive scale.[39] This included the systematic confiscation of art and cultural objects in public and private collections across continental Europe.[40] Scholars have noted that "as many works of art were displaced, transported, and stolen as during the entire Thirty Years War or all the Napoleonic Wars."[41] It has been estimated that "[o]ne-third of all of the art in private hands had been pillaged by the Nazis."[42] Ronald Lauder, former U.S. ambassador to Austria and former Museum of Modern Art chairman, has noted that "more than 100,000 pieces of art, worth at least $10 billion in total, are still missing from the Nazi era."[43]

---

[39] *See, e.g., How Is Nazi-Looted Art Returned?* THE ECONOMIST (Jan. 12, 2014), *available at* http://www.economist.com/blogs/economist-explains/2014/01/economist-explains (stating that "Between 1933 and 1945 the Nazis engaged in the biggest art theft in history. They amassed millions of works from mostly Jewish collectors and the museums of occupied territories.").

[40] *See, e.g.,* Bert Demarsin, *Let's Not Talk About Terezin: Restitution of Nazi Era Looted Art and the Tenuousness of Public International Law*, 37 BROOK. J. INT'L L. 117, n1 (2011) ("'Nazi era looted art' refers to art objects that were stolen or otherwise seized from their owners between the moment of Hitler's rise in 1933 and the fall of the regime in 1945. . . . . [F]or works created prior to 1933, Sotheby's requires full provenance information from 1933 to 1948. . . . [And] the American Association of Museums ["AAM"] considers 1951, with the closing of the Munich Central Collecting Point, as the final year."). *See also* National Gallery of Art website, Munich Central Collecting Point Archive, *available at* http://www.nga.gov/content/ngaweb/research/library/imagecollections/core-collection/munich-central.html (explaining that "The Munich Central Collecting Point was established to accommodate repositories of Nazi-confiscated works of art and other cultural objects, hidden throughout Germany and Austria, which were discovered by the Allies at the close of World War II. At the central collecting points of Marburg, Wiesbaden, Munich, and the Offenbach Archival Depot, objects were identified, photographed, and restituted to their countries of origin. The works of art that passed through the Munich Central Collecting Point originated from many European museums and from private collections, a large percentage of which were French and Dutch. The recovered objects comprised a wide variety of media, from painting and sculpture to textiles and metalwork. The Munich Central Collecting Point ceased its restitution activities in 1951.").

[41] HECTOR FELICIANO, THE LOST MUSEUM 23 (1997).

[42] *Id.* at 4.

[43] Jennifer Anglim Kreder, *Guarding the Historical Record from the Nazi-Era Art Litigation Tumbling Toward the Supreme Court*, 159 U. PA. L. REV. 253, 255 (2011). *See also* Kelly Ann Falconer, *When Honor Will Not Suffice: The Need for a Legally Binding International Agreement Regarding Ownership of Nazi-Looted Art*, 21 U. PA. J. INT'L ECON. L. 383, 383-84 (2000) (stating that "It has been estimated that German forces and other Nazi agents before and during WWII seized or coerced the sale of one-fifth of all Western art then in existence."); MICHAEL J. BAZYLER, HOLOCAUST JUSTICE: THE BATTLE FOR RESTITUTION IN AMERICA'S COURTS 202 (2003) (stating that "The value of Nazi-era looted art has been estimated at $2.5 billion or approximated $20.5 billion at today's values."); The National Archives of the United States, DOCUMENTING NAZI PLUNDER OF EUROPEAN ART, GREG BRADSHER (Nov. 1997), *available at* http://www.archives.gov/research/holocaust/records-and-research/documenting-nazi-plunder-of-european-art.html (stating that "More than 100,000 Nazi-looted artworks have been located, but not restituted to their original owners or heirs. . . . Philip Saunders, editor of Trace, the stolen art register, stated that 'there are at least 100,000 works of art still missing from the Nazi occupation'.").

The dislocation of cultural objects during this period took many forms—direct confiscation (seized by government officials and agents), "abandoned" objects (seized after being left behind as their owners fled persecution),[44] forced sales,[45] and what are sometimes called "fluchtgut" or "fluchtkunst"[46] ("flight goods" or "flight art," which are cultural objects sold, generally at a steep discount, by owners desperate to finance their escape from Nazi-occupied or threatened areas). In many instances, claims for the restitution of *fluchtgut* raise many of the same issues as more usual cases of forced sales, and can be viewed as an extension of those cases.

The Third Reich's policy of seizing works of art to build the collection of a planned Fuhrermuseum to be constructed in Linz, Austria, (for the modern works the regime deemed "*entartete Kunst*" [degenerate art]) is, by now, well-known. *The Rape of Europa* (Lynn H. Nicholas, 1994), *The Lost Museum* (Hector Feliciano, 1995), and *The Monuments Men* (Robert M. Edsel, 2009) have given detailed accounts of Nazi art looting for a popular audience.

Although the Nazis' formal cultural plunder program carried out by the *Einsatzstab Reichsleiter Rosenberg* (the ERR) was not established until 1940, forced sales and outright theft of works began much earlier. "Forced sales" are transactions in which businesses or assets were "aryanized" and the purchase price was paid into a blocked bank account to which the former property owners had no access. A similar concept is that of fluchtgut or fluchtkunst, which were acquired by the regime or its agents from property owners for a fraction of their market price (or for no payment) in circumstances where the owners, frequently but not exclusively Jews, were desperate to secure exit visas or to raise funds for travel costs to

---

44 *See, e.g.*, Menzel v. List, 267 N.Y.S.2d 804 (N.Y. 1966)(seeking to recover a painting by Marc Chagall that hung in the Menzel's Brussels apartment when they fled Belgium before the Nazi occupation). The Menzel court rejected the defendant's argument that the Menzels had abandoned the painting.

45 *See, e.g.*, Vineberg v. Bissonette, 529 F.Supp.2d 300, 307 (D.R.I. 2007) (noting that "the Nazi government forced Dr. Stern to liquidate inventory in his art gallery and controlled the manner of the forced sale," and concluding that "Dr. Stern's surrender of the painting to [the auction house] for auction was ordered by the Nazi authorities and therefore the equivalent of an official seizure or a theft."). *But see* Orkin v. Swiss Confederation, 770 F.Supp.2d 612, 616 (S.D.N.Y. 2011) (dismissing the action for lack of jurisdiction, because "[p]laintiff does not allege that Reinhart acted in any capacity other than as a private individual." The court noted that "[i]n 1933, [Plaintiff's grandmother] sold the drawing to Swiss art collector Oskar Reinhart for 8,000 Reichsmarks to help fund her family's escape from the Nazis' persecution of German Jews.").

46 *See, e.g.*, Florian Weiland, *Ist Fluchtkunst dasselbe wie Raubkunst?* (Is flight art the same as looted art?), SUDKURIER (Sept. 3, 2014), *available at* http://www.suedkurier.de/nachrichten/kultur/themensk/Ist-Fluchtkunst-dasselbe-wie-Raubkunst;art410935,7218364.

escape Nazi-controlled territories. At times such forced sales were given the formal appearance of licit transactions. Before the war's end, the Allies and the governments-in-exile issued the London Declaration,[47] invalidating "any transfers of, or dealings with, property, rights and interests of any description whatsoever which are, or have been, situated in the territories which have come under the occupation or control" of the Axis power. The policy articulated in the London Declaration applied "whether such transfers of dealings have taken the form of open looting or plunder, or of transactions apparently legal in form, even when they purport to be voluntarily effected."

After the war, efforts to identify Nazi-looted works had mixed success. Formal restitution to original owners also met with mixed success. The first United States decision awarding restitution to original owners of Nazi-looted art—Marc Chagall's *Le Paysan a L'echelle*—was in 1966 (*Menzel v. List*, 267 N.Y.S.2d 804 (N.Y. 1966).[48] The *Menzel* decision was followed by *U.S. v. Portrait of Wally, A Painting by Egon Schiele, Defendant in Rem*, 2002 No. 99 Civ. 9940, 2002 WL 55352 (S.D.N.Y. 2002); *Vineberg v. Bissonnette*, 529 F. Supp.2d 300 (D.R.I. 2007)(a decision based on a forced sale); and *Republic of Austria v. Altmann*, 541 U.S. 677 (U.S. 2007),[49] among others. However, much of the art looted by the Nazis remains missing, and efforts by museums and governments have been criticized for lacking transparency.

1. The Challenges of Restitution

The challenges original owners (or their heirs) face in securing the return of objects taken from them in this manner are typically quite complex, since many decades have passed and the circumstances of the taking may be difficult to establish. As one scholar has noted, the Nazis not only plundered Europe's art collections:

> As part of a genocide of unparalleled scale, they also murdered (or forced into exile) many owners of that property. Thus, at the end of World War II, most of those best positioned to establish claims for restitution of

---

[47] *Inter-Allied Declaration against Acts of Dispossession committed in Territories under Enemy Occupation and Control, available at* http://www.lootedartcommission.com/inter-allied-declaration.

[48] Menzel v. List, 267 N.Y.S.2d 804 (N.Y. 1966), *available at* http://www.kentlaw.edu/faculty/sharding/classes/HardingPropandCultureF2009/CourseDocs/MenzelEdit.pdf.

[49] Republic of Austria v. Altmann, 541 U.S. 677 (U.S. 2007), *available at* http://www.oyez.org/cases/2000-2009/2003/2003_03_13.

their stolen property were unlikely to have survived. For those who did survive, or for their heirs, the practicalities of locating property and compiling evidence to support a claim for restitution were daunting. Indeed, relatively few claims for restitution of Holocaust art were filed in United States courts until more than fifty years following the close of World War II.[50]

2. A Developing International Consensus: The Washington Conference Principles

In 1998, the U.S. Department of State convened the Washington Conference on Holocaust Era Assets.[51] Representatives of 44 countries gathered at the U.S. Holocaust Memorial Museum. In his opening remarks, Elie Wiesel asked "[w]hy is [the discussion of how to address restitution of assets] taking place at such a late date under the moral pressure of public opinion?" His answer is important. "In truth," he explained,

> the search for the missing monies, apartments and collections of art should have been initiated long ago and more elegantly, with a greater measure of grace—by banks and governments themselves. And I speak of neutral countries, as well as of countries which had been occupied by the Germans. Now we know that some did that, some were gracious—but for the wrong reasons. More precisely, for the benefit of the wrong people. Almost under duress, efforts were being made to ask for the restitution of what had been stolen. In some places, because Jews had asked for the restitution, a new wave of anti-Semitism swept the country.[52]

Wiesel's statement encapsulates the problem that ongoing efforts at restitution are meant to address—not only to see justice done, but also to ensure that history and the public record are not defaced.

What emerged from the Washington Conference was a set of nonbinding principles (the "Washington Conference Principles"),[53] which

---

50 Stephen K. Urice, *Elizabeth Taylor's Van Gogh: An Alternative Route to Restitution of Holocaust Art?* 22 DEPAUL J. ART, TECH. & INTELL. PROP. L. 1, 1–2 (2011).

51 Washington Conference on Holocaust-Era Assets, *Proceedings, available at* http://fcit.usf.edu/holocaust/resource/assets/index.HTM.

52 *Id.*

53 U.S. Dept. of State & U.S. Holocaust Memorial Museum, *Proceedings of the Washington Conference Principles on Nazi-Confiscated Art,* app. G 1-11, at 971–72 (1998), *available at* http://www.state.gov/p/eur/rt/hlcst/122038.htm.

are guidelines for countries to incorporate into their national laws and legal and ethical approaches for the just handling of Nazi-era claims. The Washington Conference Principles are explicitly intended to reflect the consensus reached among the 44 countries participating in the conference. The principles state, in part, that "if the pre-War owners of art that is found to have been confiscated by the Nazis and not subsequently restituted, or their heirs, can be identified, steps should be taken expeditiously to achieve a just and fair solution, recognizing that this may vary according to the facts and circumstances surrounding a specific case."

National and international support for the *Washington Conference Principles* were reiterated and reinforced by the *Declaration of the Vilnius International Forum on Holocaust-Era Looted Cultural Assets* (2000),[54] issued by 38 countries, and the *Terezin Declaration on Holocaust Era Assets and Related Issues* (2009),[55] issued by 46 countries. Commentators have noted that the *Washington Conference Principles* and the *Terezin Declaration* "do not grant either party—the art's possessor or its claimant—presumptions of correctness. Rather, they allow for the fact that while Holocaust victims (or heirs) and museums often face unique factual circumstances for each claim, not all claims are equal."[56]

The effect of the Washington Conference Principles on museum practice has been profound. The most important museum professional organizations have issued ethics guidelines concerning museums' handling of potential Nazi-era looted objects in their collections. The International Council of Museums (ICOM) issued its Recommendations concerning the Return of Works of Art Belonging to Jewish Owners (1999),[57] the American Alliance of Museums (AAM) issued its Standards Regarding the Unlawful Appropriation of Objects During the Nazi Era,[58] and the Association of Art Museum Directors (AAMD) issued its Resolution of Claims

---

[54] *Vilnius Declaration, available at* http://www.lootedartcommission.com/vilnius-forum.

[55] U.S. Dept. of State Bureau of European & Eurasian Affairs, *Prague Holocaust Era Assets Conference: Terezin Declaration* (June 30, 2009), *available at* http://www.lootedartcommission.com/NPNMG484641.

[56] Simon J. Frankel and Ethan Forrest, *Museums' Initiation of Declaratory Judgment Actions and Assertion of Statutes of Limitations in Response to Nazi-Era Art Restitution Claims—A Defense*, 23 DePaul J. Art. Tech. & IP Law 279, 295–96 (2013).

[57] International Council of Museums Recommendations concerning the Return of Works of Art Belonging to Jewish Owners, *available at* http://www.lootedartcommission.com/OXSHQE36019.

[58] American Alliance of Museums Standards Regarding the Unlawful Appropriation of Objects During the Nazi Era, *available at* http://www.aam-us.org/resources/ethics-standards-and-best-practices/collections-stewardship/objects-during-the-nazi-era.

for Nazi-Era Cultural Assets.[59] These professional ethics guidelines offer similar recommendations, drawn from the Washington Conference Principles—museums should (i) review their collections for potentially Nazi-looted objects, (ii) establish provenance research procedures, (iii) publish information concerning objects of doubtful provenance in their collections, and (iv) resolve claims by original owners and their heirs to potentially looted objects in their collections in an equitable and appropriate manner. Many museums have assessed their collections for potential Nazi-era confiscated objects and have publicized on their websites objects whose provenance contains gaps during the relevant period or otherwise raises questions.[60] In fact, some museums, notably the Museum of Fine Art, Boston, have established a curator of provenance to evaluate these and other issues.[61] Notably, the Samuel H. Kress Foundation has established the Kress Provenance Research Project to support museum best practices in provenance research.[62] The major auction houses have similarly focused resources on provenance research.

The AAMD spoliation report recommends that "member museums consider using mediation wherever reasonably practical to help resolve claims regarding art illegally confiscated during the Nazi/World War II era and not restituted."[63] The AAM Standards, however, provide more particularized recommendations to museums in how they should address claims to potentially Nazi-looted objects in their collections, noting that "in order to achieve an equitable and appropriate resolution of claims, museums may elect to waive certain available defenses."

Fifteen years after the Washington Conference, serious questions continue to be raised as to whether countries, museums, and others are living up to Washington Conference principles. In September 2014, the

---

59 Association of Art Museum Directors Art Museums and the Identification and Restitution of Works Stolen by the Nazis, *available at* https://aamd.org/sites/default/files/document/Nazi-looted%20art_clean_06_2007.pdf.

60 These museums include The Metropolitan Museum of Art (http://www.metmuseum.org/research/provenance-research-project); The Art Institute of Chicago (http://www.artic.edu/aic/collections/provenance); Museum of Fine Arts Boston (http://www.mfa.org/collections/provenance); The Museum of Modern Art (http://www.moma.org/collection/provenance/); The Frick Collection (http://www.frick.org/collection/provenance); and The Smithsonian Institution (http://provenance.si.edu/jsp/index.aspx).

61 *See* Geoff Edgers, *A Detective's Work at the MFA*, THE BOSTON GLOBE (Dec. 11, 2011), *available at* http://www.bostonglobe.com/arts/2011/12/11/detective-work-mfa/6iaei4YOQOj83s9u3YfDXO/story.html.

62 Kress Provenance Research Project, *available at* http://www.kressfoundation.org/provenance/.

63 Report of the American Association of Museum Directors Task Force on the Spoliation of Art during the Nazi/World War II Era, *available at* https://aamd.org/document/report-of-the-aamd-task-force-on-the-spoliation-of-art-during-the-nazi/world-war-ii-era.

Conference on Jewish Material Claims Against Germany and the World Jewish Restitution Organization issued a report, "Holocaust-Era Looted Art: A Current World-Wide Overview,"[64] which provides a 50-country survey of restitution efforts. Increasingly, restitution claims arise in connection with governments' allegedly inadequate or unjust post-war internal restitution efforts.

3. Museums' Use of Technical Defenses

The question of museums waiving defenses, as the AAM Standards suggest, has emerged as an important point of conflict in Nazi-era restitution cases. In a few instances, museums have filed quiet title actions against restitution claimants, asking courts to issue declaratory judgments that the museums have good title to the objects and/or the claimants' rights have been lost due to statutes of limitations or laches.[65] Such cases remain rare and are controversial.[66] However, museums' asserting statutes of limitations and laches defenses—what have become known as "technical defenses"—rather than allowing cases to be decided solely on the merits is not less controversial.[67]

---

[64] *Holocaust-Era Looted Art: A Current World-Wide Overview, available at* http://art.claimscon.org/wp-content/uploads/2014/09/Worldwide-Overview.pdf.

[65] *See, e.g.*, Toledo Museum of Art v. Ullin, 477 F. Supp. 2d 802 (N.D. Ohio 2006); Detroit Inst. of Arts v. Ullin, No. 06-10333, 2007 WL 1016996, at *1 (E.D. Mich. Mar. 31, 2007); Museum of Fine Arts, Boston v. Seger-Thomschitz, Case No. 08-10097-RWZ, 2009 WL 6506658 (D. Mass. June 12, 2009); Museum of Fine Art v. Schoeps, 549 F.Supp.2d 543 (S.D.N.Y. 2008).

[66] *See, e.g.*, Grosz v. Museum of Modern Art, 772 F.Supp.2d 473 (S.D.N.Y. 2010); Simon J. Frankel & Ethan Forrest, *Museums' Initiation of Declaratory Judgment Actions and Assertion of Statutes of Limitations in Response to Nazi-Era Restitution Claims—A Defense*, 23 DePaul J. Art, Tech. & Intell. Prop. L. 279, 281 (2013).

[67] *See, e.g.*, Jessica Schubert, *Prisoners of War: Nazi-Era Looted Art and the Need for Reform in the United States*, 30 Touro L. Rev. 675 (2014); Jessica Mullery, *Fulfilling the Washington Principles: A Proposal for Arbitration Panels to Resolve Holocaust-Era Art Claims*, 11 Cardozo J. Conflict Resol. 643 (2010); Benjamin E. Pollock, *Out of the Night and Fog: Permitting Litigation to Prompt an International Resolution to Nazi-Looted Art Claims*, 43 Hous. L. Rev. 193 (2006); Rachel Durbin, *Museums and Self-Regulation: Assessing the Impact of Newly Promulgated Guidelines on the Litigation of Cultural Property*, 18 U. Miami Bus. L. Rev. 101 (2010); Emily A. Graefe, *The Conflicting Obligations of Museums Possessing Nazi-Looted Art*, 51 B.C. L. Rev. 473 (2010); Jennifer Anglim Kreder, *Guarding the Historical Record from the Nazi-Era Art Litigation Tumbling Toward the Supreme Court*, 159 U. Pa. L. Rev. 253 (2011); Katherine N. Skinner, *Restituting Nazi-Looted Art: Domestic, Legislative, and Binding Intervention to Balance the Interests of Victims and Museums*, 15 Vand. J. Ent. & Tech. L. 673 (2013).

Statute of limitations and laches[68] defenses are commonplace in stolen art litigation.[69] The propriety of museums' use of such technical defenses is highlighted in *Von Saher v. Norton Simon Museum of Art at Pasadena*.[70] Before the Second World War, Jacques Goudstikker was a preeminent Amsterdam art dealer.[71] When the Nazis invaded the Netherlands in 1940, the Goudstikkers, as Jews, were endangered. They fled the country, leaving behind their possessions, including the contents of Jacques's art gallery, which included more than 1,400 objects, including two life-size sixteenth-century panels by Lucas Cranach the Elder, titled *Adam* and *Eve*. Jacques Goudstikker had purchased the Cranach panels at auction in 1931. The auction was titled "The Stroganoff Collection," and included objects that had been expropriated by the Soviet government from the Stroganoff family, as well as from other owners within the U.S.S.R.

After the Nazis occupied Amsterdam, the Goudstikkers' possessions were confiscated, with Hermann Goering selecting roughly 800 objects for his personal collection. Many of the Goudstikker objects were retrieved by Allied forces at the end of the war and were sent to the Central Collecting Point in Munich for cataloging and processing. Allied policy was to return Nazi-looted objects to the governments of the countries from which they had been taken, reasoning that those countries were in the best position to locate the original owners and return the objects to them or to their heirs. Along with other Goudstikker objects, the Allies restituted the Cranach panels to the government of the Netherlands. However, in 1961, an heir of the Stroganoff family filed a claim against the Cranachs, and Netherlands restituted the panels to him. The heir sold the Cranach panels to the Norton Simon Museum of Art at Pasadena in the early 1970s.

With *Von Saher* the question of whether a statute of limitations defense is appropriate in the case of Nazi-looted objects has been extensively litigated. Concerned that California's three-year statute of limitations

---

68 Laches is an equitable defense "designed to promote diligence and prevent enforcement of stale claims" by those who have "'slumber[ed] on their rights.'" Gull Airborne Instruments, Inc. v. Weinberger, 694 F.2d 838, 843 (D.C.Cir.1982). To invoke the defense of laches to bar a claim, a defendant must demonstrate that (1) "the plaintiff has unreasonably delayed" in asserting its claim, and (2) "there was 'undue prejudice' to the defendant as a result of the delay." Jeanblanc v. Oliver Carr Co., No. 94-7118, 1995 WL 418667, at *4 (D.C. Cir. June 21, 1995).

69 For a discussion of statutes of limitations and related issues in stolen art cases, see my earlier discussion in *Restitution of Stolen Cultural Objects*, *available at* http://www.gtlaw-culturalassets.com/2015/02/restitution-repatriation-and-return-when-objects-go-back/.

70 Von Saher v. Norton Simon Museum of Art at Pasadena, 754 F.3d 712 (9th Cir. 2014).

71 *See Reclaimed: Paintings from the Collection of Jacques Goudstikker*, exhibition March 15—August 2, 2009, Jewish Museum website, *available at* http://thejewishmuseum.org/exhibitions/reclaimed-paintings-from-the-collection-of-jacques-goudstikker.

was presenting an unfair burden on claimants with respect to Holocaust and in Nazi-era looting cases, the California legislature extended that statute of limitations, but only for such Holocaust and Nazi-era looting claims. Marei Von Saher, the heir of Jacques Goudstikker, filed a replevin action in California in May 2007 against the museum, and the museum filed a motion to dismiss, arguing that the California statute extending the limitations period unconstitutionally intruded upon the federal government's "exclusive power to make and resolve war, including the procedure for resolving war claims."[72] The district court agreed, and dismissed the case. Ms. Von Saher appealed the decision to the 9th Circuit Court of Appeals, which issued a decision finding the California extension of its statute of limitations unconstitutional but allowing Ms. Von Saher leave to amend her complaint to allege that her claim was brought within the existing three-year statute of limitations measured by the discovery rule.[73] That decision was reheard *en banc*, with the full court again holding the extended limitations period to be unconstitutional, and remanding the case to the district court to allow the plaintiff to amend her complaint.[74]

Following the 9th Circuit's decision, Ms. Von Saher filed an amended complaint. The California legislature amended its statute of limitations, this time avoiding the foreign affairs conflict, and providing generally that claims for the recovery of artworks must be brought within six years after "actual discovery" by the plaintiff of the current location and current possessor of the object (provided that the object has been taken within the last 100 years). The constitutionality of this limitations period was challenged in a wholly separate Nazi-confiscated art case, and the statute was upheld.[75] However, the district court granted the museum's second motion to dismiss the case, holding that Ms. Von Saher's claims were preempted by the foreign affairs doctrine.[76] Quoting the solicitor general's brief with approval, the district court found that "[w]hen a foreign nation, like the Netherlands here, has conducted bona fide post-war internal restitution proceedings following the return of Nazi-confiscated art to that nation under the external restitution policy, the United States has a substantial interest in respecting the outcome of that nation's proceedings."[77]

---

72 Von Saher v. Norton Simon Museum of Art at Pasadena, Case No. CV-07-2866-JFW, 2007 WL 4302726 (C.D. Cal. Oct. 18, 2007).

73 Von Saher v. Norton Simon Museum of Art at Pasadena, 578 F.3d 1016 (2009).

74 Von Saher v. Norton Simon Museum of Art at Pasadena, 592 F.3d 954 (2010).

75 Cassirer v. Thyssen-Bornemisza Collection Foundation, 737 F.3d 613 (9th Cir. 2013).

76 Von Saher v. Norton Simon Museum at Pasadena, 862 F.Supp.2d 1044 (2012).

77 *Id.* at 1051.

On appeal, the 9th Circuit reversed that decision, finding that the Dutch post-war internal restitution proceedings that resulted in the Cranachs being given to the Stroganoff heir were not adequate, and were, in fact, criticized and disavowed by the Netherlands in a reassessment in the 1990s. The court further found that the later Dutch restitution proceedings concerning objects from the Goudstikker collection (which resulted in the return to Ms. Von Saher of several hundred objects) were not internal restitution proceedings with respect to the Cranach panels, since those panels were no longer located within the Netherlands at that time and could not be returned.

The 9th Circuit rejected the solicitor general's position that United States policy supported the finality of countries' internal restitution decisions, without further considerations. Rather, the court stated:

> U.S. policy on the restitution of Nazi-looted art includes the following tenets: (1) a commitment to respect the finality of 'appropriate actions' taken by foreign nations to facilitate the internal restitution of plundered art; (2) a pledge to identify Nazi-looted art that has not been restituted and to publicize those artworks in order to facilitate the identification of prewar owners and their heirs; (3) the encouragement of prewar owners and their heirs to come forward and claim art that has not been restituted; (4) concerted efforts to achieve expeditious, just and fair outcomes when heirs claim ownership to looted art; (5) the encouragement of everyone, including public and private institutions, to follow the Washington Principles; and (6) a recommendation that every effort be made to remedy the consequences of forced sales."[78]

Museums and their trustees have a duty to protect and preserve the objects in their collections, as well as an obligation to evaluate claims made against objects that they hold.[79] Nevertheless, the *Von Saher* case has become a touchstone for critics of museums' use of technical defenses to delay or foreclose resolution of bona fide claims on their merits.

---

[78] Von Saher v. Norton Simon Museum of Art at Pasadena, 754 F.3d at 721.

[79] *See, e.g.*, Patty Gerstenblith, *Acquisition and Deacquisition of Museum Collections and the Fiduciary Obligations of Museums to the Public*, 11 CARDOZO J. INT'L & COMP. L. 409 (2003) (noting that "Use of either the laches defense or the discovery rule will necessitate a lengthy trial that would consume museum resources. It will lead to losses in terms of finances, efforts of staff, and, in many cases, negative publicity. It is thus reasonable for a board of trustees to determine that its chances of retaining an art work through litigation and use of these affirmative defenses are not likely to succeed and thus to seek settlement, while saving the expense of litigation.").

4. Objects Held by Foreign Museums: The Foreign Sovereign Immunities Act

Most United States museums are private charitable organizations, but that is not the norm in most other parts of the world, where museums are state-owned or state-affiliated. That means that parties asserting claims for the restitution of objects held in foreign museums frequently involve questions of foreign sovereign immunity.

Generally, a foreign state is immune from the jurisdiction of federal and state courts in the United States.[80] However, the Foreign Sovereign Immunities Act (FSIA)[81] allows United States courts to exercise jurisdiction over foreign sovereigns and their agencies and instrumentalities, but only within certain statutorily-defined exceptions. Although the FSIA was not enacted until 1976, it applies to all cases filed after its enactment, regardless of when the alleged wrongdoing occurred.[82] Under the FSIA, state-owned or state-affiliated museums are considered agencies or instrumentalities of their foreign sovereigns.[83]

The most commonly applied FSIA exception in cultural property restitution cases is the "expropriation exception."[84] Under the expropriation exception, a foreign sovereign (or its agency or instrumentality) is amenable to suit in United States courts where property has been taken in violation of international law and either (1) "that property or any property exchanged for such property is present in the United States in connection with a commercial activity carried on in the United States by the foreign state," or (2) that property or any property exchanged for such property is

---

[80] *See* Verlinden B.V. v. Cent. Bank of Nigeria, 461 U.S. 480, 486 (1983).

[81] 28 §§ U.S.C. 1602–1611.

[82] *See* Republic of Austria v. Altmann, 541 U.S. 677, 700 (2004) (holding that the FSIA applies to conduct "that occurred prior to 1976 and, for that matter, prior to 1952 when the State Department adopted the restrictive theory of sovereign immunity.").

[83] *See* Cassirer v. Kingdom of Spain, 461 F.Supp.2d 1157, 1163–64 (C.D. Cal. 2006) (holding that the Thyssen-Bornemisza Collection Foundation is an agency or instrumentality of the Kingdom of Spain, because it arranged and was a party to the original loan of the artworks, contributed toward the purchase price paid for the artworks, provided a facility to house the artworks, paid the cost of refurbishing that facility, and Spain's governmental ministers were required to form part of the Collection's directors); de Csepel v. Republic of Hungary, 714 F.3d 591, (D.C. Cir. 2013) (the Hungarian National Gallery); Agudas Chasidei Chabad of United States v. Russian Federation, 528 F.3d 934 (D.C. Cir. 2008) (Russian State Library and Russian State Military Archive); and Altmann v. Republic of Austria, 142 F.Supp.2d 1187 (C.D. Cal. 2001) (Austrian Gallery which was formerly an agency or instrumentality of Austria and was subsequently privatized).

[84] *See, e.g.* Altmann v. Republic of Austria, 317 F.3d 954, (9th Cir. 2002), aff'd, 541 U.S. 677 (2004); Cassirer v. Kingdom of Spain, 580 F.3d 1048, (9th Cir. 2009); Agudas Chasidei Chabad of United States v. Russian Federation, 528 F.3d 934 (D.C. Cir. 2008); Malewicz v. City of Amsterdam, 362 F.Supp.2d 298 (D.D.C. 2005).

owned or operated by an agency or instrumentality of the foreign state and that agency or instrumentality is engaged in a commercial activity in the United States."[85]

5. Foreign Sovereign-Owned Property in the U.S.

The first prong of the expropriation exception has typically been applied in cases where objects owned by foreign museums are temporarily located in the United States. For example, in *Malewicz v. City of Amsterdam*,[86] the heirs of artist Kazimir Malewicz sought the return of 14 Malewicz paintings from the City of Amsterdam, whose Stedelijk Museum had placed the paintings on temporary loan to the Solomon R. Guggenheim Museum and the Menil Collection. Amsterdam argued that because the paintings on loan were immune from seizure under the U.S. Department of State's Mutual Educational and Cultural Exchange Program, the court should dismiss the case. The court, however, disagreed, holding that "[i]mmunity from seizure is not immunity from suit for a declaration of rights or for damages arising from an alleged conversion if the other terms for FSIA jurisdiction exist."[87]

The court found that the requirements for FSIA jurisdiction were satisfied, because (1) the museum's taking of the paintings violated international law, and (2) the paintings were present in the United States in connection with commercial activity. For purposes of determining whether jurisdiction exists under the FSIA, the court "need not decide whether the taking actually violated international law; as long as a claim is substantial and nonfrivolous, it provides a sufficient basis for the exercise of [the court's] jurisdiction." For purposes of the FSIA, a taking violates international law if it is not for a public purpose, or is discriminatory, or does not provide for just compensation. The City of Amsterdam argued that FSIA takings jurisdiction cannot exist unless the plaintiffs have first exhausted local remedies. The court, however, agreed with the heirs that exhaustion of local remedies was not required because no local remedies were available to the heirs since, under Dutch law, no claim for the return of property (or damages for its taking) can be brought later than 30 years after the date of the taking. Therefore, the heirs had no remedy available to them

---

85 28 U.S.C. § 1605(a)(3).

86 Malewicz v. City of Amsterdam, 362 F.Supp.2d 298 (D.D.C. 2005); Malewicz v. City of Amsterdam, 517 F.Supp.2d 322 (D.D.C. 2007).

87 *Id.* at 312.

in Dutch courts. The court found that the museum's loan of the paintings to the United States museums satisfied the commercial activity requirement.

6. Foreign Sovereign-Owned Property Outside the U.S.

The expropriation exception's second prong has proven to be an even more powerful tool in cultural property restitution cases, and has provided the basis for United States jurisdiction in many of the highest-profile cases of the last decade. They have included the restitution from the Austrian state museum of several Gustav Klimt paintings, the best-known of which is his portrait of *Adele Bloch-Bauer I* (which was then acquired by the Neue Galerie[88] for $135 million), to the heir of the Bloch-Bauers.[89] The *Altmann* case went to the U.S. Supreme Court and established the principle that jurisdiction under the FSIA applies to cases filed after enactment of the FSIA, regardless of when the actions that give rise to the case occurred. In fact, these cases have been instrumental in the development of FSIA jurisprudence. The case has been the subject of numerous articles and books, and is the basis for a film, "Woman in Gold," with Helen Mirren as Maria Altmann.[90]

While the Altmann case was ultimately resolved by settlement, many cases seeking restitution of cultural objects held by foreign state museums or entities are ongoing. These include actions by (i) heirs seeking return of a Nazi-confiscated painting currently owned by a Spanish state-affiliated museum[91] (which established the principle that the foreign state against whom suit is brought need not be the same foreign sovereign responsible for taking the property); (ii) heirs for the return of a collection of paintings, including works by Lucas Cranach the Elder, El Greco, Francisco de Zurbaran, and Gustave Courbet, from the Hungarian National Gallery (which relies upon the breach of a post-war bailment agreement between the family and the museum);[92] (iii) a religious organization for return of a religious library and archive from the Russian

88 Neue Galerie website, *available at* http://www.neuegalerie.org/.

89 Altmann v. Republic of Austria, 142 F.Supp.2d 1187 (C.D. Cal. 2001); Altmann v. Republic of Austria, 317 F.3d 954, (9th Cir. 2002), aff'd, 541 U.S. 677 (2004).

90 *Woman in Gold* (2015), Internet Movie Database, *available at* http://www.imdb.com/title/tt2404425/.

91 Cassirer v. Kingdom of Spain, 461 F.Supp.2d 1157, 1163–64 (C.D. Cal. 2006); Cassirer v. Kingdom of Spain, 616 F.3d 1019, 1032 (9th Cir. 2010); Cassirer v. Thyssen-Bornemisza Collection Foundation, No. CV 05-03459 GAF, 2014 WL 5510996, *5 (C.D. Cal. Oct. 31, 2014).

92 de Csepel v. Republic of Hungary, 714 F.3d 591, (D.C. Cir. 2013).

State Library and Russian State Military Archive, whose objects were first confiscated by the Nazis and later seized by Soviet troops and taken back to the Soviet Union (where the organization brought suit in the United States after Russia frustrated litigation there). The organization obtained a default judgment against Russia, and has imposed sanctions of $50,000 per day for Russia's failure to comply with the court's order directing it to return the objects.[93]

The Washington Conference Principles, the museum ethics guidelines and standards, and the succession of court decisions (particularly those brought under the FSIA) not only have significantly transformed the law in the area of cultural property restitution, but perhaps more importantly, have transformed awareness and behavior. These developments have the potential to affect a normative shift that extends beyond the historical specifics of World War II, and to change the way we think of rights and ownership of cultural property in a wide range of contexts. They are, and will continue to be, touchstones in a broader and continuing discussion.

7. Statutes of Limitation

The tension between repose and return has not abated. If anything, it has grown more heated, and nowhere more than in the controversy over whether statutes of limitations barring claims after a period of time should be applied in Nazi-confiscated art cases. Klaus Albrecht Schröder, director of Vienna's Albertina Museum,[94] made headlines by calling for a time limit to be placed on restitution claims against public institutions concerning Nazi-confiscated art.[95] In Schröder's view, museums have largely followed the Washington Conference Principles, and he called for an outer time limit (or 20 or 30 years from the present date) after which future claims would be barred. In support of such a limit, Schröder points out that cultural objects taken during other periods are not exempted from statutes of limitations. "If we don't set a time limit of around 100 years after the end of the Second World War," he noted, "then we should ask ourselves why claims regarding crimes committed during the First

---

93 Agudas Chasidei Chabad v. Russian Federation, 466 F.Supp.2d 6, 16 (D.D.C. 2006); Agudas Chasidei Chabad of U.S. v. Russian Fed'n, 528 F.3d 934, 948 (D.C. Cir. 2008).

94 *See* http://www.albertina.at/.

95 Flavia Foradini, *Vienna Museum Director Calls for Time Limit on Nazi-Loot Restitution Claims*, The Art Newspaper (Mar. 30, 2015), *available at* http://www.theartnewspaper.com/articles/Vienna-museum-director-calls-for-time-limit-on-Naziloot-restitution-claims/37391.

World War should not still be valid; why we don't argue anymore about the consequences of the 1870–1871 Franco-Prussian war, and why we don't claim restitution of works of art that have been stolen during previous wars?"

Ronald Lauder[96] rejected any limitations period. "There should be no statute of limitations in the case of Nazi-looted art," Lauder wrote, "just as there is no statute of limitations for genocide, because for almost every stolen painting, a felony murder was committed and a family was destroyed. The crimes of the Nazis were unique. Seventy years after the end of World War II, there is a moral obligation for museums and countries to do the right thing. These families have waited long enough."[97]

This tension between repose and return is at the heart of several current Nazi-confiscated art restitution cases, and none more prominently than that brought by Marei von Saher, the heir of Dutch Jewish art dealer Jacques Goudstikker, against the Norton Simon Museum of Art at Pasadena for the return of two paintings by Lucas Cranach the Elder, titled *Adam and Eve.* For background on the case, see my earlier discussion in this chapter.[98]

United States courts typically articulate the policy behind statutes of limitations as encouraging diligence and timely prosecution of claims, often referred to as the avoidance of stale claims. As the New Jersey Supreme Court observed, "[t]he purpose of a statute of limitations is to 'stimulate to activity and punish negligence' and 'promote repose by giving security and stability to human affairs.'. . . A statute of limitations achieves those purposes by barring a cause of action after the statutory period."[99] The key issue for the application of a statute of limitations is when the cause of action "accrues," which is the date from which the limitations period runs. In actions for the return of stolen cultural property, there are, broadly-speaking, four distinct approaches to the question of accrual: (1) at the time the theft occurs (Louisiana); (2) at the time the original owner knows, or should know, the location of the stolen property and the identity of the current possessor (the "discovery rule") (most states); (3) a modified discovery rule requiring the original owner to exercise due diligence (New Jersey); and (4) at the time when the

---

96 *See* https://lauderfoundation.com/president.

97 Ronald S. Lauder, *Much Unfinished Business*, THE WALL STREET JOURNAL (April 7, 2015), *available at* http://www.wsj.com/articles/much-unfinished-business-1428441748.

98 *See* http://www.gtlaw-culturalassets.com/2015/03/restitution-of-cultural-objects-taken-during-world-war-ii-part-ii/#more-1751.

99 O'Keeffe v. Snyder, 83 N.J. 478, 490 (N.J. 1980).

original owner makes demand upon the current possessor for the return of the object and the current possessor refuses to return it (the "demand and refusal" rule)(New York). Accrual at the time of the theft favors the current possessor, and is often regarded as harsh for original owners. The demand and refusal rule, on the other hand, favors the original owner, and is regarded by some as harsh for good faith purchasers.

In adopting the demand and refusal rule, the New York Court of Appeals believed that it was best to place the burden of due diligence on the purchaser, explaining:

> To place the burden of locating stolen artwork on the true owner and to foreclose the rights of that owner to recover its property if the burden is not met would, we believe, encourage illicit trafficking in stolen art. Three years after the theft, any purchaser, good faith or not, would be able to hold onto stolen art work unless the true owner was able to establish that it had undertaken a reasonable search for the missing art. This shifting of the burden onto the wronged owner is inappropriate. In our opinion, the better rule gives the owner relatively greater protection and places the burden of investigating the provenance of a work of art on the potential purchaser.[100]

California has long been a discovery rule jurisdiction, but just how the discovery rule applies has been the subject of considerable discussion. A seminal case in the development of California's statute of limitations has been *Von Saher v. Norton Simon Museum of Art at Pasadena*, which has been litigated now for 8 years chiefly on the question of whether the case should be barred by a statute of limitations defense. The case has had a tremendous (and tremendously important) impact on California's statute of limitations for actions to recover stolen artwork. In the most recent decision in the case, the United States District Court for the Central District of California on April 2, 2015, issued an order denying the museum's latest motion to dismiss.[101] In doing so, however, the court answered a question on the application of California's statute of limitations for stolen art that has important implications for art transactions. The court held that California's 6-year statute of limitations for claims for the return of

---

[100] Solomon R. Guggenheim Foundation v. Lubell, 77 N.Y.2d 311, 320 (N.Y. 1991).

[101] Von Saher v. Norton Simon Museum of Art at Pasadena, Case No. CV 07-2866-JFW (C.D. Cal. April 2, 2015).

stolen art begins to run anew each time the work is transferred, even if the statute of limitations has already expired on claims against the seller or transferor.

California has modified its statute of limitations for actions to recover stolen art three times since 1983. Before 1983, the state had a 3-year statute of limitations that applied across the board to all actions to recover stolen property, including artwork. Since the statute did not state when a cause of action for return of stolen property accrued (i.e., what conditions were necessary to set the limitations clock running), courts variously interpreted it to mean that the statute of limitations began to run at the time of the theft or, alternatively when the rightful owner discovered where the object was located and the identity of its present possessor (the discovery rule). In 1983, the state amended its statute of limitations to adopt the "discovery rule" for accrual of causes of action for the recovery of stolen artwork. In *Naftzger v. the American Numismatic Society*,[102] the California Court of Appeal held that even the pre-1983 statute had an implied discovery rule. The court noted that "[t]he discovery rule protects those who are ignorant of their cause of action through no fault of their own. It permits delayed accrual until a plaintiff knew or should have known of the wrongful conduct at issue."[103]

In 2002, responding to concerns that the statute of limitations was unfairly frustrating efforts by parties seeking the return of Nazi-confiscated artworks, the California legislature enacted Section 354.3 of the California Code of Civil Procedure, which extended the statute of limitations until December 31, 2010, to allow "any owner, or heir or beneficiary of an owner, of Holocaust-era artwork, [to] bring an action to recover Holocaust-era artwork from . . . any museum or gallery that displays, exhibits or sells any article of historical, interpretive, scientific, or artistic significance."[104] However, the U.S. Court of Appeals for the Ninth Circuit struck down Section 354.3 as unconstitutional, reasoning that the statute is preempted under the foreign affairs doctrine, since it impermissibly intrudes "into a field occupied exclusively by the federal government."[105]

---

102 42 Cal.App.4th 421, 435 (Cal. App. 1996).
103 *Id.* at 428.
104 Cal. C.C.P. § 354.3, quoted in Von Saher v. Norton Simon Museum of Art at Pasadena, 592 F.3d 954, 958 (9th Cir. 2010).
105 *Id.* at 968.

Shortly after the Ninth Circuit issued its decision, the California legislature amended Section 338 to provide for a 6-year statute of limitations for actions to recover stolen artwork (not only Holocaust-era artwork), but only when the claim is made against a museum, gallery, auctioneer, or dealer. However, actions are limited to those for the return of artworks that were taken "within 100 years prior to enactment of this statute."[106] Under revised Section 338, the cause of action accrues upon the *actual* discovery by the plaintiff of the location of the object and the identity of the current possessor. The revised statute provides that:

> an action for the specific recovery of a work of fine art brought against a museum, gallery, auctioneer, or dealer . . . of a work of fine art, including a taking or theft by means of fraud or duress, shall be commenced within six years of the actual discovery by the claimant or his or her agent, of both of the following:
>
> (i) The identity and the whereabouts of the work of fine art. In the case where there is a possibility of misidentification of the object of fine art in question, the identity can be satisfied by the identification of facts sufficient to determine that the work of fine art is likely to be the work of fine art that was unlawfully taken or stolen.
>
> (ii) Information or facts that are sufficient to indicate that the claimant has a claim for a possessory interest in the work of fine art that was unlawfully taken or stolen.[107]

Significantly, the amendment also exempts actions for the recovery of stolen artwork brought against museums, galleries, auctioneers, and dealers from the application of Section 361, which disallows suits where the cause of action has arisen in another jurisdiction if the statute of limitations for bringing the action in that jurisdiction has already run.[108] So, under revised Section 338 (c)(3)(A), restitution actions may be brought against museums, galleries, auctioneers, and dealers within 6 years after the claimant actually discovers the identity and whereabouts of the stolen

---

106 Cal. C. C. P. § 338(c)(3)(B).

107 Cal. C. C. P. § 338(c)(3)(A).

108 *See* Cal. C. C. P. § 361, which states that "When a cause of action has arisen in another State, or in a foreign country, and by the laws thereof an action thereon cannot there be maintained against a person by reason of the lapse of time, an action thereon shall not be maintained against him in this State, except in favor of one who has been a citizen of this State, and who has held the cause of action from the time it accrued."

work, and can be brought irrespective of whether the statute of limitations has run in the jurisdiction where the cause of action arose.

In its amended motion to dismiss, the museum argued that Ms. von Saher's cause of action was time-barred by the statute of limitations, even as amended. Ms. von Saher's cause of action, the museum argued, accrued between 1946 and 1952, when Desi Goudstikker, Jacques's widow, actually discovered that the paintings were then in the possession of the Dutch government. The museum argued that Ms. Von Saher, as plaintiff, stands in the shoes of Desi Goudstikker, Ms. von Saher's predecessor-in-interest. Ms von Saher argued that the statute of limitations applies only to the current claimant, not to predecessors-in-interest.

The district court disagreed with Ms. Von Saher, holding that heirs are subject to their ancestors' knowledge and actions with respect to statutes of limitations. However, the district court disagreed with the museum that the mere fact that the statute of limitations would have run with respect to Desi Goudstikker's claim against the Dutch government would also mean that Ms. von Saher's action against the museum is likewise time-barred. The court noted that if it were to accept Ms. von Saher's position that the statute of limitations runs with respect to each claimant, "[a]n expired claim would be revived any time a claimant died and passed that claim to an unknowledgable heir or the claimant assigned that claim to an ignorant third party. Such a result would eviscerate the purpose of a statute of limitations."[109]

However, the court went on to consider when Ms. Von Saher's cause of action against the museum accrued. The museum's position was that the cause of action that accrued at the time Desi Goudstikker discovered the whereabouts of the paintings then in the possession of the Dutch government was continued in the museum's later possession (a concept in United States law known as "tacking"). [110] There is a certain appeal of symmetry in this, since if Ms. von Saher is the successor-in-interest of Desi Goudstikker, why wouldn't the museum be the successor-in-interest

---

[109] Von Saher v. Norton Simon Museum of Art at Pasadena, Case No. CV 07-2866-JFW, at *7 (C.D. Cal. April 2, 2015).

[110] *See, e.g.*, Patty Gerstenblith, *The Adverse Possession of Personal Property*, 37 BUFF. L. REV. 119, 146–147 (1988/1989)("The ability of a possessor to add his or her time of possession to that of a prior possessor so that the total comprises the time period required for the running of the statute of limitations is known as 'tacking' and is applied in the doctrine of adverse possession of real property. . . . Although tacking is almost universally accepted for adverse possession of real property, this has not been the case for personal property.").

of the Dutch government? The answer, the district court held, lay in the nature of title to stolen property.

In most common law jurisdictions (the United States, the United Kingdom, and others) a thief cannot transfer title to stolen property, and, as a result, the stolen property remains tainted in the hands of all subsequent possessors. Moreover, as the court stated, California law has long recognized that "each time stolen property is transferred to a new possessor, a new tort or act of conversion has occurred," and so "the statute of limitations . . . begins to run anew against each subsequent purchaser."[111] The new or subsequent possessor, even if he or she purchased the stolen property in good faith and without knowledge of the theft, nevertheless "commits a new act of conversion, and a new statute of limitations begins to run, even if the new possessor purchases the property honestly and in good faith."[112]

The question for the district court, however, was whether a purchaser who acquires a stolen artwork after the limitations period has run is subject to a new statute of limitations. That is, if the statute of limitations has expired and the possessor then sells the artwork, does the statute of limitations begin to run anew against the buyer/new possessor? Although several courts had previously raised this question, none had yet answered it.[113] The district court noted that "it is an open question in California whether a subsequent possessor who acquires stolen property after the statute of limitations has already expired is subject to a renewed limitations period."[114]

Quoting a late 19th-century decision, *Harpending v. Meyer*, 55 Cal. 555 (Cal. 1880), the district court stated:

> [I]t is distinctly held that where the possession of property is obtained from one who had no right to transfer it, a right of action by the owner against the transferee accrues as soon as the latter acquires possession of

---

111 *Id.* at *8.

112 *Id.*

113 *Id.* at *9 (*citing* Soc'y of California Pioneers v. Baker, 43 Cal. App. 4th 774, 783 n.4 (1996)("[W]e need not decide whether a purchaser who acquired the item after the statute expired would be subject to renewal of the limitations period."); and Naftzger v. American Numismatic Soc'y, 42 Cal. App. 4th 421, 433 (1996) ("We do not decide, for example, if an owner who fails to file a lawsuit under the prior version of section 338, subdivision (c) within three years of discovering the property's whereabouts will be time barred if the thief or subsequent possessor later moves the stolen property to an unknown location, sells, or continues to withhold the stolen property.")).

114 *Id.* at *8–9.

> it; that the bare taking of possession under such circumstances constitutes a new conversion on the part of the person taking it, and that from the time of the commission of that act, the statute will commence running.[115]

The district court reasoned that the expiration of the statute of limitations "merely extinguishes the owner's right to seek a remedy from the thief or possessor; it does not thereby divest the owner of title or convey title to the thief or possessor. . . . Accordingly, because the thief cannot convey valid title no matter how much time has passed, the subsequent possessor's acquisition of stolen property constitutes a new conversion. Because a new tort has occurred, the owner is entitled to a new limitations period."[116] So, for stolen artwork, even when the statute of limitations has expired as to one owner, if that owner sells or transfers the work to someone else, the statute of limitations begins to run fresh against the new owner.

The district court addressed the question of the fairness of allowing the statute of limitations to run anew against a subsequent purchaser or transferor, noting that:

> there is nothing unfair about affording Plaintiff an opportunity to pursue the merits of her claims against Norton Simon. As the California Legislature recognized by enacting AB 2765, museums are sophisticated and are well-equipped to trace the provenance of the fine art that they purchase. After carefully weighing the equities, the Legislature determined that the importance of allowing victims of stolen art an opportunity to pursue their claims supersedes the hardship faced by museums and other sophisticated entities in defending against potentially stale ones.[117]

---

[115] *Id.* at *8.
[116] *Id.* at 10.
[117] *Id.* at 11.

CHAPTER 7

Restrictions on Materials

A. Overview

A further risk in art transactions is regulatory impairment or restriction with respect to materials, which arises on both national and international levels. Many such restrictions derive from conservation and preservation efforts. A notable example is the dispute that arose between the estate of gallerist Ileana Sonnabend and the IRS over the valuation of Robert Rauschenberg's *Canyon* (1959).[1] The painting, one of Rauschenberg's combines, incorporates as one of its elements a stuffed bald eagle. Under the Bald and Golden Eagle Protection Act[2] it is prohibited to "take, possess, sell, purchase, barter, offer to sell, purchase or barter, transport, export or import, at any time or any manner, any bald eagle . . . [or any golden eagle], alive or dead, or any part, nest, or egg thereof." As with many similar conservation statutes, violations of the act may result in the imposition of fines and/or criminal sanctions. The IRS argued that even though the painting could not be legally sold in the United States, its value for estate tax purposes nevertheless would be based upon a market value, even if that market was a black market. The estate and the IRS eventually settled the matter, and the painting was donated by the estate to the Museum of Modern Art.

Similar restrictions on the ownership and transfer of different types of art and cultural property materials arise in many other contexts. The recent modifications to the U.S. Fish and Wildlife Service's regulation on

---

[1] *See* http://www.moma.org/collection/works/165011.

[2] 16 U.S.C. §§ 668-668c. For a brief discussion of the Bald and Golden Eagle Protection Act, see the U.S. Fish & Wildlife Agency's description of the act and its reach, *available at* http://www.fws.gov/midwest/MidwestBird/EaglePermits/bagepa.html.

the importation and sale of African elephant ivory have been an important art and cultural property trade flashpoint, and the extended discussion below of the nature and background of ivory regulation provides an introduction not only to how such materials restrictions apply in the case of African elephant ivory, but also to how they apply to a variety of other types of materials, including many types of flora and fauna. In all such instances, documentation (especially provenance and conservation documentation) becomes absolutely critical.

B. Ivory

In response to concerns that poaching of African elephants is rapidly driving the species to extinction, the United States federal government has tightened restrictions on the import, export, transfer, and sale of African elephant ivory and rhinoceros horn.[3] The revised restrictions followed on President Obama's July 2013 executive order[4] committing the United States to increase its efforts to halt wildlife trafficking. As reported by the Wildlife Conservation Center, "[t]here were an estimated 1.2 million African elephants in 1980, but now the population is down to less than 420,000. . . . For forest elephants, a separate species from the savannah elephant, the news is worse. Ten percent of the population was killed in 2012, and another 10 percent in 2013. . . . With fewer than 100,000 left, extinction could be only 10 years away."[5] Wildlife conservationists argue that a complete ban on the sale of ivory is necessary, and is the only way to stop poaching of elephants.[6] Some have suggested that a complete ban on ivory actually facilitates further looting and an illicit ivory market, and have urged the creation of a limited, regulated, licit market in ivory.[7]

---

[3] Import and export of Asian elephant ivory is allowed for noncommercial purposes either with an ESA permit or if the specimen qualifies as pre-ESA or as an antique under the ESA.

[4] *Executive Order, Combatting Wildlife Trafficking* (July 1, 2013), *available at* http://www.whitehouse.gov/the-press-office/2013/07/01/executive-order-combating-wildlife-trafficking.

[5] Gil Aegerter, *Saving the Elephants? State Bans on Ivory Trade Gather Steam*, NBC News (Aug. 12, 2014), *available at* http://www.nbcnews.com/science/environment/saving-elephants-state-bans-ivory-trade-gather-steam-n179121.

[6] *See* Christina Russo, *Can Elephants Survive a Legal Ivory Trade? Debate Is Shifting Against It*, National Geographic (Aug. 29, 2014), *available at* http://news.nationalgeographic.com/news/2014/08/140829-elephants-trophy-hunting-poaching-ivory-ban-cities/.

[7] *See* Daniel Stiles, *Can Elephants Survive a Continued Ivory Trade Ban*, National Geographic (Sept. 15, 2014), *available at* http://voices.nationalgeographic.com/2014/09/15/opinion-can-elephants-survive-a-continued-ivory-trade-ban/.

The revised rule's most controversial change has been its limitation of the antique exception to the general ban on ivory, which previously allowed commercial *and* noncommercial import, export, transfer, and sale of objects at least 100 years old that were either made of ivory or included ivory elements. The original version of the amended rule eliminated the antiques exception in all commercial contexts and substantially limited it in noncommercial contexts.[8] New York,[9] New Jersey,[10] California and Hawaii have similarly tightened their existing restrictions on the trade in and transfer of ivory.[11]

Response to this change was swift and, from many sectors, strongly negative, questioning what the revised rule would mean for the trade in art, antiques, musical instruments,[12] antique guns,[13] and other objects either made of ivory or containing ivory elements.[14] Collectors, museums, orchestras, and musicians pointed out that the revised rule would ban much long-standing collecting and cultural exchange activity. The policy was modified in May, in response to these objections, to clarify and provide some protection for noncommercial cultural activities.[15] Despite that modification, many in the arts community remain concerned that even for activities that are apparently authorized by the revised rule, the

---

8 *Director's Order No. 210: Administrative Actions to Strengthen U.S. Trade Controls for Elephant Ivory, Rhinoceros Horn, and Parts and Products of Other Species Listed Under the Endangered Species Act, U.S. Fish & Wildlife Service* (Feb. 25, 2014), *available at* http://www.fws.gov/policy/do210.html.

9 *See New York State Passes Historic Ban on Sale of Elephant Ivory and Rhino Horn, Wildlife Conservation Society* (June 20, 2014), *available at* http://www.wcs.org/press/press-releases/ny-state-ivory-ban-passes.aspx; *see also* Patrick Clark, *Antique Shops Threaten to Leave New York Over Ivory Ban*, Bloomberg BusinessWeek (Aug. 18, 2014), *available at* http://www.businessweek.com/articles/2014-08-18/new-yorks-ivory-ban-has-antique-shops-threatening-to-flee.

10 *See* Assembly Bill No. 3128, *available at* http://www.njleg.state.nj.us/2014/Bills/A3500/3128_I1.HTM, and Senate Bill No. S 2012, *available at* http://legiscan.com/NJ/bill/S2012/2014; *see also Governor Christie Signs Bipartisan Legislation to Crack Down on Black Market Ivory Trafficking* (Aug. 5, 2014), *available at* http://www.state.nj.us/governor/news/news/552014/approved/20140805c.html.

11 *See, e.g., Ivory Ban Now in Place*, California Department of Fish and Wildlife News (July 1, 2016), *available at* https://cdfgnews.wordpress.com/2016/07/01/california-ivory-ban-now-in-effect/; Geles times (Sept. 2, 2014), *available at* http://www.latimes.com/business/la-fi-ivory-bans-; Chris D'Angelo, *One of America's Largest Ivory Markets Just Banned Sales*, The Huffington Post (Mar. 7, 2016), *available at* http://www.huffingtonpost.com/entry/ivory-ban-hawaii_us_56d8ead8e4b0000de40403d4.

12 *See Ivory Ban Impact on American Orchestras* (Oct. 23, 2014), *available at* http://americanorchestras.org/advocacy-government/travel-with-instruments/endangered-species-material/ivory-ban-impact-on-orchestras.html.

13 *See* Tim Devaney, *Senators Seek Answers on Ivory Ban*, The Hill (Aug, 8, 2014), *available at* http://thehill.com/regulation/214590-senators-seek-answers-on-ivory-ban.

14 *See*, e.g., Allison Meier, *Museums, Musicians, and Antiques Dealers Resist Harsh New Ivory Restrictions*, HyperAllergic (June 26, 2014), *available at* http://hyperallergic.com/134867/museums-musicians-and-antique-dealers-resist-harsh-new-ivory-restrictions/; Tom Mashberg, *Limits on Ivory Sales, Meant to Protect Elephants, Set Off Wide Concerns*, New York Times (March 20, 2014), *available at* http://www.nytimes.com/2014/03/21/arts/design/new-limits-on-ivory-sales-set-off-wide-concerns.html?_r=0#;.

15 Director's Order No. 210, Amendment 1, U.S. Fish & Wildlife Service, May 15, 2014, *available at* http://www.fws.gov/policy/a1do210.pdf.

procedures and actual implementation remain uncertain. When antique objects of cultural and historic importance are at issue, many are understandably wary of placing those objects at risk of being detained or perhaps seized and destroyed.

Critics found even the revised rule to be overly broad, jeopardizing our understanding of the past by imposing current standards of behavior, effectively editing the past to suit contemporary tastes. "It is wrong, and foolish, to project our scruples on to the past," Jonathan Jones wrote in *The Guardian*. "There is no reason to abhor the wonderful masterpieces created by past generations with a technique we no longer 'approve of,' or to deny ourselves the pleasure of these artistic marvels. This is why American antiques dealers are right to demand clarification of current restrictions that seem to potentially ban the sale of bona fide historical objects."[16]

On July 10, 2014, companion bills were introduced in the Senate (S. 2587)[17] and House of Representatives, (H.R. 5052),[18] the "Lawful Ivory Protection Act of 2014," which would have prevented the new ivory rules from going into effect. The proposed bills would have amended the Endangered Species Act (discussed below) to prohibit any regulation going into effect after February 24, 2014, that would (i) prohibit or restrict the possession, sale, delivery, receipt, shipping, or transportation of elephant ivory that has been lawfully imported; (ii) change any methods of, or standards for, determining if ivory has been lawfully imported; or (iii) prohibit or restrict the importation or possession of ivory that was lawfully importable or possessable on that date. These bills were not passed.

Amid this storm over the new rule, it is important to attempt to clarify for collectors, museums, musicians, and others what activities are permitted under the revised rule and what activities are forbidden.

1. Background to the Regulation of Ivory

Ivory regulation has long been complex, "arising from the intersection of federal statutory law, executive-branch orders, and the guidelines imposed by international conservation treaties. As animal populations fluctuate,

---

16 Jonathan Jones, *Ivory: The Elephant in the Art Gallery*, The Guardian (May 15, 2014), *available at* http://www.theguardian.com/artanddesign/jonathanjonesblog/2014/may/15/ivory-elephant-artworks-banned-cultural-legacy.

17 S. 2587, *available at* https://www.congress.gov/bill/113th-congress/senate-bill/2587/text.

18 H.R. 5052, *available at* https://www.congress.gov/bill/113th-congress/house-bill/5052?q=%7B%22search%22%3A%5B%22hr5052%22%5D%7D.

so do the laws."[19] In United States domestic law, the protections and obligations with respect to ivory that have been promulgated under the Convention on International Trade in Endangered Species of Wild Fauna and Flora (CITES)[20] are implemented through the Endangered Species Act (the ESA) (which lists both Asian and African elephants as endangered, and provides that artifacts carved of elephant ivory ["worked elephant ivory," in contrast to unworked or "raw" ivory] may travel legally if accompanied by documentation proving that their provenance pre-dates the ESA)[21] and the African Elephant Conservation Act (the AECA, which broadly prohibits the import of raw or worked ivory).[22] The Lacey Act provides for both civil and criminal penalties for trade in wildlife that has been taken in violation of any state or foreign wildlife law or regulation.[23]

CITES attempts to eliminate the illegal trade in animals and plants, their parts, and associated products (including ivory), by means of a variety of mechanisms, including domestically implemented trade bans and licensing regimes. The convention entered into force on July 1, 1975, and presently has 180 state parties.[24] In 1989, CITES was amended to ban the sale of new ivory. Critics of the CITES ivory ban have pointed out that demand for new ivory remains strong in Asia, particularly China, and that the net effect of the ban has been to greatly increase the price poachers are able to obtain for illicit ivory.[25]

---

19 *See* Ben Phelan, *An Overview of Current Ivory Law* (August 11, 2014), *available at* http://www.pbs.org/wgbh/roadshow/fts/chattanooga_200804A10.html.

20 Convention on International Trade in Endangered Species of Wild Fauna and Flora (1973, as amended), *available at* http://www.cites.org/eng/disc/text.php.

21 Endangered Species Act, 7 U.S.C. § 136, 16 U.S.C. § 1531 *et seq.* (1973), *available at* http://www.fws.gov/endangered/laws-policies/.

22 African Elephant Conservation Act, 16 U.S.C. §§4201–4203 (1988), *available at* http://www.fws.gov/international/wildlife-without-borders/multinational-speicies-conservation-acts-african-elephant.html.

23 The Lacey Act, 18 U.S.C. §§ 42–43, 16 U.S.C. §§ 3371–3378 (1900 and later amendments), *available at* http://www.fws.gov/international/laws-treaties-agreements/us-conservation-laws/lacey-act.html.

24 Convention on International Trade in Endangered Species of Wild Fauna and Flora (1973, as amended), *available at* http://www.cites.org/eng/disc/parties/index.php.

25 *See* Doug Bandow, *The Administration's New Ivory Ban: I'm From the Government and I'm Here to Kill Elephants and Treat Americans as Criminals* (Mar. 17, 2014), *available at* http://www.cato.org/publications/commentary/administrations-new-ivory-ban-im-government-im-here-kill-elephants-treat. *See also* Darryl Fears, *Overwhelmed U.S. Port Inspectors Unable to Keep Up with Illegal Wildlife Trade*, THE WASHINGTON POST (Oct. 17, 2014), *available at* http://www.washingtonpost.com/national/health-science/overwhelmed-us-port-inspectors-unable-to-keep-up-with-illegal-wildlife-trade/2014/10/17/2fc72086-fe42-11e3-b1f4-8e77c632c07b_story.html (reporting that "international wildlife trafficking has grown from a small concern into a criminal colossus worth an estimated $20 billion per year, police and economists say—the fourth-largest global black market behind the trades for drugs, guns and humans for sex.").

2. The Antique Exception

Before the revised rule went into effect, objects at least 100 years old that are either made of African elephant ivory or include ivory components were exempt from the general ESA and CITES ivory prohibition.[26] This changed dramatically under the original version of the rule that was issued in February 2014, which (i) wholly eliminated the antique exception for commercial transactions (i.e., sales), and (ii) retained the antique exception for noncommercial transactions only if the object has not been sold after February 26, 1976. Recognizing that the "noncommercial movement of musical instruments and certain other CITES pre-Convention" objects are not "contributing to the poaching crisis or to illegal trade," the service amended its earlier order.[27]

As modified in May 2014, the revised rule allows qualified antiques to be imported for noncommercial purposes (loans, traveling exhibitions, etc.). However, *no* commercial importation of *any* African elephant ivory is allowed, even if those objects would otherwise qualify as antique.

To qualify for the noncommercial antique exception, the importer or exporter must show (through appropriate documentation) that the object:

(i) is at least 100 years old;

(ii) is composed in whole or in part of an ESA-listed species;

(iii) has not been repaired or modified with any ESA-listed species after December 27, 1973; and

(iv) is being or was imported through a designated endangered species "antique port."

The United States established thirteen "antique ports" on September 22, 1982, and required that all imports of ESA-listed species be made exclusively through those designated ports. These antique ports are Boston, New York, Baltimore, Philadelphia, Miami, San Juan, New Orleans, Houston, Los Angeles, San Francisco, Anchorage, Honolulu, and Chicago. Objects that were imported before September 22, 1982 (and so before the antique ports were established), may still qualify for the antique exception,

---

[26] Most European countries, by contrast, exempted such objects that were only 50 years old.
[27] U.S. Fish & Wildlife Service, *Ivory FAQ*, *available at* http://www.fws.gov/international/travel-and-trade/ivory-ban-questions-and-answers.html.

but the documentation accompanying such objects must satisfy the first three of the above-listed criteria.[28]

3. Commercial Import, Export, and Interstate Sales

No commercial importation of African elephant ivory is permitted (effective February 25, 2014). Commercial export of worked African elephant ivory is permitted, provided that the ivory is accompanied by a CITES pre-Convention certificate showing that it was removed from the wild no later than February 26, 1976. Raw African elephant ivory may not be exported.

Interstate sale of African elephant ivory is permitted, but only if the seller shows (through appropriate documentation) that (i) the object was lawfully imported prior to January 18, 1990 (the date that the African elephant was listed in CITES Appendix I), or (ii) the object was (or its ivory components were) imported under a CITES pre-Convention certificate.[29] Since interstate commerce in ivory derived from species other than African elephants is separately regulated, anyone attempting to sell any ivory in interstate transactions must be able to document the species the applicable ivory is derived from.

Forms of ivory are, in fact, derived from many different species, a number of which fall within different regulatory schemes. For instance, ivory is derived from walruses, warthogs, hippopotami, mammoths, mastodons, and narwhals.[30] Whale tooth ivory is regulated not only by the ESA and CITES, but also by the Marine Mammal Protection Act.

While it is possible to identify elephant ivory from other types of ivory, it is not possible "to distinguish between African and Asian elephant ivory visually or by most analytical methods, with the exception of DNA analysis."[31] Moreover, "[a]s ivory desiccates it loses its surface luster and becomes harder. With the passage of time, these changes can make visual identification more difficult. Indeed, ancient ivory, bone, and wood (as from archaeological contexts) can appear quite similar, requiring the use of analytical testing for identification."[32] The difficulty of

---

28 *Id.*

29 Asian elephant ivory sold in interstate commerce within the United States must meet the criteria of the antique exception.

30 Stephanie Hornbeck, *Ivory: Identification and Regulation of a Precious Material,* Smithsonian National Museum of African Art Conservation Law, *available at* http://www.caryatid-conservation.com/Documents/ivory%20identification%20and%20regulation.pdf.

31 *Id.*

32 *Id.*

distinguishing ivory species and ivory age by visual inspection alone makes maintaining full and accurate documentation of ivory and ivory-containing objects essential. Such documentation should include any CITES permits or certificates, certified appraisals, bills of sale, and documentation of the place and date the object was manufactured. Unfortunately, many objects in private and public collections either wholly lack this documentation or are incompletely documented. This lack of documentation may render ivory and ivory-containing objects unsalable and may also preclude their export.

4. Personal Ownership and Personal Use

The revised rule does not prohibit personal ownership of either worked or raw African elephant ivory, but the general rule prohibiting its commercial importation does apply. Therefore, it is not possible for an individual to purchase either raw or worked African elephant ivory abroad and bring it to the United States.

There are, however, three circumstances in which such ivory may be imported for noncommercial personal use. The first two of these circumstances have common requirements. Worked African elephant ivory may be imported for personal use either (a) as part of a household move, or (b) as part of an inheritance. In each case, importation is permitted only if (i) the ivory was legally acquired before February 26, 1976, (ii) the ivory has not been transferred from one person to another person "in pursuit of financial gain or profit" after February 25, 2014, and (iii) the item is accompanied by a valid CITES pre-Convention certificate.

The third circumstance in which importation is allowed is for sport-hunted trophies. African elephant ivory (either worked or raw) may also be imported as part of a sport-hunted trophy.

5. Museum Acquisitions and Loans

The revised ivory rule has striking impacts on museum acquisitions and loans. In a presentation to the U.S. House of Representatives Subcommittee on Fisheries, Wildlife, Oceans and Insular Affairs, the Association of Art Museum Directors warned that "two vital components of museum activities have been impacted [by the new ivory rule]: the ability of American Art Museums to acquire new works and the ability of American Art Museums to take part in exchanges of international exhibitions and direct loans with foreign lenders."[33]

Before the revised rule was issued in February, United States museums could acquire antique ivory and objects containing ivory from sellers abroad and import them. As of February 25, 2014, museums may only acquire ivory in interstate sales within the United States.[34] Gifts to museums of ivory objects are permitted, provided the objects have proper documentation. Ivory-containing objects in United States museum collections whose importation would now be prohibited (assuming that their ivory elements are African elephant ivory) include (i) an Etruscan bronze chariot inlaid with ivory (Metropolitan Museum of Art),[35] (ii) a 6th-century Byzantine Ivory Pyx (Box) (Cleveland Museum of Art),[36] (iii) a 14th-century French Diptych (Detroit Institute of Arts),[37] and (iv) an 18th-century German sculpture, Christ Crucified (National Gallery of Art).[38]

Worked African elephant ivory and objects containing such ivory may be imported for museum exhibitions only if the following criteria are satisfied: (i) the ivory was legally acquired prior to February 26, 1976, (ii) the ivory has not been transferred from one person to another in the pursuit of financial gain or profit after February 25, 2014, (iii) the person or group seeking to import the object qualifies for a CITES traveling exhibition certificate, and (iv) the object is accompanied by a valid CITES traveling exhibition certificate[39] or an equivalent CITES document. Raw African elephant ivory cannot be imported, even for museum loans.

---

33 Association of Art Museum Directors, *Presentation to Subcommittee on Fisheries, Wildlife, Oceans and Insular Affairs* (June 24, 2014), *available at* https://aamd.org/sites/default/files/key-issue/FINALS~1.DOC.

34 *See* Lee DeVito, *Punishing the DIA for Ivory Trade Does Nothing to Stop Illegal Poaching of Elephants,* MetroTimes (Nov. 12, 2014), *available at* http://www.metrotimes.com/Blogs/archives/2014/11/12/punishing-the-dia-for-ivory-trade-does-nothing-to-stop-the-illegal-poaching-of-elephants; *see also* Graham W.J. Beal, *Director's Letter, Detroit Institute of Arts* (Nov. 2014), *available at* http://archive.constantcontact.com/fs100/1102135368424/archive/1119032137073.html.

35 Etruscan Bronze Chariot Inlaid with Ivory (2d quarter of the 6th century B.C.), see Metropolitan Museum of Art website, *available at* http://www.metmuseum.org/collection/the-collection-online/search/247020.

36 Byzantine Ivory Pyx (Box) (6th century), see Cleveland Museum of Art website, *available at* http://www.clevelandart.org/art/1951.114.

37 French 14th Century Diptych, see Detroit Institute of Arts website, *available at* http://www.dia.org/object-info/8e5cc938-2e96-4bf4-83a1-a65468127ab6.aspx?position=28.

38 Christ Crucified (18th century German), see National Gallery of Art website, *available at* http://www.nga.gov/content/ngaweb/Collection/art-object-page.101681.html.

39 To view the application form for a U.S.-issued CITES traveling exhibition certificate, see U.S. Fish & Wildlife Service Form 3-200-30, *available at* http://www.fws.gov/forms/3-200-30.pdf; *see also* Model Traveling-Exhibition Certificate, CITES website, *available at* http://www.cites.org/eng/res/12/E12-03R14A3.pdf ; *CITES Document Requirements: Guidance for U.S. Importers and Exporters,* U.S. Fish & Wildlife Service website, *available at* http://www.fws.gov/le/pdf/CITESDocumentRequirements11142007.pdf.

The effects of the revised rule on museum loans were immediately felt. In October 2014, several mummies and their associated funerary objects that were being imported for an exhibition, "Afterlife: Tombs and Treasures of Ancient Egypt," were detained by customs officials in Miami. The funerary objects included ivory vessels and jewelry, which required examination and confirmation.[40] While the mummies and ivory objects were ultimately released to the museum, the museum community remains concerned about the uncertainty and unpredictability of the process, and the possible risks to fragile and irreplaceable objects.

6. Musical Instruments

Musicians are also feeling the effects of the revised rule. Many musical instruments, particularly antique musical instruments, contain ivory elements. "[V]iolin bows from the 18th and 19th centuries," for example, and many keyboard instruments, "such as pianos, harpsichords and organs . . . have ivory fittings."[41] As with museum acquisitions of antique ivory objects, musicians also are now prohibited from importing any instruments purchased abroad that contain African elephant ivory.

Musical instruments containing worked African elephant ivory may be imported and exported in noncommercial (nonsales) transactions, but only if (i) the ivory was legally acquired prior to February 26, 1976, (ii) the ivory has not been transferred from one person to another person in pursuit of financial gain or profit after February 25, 2014, and (iii) the item is accompanied by a CITES musical instrument passport or CITES traveling exhibition certificate.[42]

---

[40] *See* Garry Shaw, *Egyptian Mummies Held by Miami Customs Due to Ivory Impact Ban*, The Art Newspaper (Oct. 20, 2014), *available at* http://www.theartnewspaper.com/articles/Egyptian%20mummies%20held%20by%20Miami%20customs%20due%20to%20ivory%20import%20ban/36016.

[41] Stephanie Chase, *A Letter to Governor Christie of New Jersey Regarding Bill S.2012/A.3128* (June 24, 2014), *available at* http://violinchase.wordpress.com/2014/06/24/a-letter-to-governor-christie-of-new-jersey-regarding-bill-s-2012a-3128/.

[42] To view the application form for a U.S.-issued multi-use CITES musical instrument certificate, see U.S. Fish & Wildlife Service Form 3-200-88, *available at* http://www.fws.gov/international/pdf/permit-application-form-3-200-88.pdf; to view the application form for a U.S.-issued single-use CITES musical instrument certificate, see United States Fish & Wildlife Service Form 3-200-23, *available at* http://www.fws.gov/forms/3-200-23.pdf. To qualify, a musician or group (i) must have a primary residence in the United States, and (ii) pay an application fee. If amendment to the instrument documentation is needed after a group certificate has been issued, amendments to group certificates are available with payment of an amendment fee. The estimated period for processing of applications is 60–90 days.

7. The Critical Issue of Documentation

The revised rule for African elephant ivory reinforces the importance of full and proper documentation for collectibles. All ivory-containing objects, whether antique or not, must be accompanied by (i) all necessary CITES permits or certificates showing that the ivory was (a) legally acquired prior to February 26, 1976, or (b) legally imported after September 22, 1982, through a designated antique port; (ii) certified appraisals; (iii) bills of sale; (iv) documentation of the place and date the object was manufactured; and (v) documentation identifying the species from which the ivory was derived. Director's Order No. 210, Amendment 1, emphasizes that "[n]otarized statements or affidavits by the exporter or seller, or a CITES pre-Convention certificate alone, are not adequate proof that the article meets the ESA exception."[43]

While a lack of documentation may render objects unsaleable, insufficient documentation could also cause museums to be reluctant or unable to accept charitable donations of such objects. Even if a donation were accepted, the object's appraised value would be severely limited because no legal U.S. market for undocumented African elephant ivory exists. The donor's consternation could be compounded were the IRS's Art Advisory Panel to follow precedent and value the object based on a market value on an illicit market, resulting in an estate tax liability.[44]

---

43 Director's Order No. 210, Amendment 1, U.S. Fish & Wildlife Service, May 15, 2014, *available at* http://www.fws.gov/policy/a1do210.pdf.

44 The issue of estate tax valuation of unsaleable works of art was brought to the fore in the case of Robert Rauschenberg's "Canyon," a 1959 composition that included a taxidermied golden eagle. The painting was owned by gallerist Ileana Sonnabend, and at her death became part of her estate. Since the painting could not be sold (because the Bald and Golden Eagle Protection Act prohibits the sale of the protected species), the estate valued the work at $0. The IRS disagreed, arguing that the painting's value should be determined by its black market value, which it placed at $65 million, resulting in a $29.1 million estate tax bill. The estate appealed, and the matter was eventually settled. *See* Janet Novack, *The IRS Art Advisory Panel Has Its Head in the Clouds*, FORBES (July 22, 2012), *available at* www.forbes.com/sites/janetnovack/2012/07/22/the-irs-art-advisory-panel-has-its-head-inthe-clouds/.

CHAPTER 8

Sale Transactions

A. Overview

Within the framework of national and international commercial law, the sale of tangible, movable objects of art constitutes a sale of "goods."[1] In the United States, domestic sales of goods (including cultural property) are governed by Article 2 of the UCC.[2] Internationally, sales of goods (also including cultural property) may be governed by the United Nations Convention on

[1] Courts have held that Article 2 applies to the sale of cultural property objects. *See* Foxley v. Sotheby's Inc., 893 F. Supp. 1224 (S.D.N.Y. 1995) (holding that Article 2 applies to the sale of a painting at auction, even if the purchase price combines goods and services); Sack v. Lawton, No. 01 Civ. 285(SHS), 2003 WL 22682043 (S.D.N.Y. Aug. 28, 2003) (holding that Article 2 applies to contracts for the purchase and sale of paintings and drawings). More particularly, numerous courts have held that cultural property objects are "goods." *See, e.g.*, Balog v. Center Art Gallery-Hawaii, Inc., 745 F.Supp. 1556, 1562, n. 14 (D. Haw. 1990) (stating that "Paintings, prints and sculpture . . . fall within the [UCC] definition of goods."); Firestone & Parson, Inc. v. Union League of Philadelphia, 672 F.Supp. 819, 821–22 (E.D. Pa. 1987), judgment aff'd, 833 F.2d 304 (3d Cir. 1987)(holding that "a painting is a 'good' within the meaning of the U[CC]"). *But see* Cook v. U.S., 220 Ct. Cl. 76, 599 F.2d 400, 405, n. 8 ((1979) (stating that the IRS "assumes [incorrectly] that, if the artist's products are 'personal property' under tax sourcing rules, such products are also 'goods' covered by Article 2 of the [UCC], for purposes of determining federal income tax); Tobey v. Commissioner of Internal Revenue, 60 T.C. 227, 1973 WL 2666 (1973), acquiescence recommended, 1975 WL 38203 (I.R.S. AOD 1975) and acq., 1979-2 C.B. 1; Fink v. DeClassis, 745 F.Supp. 509 (N.D. Ill. 1990)(stating that "artwork [is an] asset [that] cannot be legitimately characterized as goods, and [no] authority . . . suggests that such assets fall within the scope of Article 2."); Insul-Mark Midwest, Inc. v. Modern Materials, Inc., 612 N.E.2d 550 (Ind. 1992)(holding that works commissioned from artists are not 'goods' for purposes of Article 2); McCulley Fine Arts Gallery, Inc. v. X Partners, 860 S.E.2d 473 (Tex. App. El Paso 1993) (Sale of Van Gogh painting Roadway in a Paris Park not a sale of goods under the UCC, and an agreement to fund its purchase outside the scope of the UCC, stating that "defendants' contention that . . . agreement to purchase [Van Gogh painting] was a 'sale of goods' in excess of $500 and that a written contract was . . . required" overturned on appeal where court held case represents a "failure to fund.").

[2] The UCC is a model law drafted as a joint project of the National Conference of Commissioners on Uniform State Laws and the American Law Institute, and is designed to harmonize the commercial laws of the United States. It was first published in 1952 and has been amended numerous times. The UCC has been enacted by all 50 U.S. states with some (mostly minor) variations. WILLIAM H. LAWRENCE, WILLIAM H. HENNING & R. WILSON FREYERMUTH, UNDERSTANDING SECURED TRANSACTIONS 4–5 (4th ed. 2007).

Contracts for the International Sale of Goods (CISG),[3] where buyer and seller have their places of business in CISG contracting countries.

Surprisingly, considering the art trade's global scope, the literature of art law, while analyzing sales under Article 2, remains largely silent on the applicability and impact of the CISG on international sales of art. While a majority of decisions addressing the sale of art have been decided under domestic law,[4] courts have been clear in holding that art also constitutes "goods" for purposes of international sales under the CISG.[5] This silence may derive from an assumption that since the CISG excludes consumer transactions and auction sales, it would not apply to sales in the art trade. While perhaps understandable, that assumption is unwarranted, and, as discussed below, unwise, since numerous types of current art sales are within the CISG's scope. Moreover, as the globalizing trend that has been evident in the trade over the last decade continues, the CISG will be relevant to an increasing number of art sales. Finally, as the art trade gains greater familiarity with the CISG's contractually flexible blend of common law and civil law concepts, it may well find that the CISG is a convenient and useful tool for meeting sellers' and buyers' expectations in certain circumstances.

B. Application of the CISG to Art Sale Transactions

Notwithstanding the silence on the CISG in art law literature, many—in fact, an increasing number of—art sale transactions are within the scope of the CISG, which, by virtue of its status as a self-executing international convention incorporated into national law,[6] will apply to such sale

---

3 The United Nations Convention on Contracts for the International Sale of Goods, S. Treaty Doc. 98-9 (1983); A/CONF.97/18 (1980); 19 ILM 668 (1980); 52 Fed. Reg. 6262–6280, 7737 (1987); 1489 UNTS 3. The CISG was drafted under the auspices of the United Nations Commission on International Trade Law (UNCITRAL), and entered into force on January 1, 1988.

4 *See, generally*, n. 2, *supra*.

5 *See* Kunsthaus Math. Lempertz OHG v. Wilhemina van der Geld, Arrondissementsrechtbank Arnheim (Netherlands, 1997), abstract *available at* http://www.unilex.info/case.cfm?pid=1&do=case&id=1098&step=Abstract (holding that a painting constituted "goods" for purposes of the CISG). Two notable exceptions to the silence on the CISG in art law literature are Yael M. Weitz and Laura Tam, International Art Transactions Under CISG, Art & Advocacy, Vol. 13 (Fall 2012), and Leila Amineddoleh, Purchasing Art in a Market Full of Forgeries: Risks and Legal Remedies for Buyers, Int. J. Cult. Prop. 22: 419-435 (2015).

6 *See, e.g.*, Jack Graves, The ABCs of the CISG 1-2 (2013) ("The CISG is federal law. . . . As such, it fully preempts state contract law within its stated scope—including a state's adoption of the Uniform Commercial Code (UCC) Article 2, as well as state common law. . . . The stated purpose of the CISG is to provide for a uniform body of sales law between commercial parties from this broad collection of Contracting States, thereby reducing potential 'frictions' inhibiting trade based on differing legal systems.")

transactions automatically, even if the parties to those transactions are unaware of the convention. Parties must be cognizant of the international nature of the CISG. One cannot assume that the rules and principles of national sales laws can be mapped directly onto the CISG or can be applied to the CISG as reliable guideposts. The CISG explicitly provides that "[i]n the interpretation of this Convention, regard is to be had to its international character and to the need to promote uniformity in its application and the observance of good faith in international trade."[7]

While national sales regimes, including UCC Article 2, will inevitably be a starting point of reference in analyzing whether parties are better served by expressly excluding the CISG from application or operating within the CISG framework, such national sales regimes cannot provide a methodology for interpreting the CISG. In interpreting the CISG, parties must look not only to the practices of national courts in construing the CISG, but also to the practices of other Contracting States in applying and construing the convention.[8] In many circumstances in cultural property sale transactions, the CISG's contractual flexibility—providing a set of default rules that generally can be tailored by the parties to fit the needs of their transaction—may offer a more useful and desirable tool than national sales regimes, such as UCC Article 2, which frequently include mandatory provisions that may ill-suit the parties' needs.[9] For instance,

---

[7] CISG, art. 7(1). Article 7(2) further provides that "[q]uestions concerning matters governed by this Convention which are not expressly settled in it are to be settled in conformity with the general principles on which it is based or, in the absence of such principles, in conformity with the law applicable by virtue of the rules of private international law." CISG, art. 7(2). *See also* Franco Ferrari, *Is the UCC Dead, or Alive and Well? International Perspectives: The Relationship between the UCC and the CISG and the Construction of Uniform Law*, 29 LOY. L.A. L. REV. 1021, 1024–1025 (April, 1996) ("[O]ne should not have recourse to any domestic concept in order to solve interpretive problems arising from the CISG. The policy behind reliance upon the autonomous interpretation also precludes recourse to domestic interpretive techniques in order to solve problems, since that would lead to results which conflict with the other premise upon which the interpretation of the CISG is to be based, namely the need to promote uniformity in its application.").

[8] *See id.* at 1027–1028 ("In order to achieve uniformity, it is . . . necessary to consider the practices of other contracting states. One must consider 'what others have already done,'—that is, one must take CISG decisions rendered by judicial bodies of other contracting states into account. Recourse to the *travaux preparatoires* and scholarly writings, as long as their underlying purposes do not conflict with the rules set forth in Article 7(1), might also help promote uniform application.").

[9] *See, e.g.*, Sarah Howard Jenkins, *Construing Laws Governing International and U.S. Domestic Contracts for the Sale of Goods: A Comparative Evaluation of the CISG and UCC Rules of Interpretation*, 26 TEMP. INT'L & COMP. L.J. 181, 182 (Fall, 2012) ("In the absence of a contrary agreement, the CISG provides default rules to govern the formation and performance of transactions for the international sale of goods. Unlike the CISG, UCC Article 2 contains a substantial number of mandatory provisions obviating the ability to opt-out of its provisions with the ease accorded by the CISG.").

UCC Article 2 includes mandatory provisions[10] governing (i) the requirement that the contract be in writing (Statute of Frauds),[11] (ii) the admissibility of parol evidence,[12] (iii) unconscionability,[13] (iv) third party beneficiaries of warranties,[14] (v) merchant buyers' duties,[15] (vi) the duty to mitigate damages,[16] (vii) liquidation or limitation of damages,[17] (viii) contractual modification or limitation of remedies,[18] and (ix) the statute of limitations in contracts for sale.[19]

1. Parties with Places of Business in Different Contracting States

The CISG governs "business-to-business transactions in goods across national borders."[20] It is "the uniform international sales law of countries that account for over three-quarters of all world trade."[21] It came into force on January 1, 1988, and, as of September 26, 2013, United Nations Commission on International Trade Law (UNCITRAL) reports that 80 Contracting States have adopted the CISG, including many countries active in the cultural property trade, among them, Brazil, China, France, German, Italy, Japan, Luxembourg, the Netherlands, Singapore, Switzerland, and the United States.[22] Notably, the United Kingdom, Ireland, India, and South Africa are not parties to the CISG.[23]

Subject to specific exclusions, the CISG will automatically apply to transactions for the sale of goods (and, unless the parties expressly opt-out from its application pursuant to CISG, art. 6, will override domestic

---

10 *See id. See also* Sarah Howard Jenkins, *Contracting Out of Article 2: Minimizing the Obligation of Performance & Liability for Breach*, 40 Loy. L.A. L. Rev. 401, 403 (2006).

11 UCC § 2-201.

12 UCC § 2-202.

13 UCC § 2-302.

14 UCC § 2-318.

15 UCC § 2-603.

16 UCC § 2-715(2)(a).

17 UCC § 2-718.

18 UCC § 2-719.

19 UCC § 2-725.

20 Jack Graves, The ABCs of the CISG 1 (2013).

21 Pace Law School CISG Database, CISG by State, Current Status, *available at* http://www.cisg.law.pace.edu/cisg/cisgintro.html#current.

22 Pace Law School CISG Database, CISG: Table of Contracting States, *available at* http://www.cisg.law.pace.edu/cisg/countries/cntries.html.

23 Jack Graves, The ABCs of the CISG at 2.

law, such as the UCC)[24] where (i) the parties to the contract have their place of business in different countries that are Contracting States,[25] (ii) the rules of private international law lead to the application of the law of a Contracting State,[26] (iii) the parties to the contract include a choice of law clause making the CISG applicable; or (iv) the CISG can be applied because it is part of the "*lex mercatoria*."[27] Pursuant to CISG, art. 1(3), "[n]either the nationality of the parties nor the civil or commercial character of the parties or of the contract is to be taken into consideration in determining the application of this Convention."[28] It is the parties' place or business (or, for individuals, habitual residence)[29] that is relevant for determining whether the CISG will apply to a transaction. For entities, the parties' state or country of formation or organization is not determinative. This means, for instance, that two companies that are formed under the laws of the same country, but which have their places of businesses in different Contracting States, would nevertheless satisfy the requirements for application of the CISG. However, for purposes of the CISG's applicability to a transaction, the location of the parties' places of business must be recognizable no later than at the time of the making of the contract by being apparent from (1) the contract; (2) dealings between the parties; or (3) information the parties have disclosed to each other.[30]

Where a party has multiple places of business, that place of business "which has the closest relationship to the contract and its performance, having regard to the circumstances known to or contemplated by the parties at any time before or at the conclusion of the contract" is deemed to

---

[24] CISG, art. 6 ("The parties may exclude the application of this Convention or, subject to article 12, derogate from or vary the effect of any of its provisions.").

[25] CISG, art. 1(1)(a) ("This Convention applies to contracts of sale of goods between parties whose places of business are in different States: when the States are Contracting States." ("Contracting States" means States that have ratified the CISG.).

[26] CISG, art. 1(1)(b) ("This Convention applies to contracts of sale of goods between parties whose places of business are in different States: when the rules of private international law lead to the application of the law of a Contracting State.").

[27] The "lex mercatoria" is sometimes referred to with respect to commercial law as part of the "general principles of international law," and is applied by arbitral panels and courts in the absence of applicable national law. *See* H.J. Berman & C. Kaufman, *The Law of International Commercial Transactions (Lex Mercatoria)*, 19 HARV. INT'L L.J. 221 (1978).

[28] CISG, art. 1(3).

[29] CISG, art. 10(b).

[30] CISG, art. 1(2) ("The fact that the parties have their places of business in different States is to be disregarded whenever this fact does not appear either from the contract or from any dealings between, or from information disclosed by, the parties at any time before or at the conclusion of the contract.").

be that party's place of business for purposes of determining whether the CISG will apply.[31]

For sales within the art trade, where sales are frequently made through intermediaries, this means that consideration potentially must be given not only to the places of business/habitual residences of the seller and the buyer, but also to the seller's and the buyer's intermediaries. The location where the sale occurs may, in fact, have limited bearing on whether or not the CISG will apply to the transaction. If the seller is a dealer whose business location is Singapore and the buyer is an art fund whose business location is New York, the CISG will apply. It may surprise some members of the trade that the location of the goods being sold may be minimally relevant to whether the CISG will govern the transaction. Similarly, if the Singapore-based seller and New York–based buyer contract for the sale of a sculpture that is located in London, the fact that the United Kingdom is not a party to the CISG does not mean that the contract would not be governed by the CISG.

In the art trade, however, the role of intermediaries can sometimes blur, so that it is not immediately clear whether the intermediary is acting as agent or as principal in the transaction. "Back-to-back" sales are common art trade practices. In a back-to-back sale, "a dealer lines up both a buyer and a seller (and sometimes other intermediate dealers) and multiple transactions are bundled into a single transaction, although the ultimate seller and the ultimate buyer may be unaware of each other's existence and, probably more important, the sale and purchase price."[32]

The art trade's extensive intermediation in sale transactions is highlighted in the circumstances that gave rise to *Edelman Arts, Inc. v. Art Int'l (UK) Ltd.*, a 2012 decision by the United States District Court for the Southern District of New York.[33] In *Edelman*, a proposed sale of a painting by Piet Mondrian between an undisclosed original seller and an (at least initially) undisclosed ultimate buyer was, in fact, made up of a series of proposed sales. Between the original seller and the ultimate buyer, there were no fewer than six intermediaries, including dealers, galleries, consultants, and agents, whose various places of business were located in France, Japan, the United States, and the United Kingdom.

---

[31] CISG, art. 10(a).

[32] Patty Gerstenblith, Art, Cultural Heritage, and the Law at 307, n. 2.

[33] Edelman Arts, Inc. v. Art Int'l (UK) Ltd., 841 F.Supp.2d 810 (S.D.N.Y. 2012).

Two distinct transactions were involved. The first was the purchase of the painting for a purchase price of $5.5 million, by Edelman Arts, Inc., whose business location was New York, from Karl Hutter Fine Arts, LLC, whose business location was California. The second transaction was Edelman's sale of the painting, for a price of $6.5 million, to Art International, whose business location was London. Although Art International was acquiring the painting on behalf of Galerie G, whose business location was in Germany, Galerie G was not a party to the sale agreement with Edelman. Edelman and Art International executed counterparts of a bill of sale, which were to be held in escrow pending closing. When Art International was unable to secure funding from Galerie G for the $6.5 million purchase price, the sale failed to close, and Edelman brought suit against Art International for breach of the sale agreement. The court was asked to decide whether the executed bill of sale was to be read and enforced as complete obligation or whether the fax cover sheets transmitted with the signed counterparts of the bill of sale, which stated that the bill of sale would be held in escrow "until monies from the buyer have been received," established a condition precedent to the bill of sale's effectiveness, whose condition was not met. The court held that the bill of sale and the fax cover sheets were to be read together as reflecting the parties' intentions, and it concluded that since the condition precedent to the effectiveness of the bill of sale had not been met, the bill of sale was not effective and so Art International had not breached any obligation due to Edelman.[34]

2. Personal Use and Auction Sale Exclusions

Although the CISG expressly excludes two areas that make up large sectors of the art trade—(i) sales for "personal, family or household use," and (ii) sales by auction—one must be careful not to overestimate the effect of those exclusions on the CISG's potential applicability in art sale transactions. As briefly noted in Chapter 4, in 2015, within the global art trade,

[34] *But see* Faggionato v. Lerner, 500 F.Supp.2d 237, 249 (S.D.N.Y. 2007) (rejecting dealer's claim to a conditional right to ownership of a painting in a back-to-back sale transaction where evidence failed to show that dealer had a right to purchase the painting from the owner and re-sell it to the buyer). *Cf.* Van Damme v. Gelber, Nahum & Gasiunasen Gallery of Palm Beach, Inc., 856 N.Y.S.2d 503, at *6 (Sup. Ct. 2008) (denying agent's motion to dismiss action against it by seller in a back-to-back sale, where agent entered into a sale agreement on behalf of its principal, which subsequently failed to perform).

approximately 47 percent of transactions by value were auction sales.[35] Of the 53 percent of sales that were not auction sales, it is unclear what percentage would qualify as consumer sales,[36] and so also potentially be excluded from CISG's scope. However, a significant number of art sale transactions do not fall within these excluded categories. Dealer-to-dealer sales, dealer-to-art-trust or art-fund sales, and dealer-to-museum sales would potentially be within the CISG's scope, as would private sales by or though auction houses to dealers, art trusts, art funds, or museums (which, while sales by or through auction houses, are not auction sales).[37]

Importantly, CISG art. 2(a) qualifies the personal use exclusion, providing that sales that are intended by the purchaser for personal use will not be excluded from the scope of the CISG if "the seller, at any time before or at the conclusion of the contract, neither knew nor ought to have known that the goods were bought for any such use."[38] Courts have considered both the personal use exclusion and the auction sale exclusion in the context of intermediated transactions, holding that such intermediated transactions may nevertheless be business-to-business sales within the scope of the CISG.

With respect to the consumer use exclusion, the Austrian Supreme Court of Justice held, in a 1997 decision,[39] that a seller could, under the express language of Article 2(a), challenge the applicability of the consumer use exception. To do so, consistent with the language of Article 2(a), the seller must show that the seller did not know and ought not to have known that buyer was purchasing the goods were for personal, family, or household use. Perhaps the richest area for such challenges would be the multiple and overlapping roles in the art trade, where the line between collector and dealer is a blurred and movable one. In some circumstances, a seller may

---

[35] *See* n. 18, *supra*. The "auction sales" figures may be misleading, since not all sales made by or through auction houses will be excluded from the CISG's scope by virtue of the auction sale exclusion.

[36] *See* TEFAF Art Market Report 2016, 27 (2016). Although 78% of dealer sales were identified as being made to private collectors, it is unclear to what extent those sales are consumer sales, made for "personal, family, or household use."

[37] *See* n. 17, *supra*. *See also* Alexandra Darraby, Art, Artifact, Architecture and Museum Law, § 5:1 (17th ed. 2014) (observing that "Historically considered a mere conduit between seller and buyer, auctions today regularly obtain proprietary or financial interests in the deal, or otherwise participate as principals in the sale. Traditional auction law, which based in common-law agency for sellers and caveat emptor for buyers no longer adequately encompasses auction activity in the markets.").

[38] CISG, art. 2(a).

[39] [Parties not listed], Oberster Gerichtshoft (Austria, 1997), abstract *available at* http://www.unilex.info/case.cfm?pid=1&do=case&id=283&step=Abstract.

well be able to show that the buyer is known to deal in goods of that kind, and that the buyer's intended personal use of the goods was not and should not have been apparent at the time of the sale.

Similarly, with respect to the auction sales exclusion, the Dutch court in *Kunsthaus Math. Lempertz OHG v. Wilhemina van der Geld*[40] distinguished between auction sales and auction consignment agreements. In that case, a Dutch seller entered into a consignment agreement with a German auctioneer to sell a painting. However, the auctioneer did not sell the painting at auction. Rather, the auctioneer sold the painting in a private sale to another German auctioneer, who subsequently offered it for sale at auction. When the painting's authenticity was challenged, however, the first auctioneer sued the seller asking to avoid the contract and for reimbursement of the purchase price. The court held that the consignment agreement between seller and auctioneer was not an auction sale. Rather, the contract between seller and auctioneer was a consignment agreement, or, as the court described it, "an order to sell by auction."[41] The *Kunsthaus* decision provides an important nuance to the elements of art sale transactions. Although a sale agreement between an auction house, on behalf of a seller, and a winning bidder at auction may fall within the auction sale exclusion, not all auction house contracts and sales are properly excluded from the CISG's scope.

3. Exclusion and Inclusion

When sale transactions fall within the scope of the CISG, the convention will automatically apply to such sale transactions unless the parties deliberately and expressly state in their contract that it will not apply.[42] Article 6 provides, very simply, "[t]he parties may exclude the application of this Convention or, subject to article 12, derogate from or vary the effect of any of its

---

[40] Kunsthaus Math. Lempertz OHG v. Wilhemina van der Geld, Arrondissementsrechtbank Arnhem (Netherlands 1997), abstract *available at* http://www.unilex.info/case.cfm?pid=1&do=case&id=355&step=Abstract, and case presentation *available at* http://cisgw3.law.pace.edu/cases/970717n1.html.

[41] *Id.* However, it should be noted that on appeal, the appellate court held that the CISG did not apply to the transaction between the seller and the auctioneer because the seller's order to sell by auction had "expressly referred to the buyer's standard terms regarding sale by auction, and the buyer's standard terms contained a provision expressly excluding the CISG and electing German law as the governing law. *See* Kunsthaus Math. Lempertz OHG v. Wilhemina van der Geld, Hof Arnhem (Netherlands 1999), abstract *available at* http://www.unilex.info/case.cfm?pid=1&do=case&id=355&step=Abstract.

[42] *See* n. 27, *supra*.

provisions."[43] However, Article 6 does not specify how definite a statement purporting to exclude the CISG from applying to the contract must be in order for the statement to be effective. Numerous courts have held that a mere choice-of-law provision electing the law of a particular jurisdiction, which does not explicitly state that the CISG is not to apply to the contract, is insufficient to exclude the CISG from application.[44] If the parties wish to exclude the CISG from applying to the transaction, they must include an explicit provision so excluding it is desirable, in order to make clear that this is the parties' intention at the time the contract is concluded. An effective exclusionary provision could read as follows: "This Agreement shall be governed by and interpreted in accordance with the laws of the State of _______, USA, without reference to any principles pertaining to conflicts of laws. However, the 1980 United Nations Convention on Contracts for the International Sale of Goods ("CISG") shall not govern or apply to this Agreement or its enforcement or to any sale made under this Agreement. The parties hereby exclude application of the CISG."[45]

If the parties instead include only in their contract a choice-of-law provision designating the law of a particular jurisdiction and fail to explicitly exclude application of the CISG, the choice-of-law provision may be ineffective, and the CISG may nevertheless apply to the contract. This is particularly true where the selected jurisdiction is a Contracting State, or a state, province, or region of a Contracting State.[46] In such circumstances,

---

[43] CISG, art. 6. The reference in article 6 to article 12 incorporates the effectiveness of a Contracting State's election under article 96 to make a declaration requiring that contracts be in writing. Where a Contracting State has made such a declaration, that writing requirement cannot be excluded or modified by the parties. However, the general rule under the CISG is that there is no writing requirement for contract formation (i.e., no equivalent of the common law and UCC Statute of Frauds). The CISG's general rule not requiring that a contract be in writing is stated in article 11.

[44] *See, e.g.*, Forestal Guarani, S.A. v. Daros Int'l, Inc., Civ. Action No. 03-4821 (JAG), 2008 WL 4560701, at *3 (D.N.J. Oct. 8, 2008)(stating that "The inclusion of an alternate choice of law provision must be announced explicitly in the contract."); Easom II, No. 06-14553, 2008 WL 1901236, at *2 (E.D. Mich. Apr. 25, 2008)(stating that "Courts have held that parties can only opt out of the CISG if their contract explicitly states this fact."); Sky Cast, Inc. v. Global Direct Dist., LLC, Civil Action No. 07-161-JBT, 2008 WL 754734, at *4 (E.D. Ky. Mar. 18, 2008) (stating that "Although parties to a contract normally controlled by the CISG may exclude the applicability of the CISG to their contract, any such exclusion must be explicit."); St. Paul Guardian Ins. Co. v. Neuromed Med. Sys. & Support., GmbH, No. 00 CIV. 9344(SHS), 2002 WL 465312, at *3 (S.D.N.Y. Mar. 26, 2002) (Holding that German law governed the contract and included the CISG, and noting that "(1) both the U.S. and Germany are Contracting States to [the CISG], and (2) neither party chose, by express provision in the contract, to opt out of the application of the CISG.").

[45] *See* William P. Johnson, *Understanding Exclusion of the CISG: A New Paradigm of Determining Party Interest*, 59 BUFF. L. REV. 213, at n. 234 (January 2011).

[46] *See id.* at 223.

"if the jurisdiction whose law is selected by the choice-of-law clause is a state within the United States or is a country that is a party to the CISG, then such choice-of-law clause generally should not by itself have the effect of excluding the CISG when the CISG is otherwise applicable. This is so because the CISG is the law of the selected jurisdiction. And for jurisdictions within the United States, this is so as a matter of United States constitutional law."

Unlike UCC Article 2, the CISG does not require a writing for contracts to arise and be effective. Moreover, the CISG allows consideration of a wide variety of courses of information about the parties' intentions, taking a more flexible approach to parol evidence. CISG, art. 11 provides that "[a] contract of sale need not be concluded in or evidenced by writing and is not subject to any other requirement as to form. It may be proved by any means, including witnesses."[47] But for parol or extrinsic evidence to be of any assistance in determining the parties' intention to exclude application of the CISG, the convention's application or exclusion must first have been in the parties' contemplation.

Conversely, when an art sale transaction is within the scope of the CISG and the parties *do not* wish to exclude application of the CISG, it may still be desirable to state this explicitly in the contract. The parties could, for instance, state that "The parties agree that this Agreement shall be governed by the 1980 United Nations Convention on Contracts for the International Sale of Goods (CISG), which shall be supplemented, as necessary, by the law of [________]."[48]

C. CISG v. UCC: Why Does It Matter?

For art sale transactions within the CISG's scope, before the parties can determine if they are best served by its exclusion or its application, they must first understand how it operates and how its operation may be significant in the context of an art sale. For art sale transactions, the CISG's distinctiveness is highlighted in three areas: (1) the absence of a writing requirement; (2) remedies for failure to deliver conforming goods; and (3) limitations periods for actions arising from breach.

---

[47] CISG, art. 11. *See also* William P. Johnson, *Understanding Exclusion of the CISG: A New Paradigm of Determining Party Interest*, 59 BUFF. L. REV. 213, 260–261 (January 2011).

[48] *See, e.g.*, JACK GRAVES, THE ABCS OF THE CISG 16 at Ex. 2-6 (2013).

It is useful first to understand the unique context of art sale transactions in the present global trade. Importantly, the norms and legal regimes that structure and govern the ownership of and trade in art have undergone tremendous change in recent decades and remain highly fluid. Significant shifts have occurred in, for instance, (i) the accrual of causes of action and application of statutes of limitations for replevin actions;[49] (ii) the rights of good faith purchasers of allegedly stolen property;[50] (iii) the rights of original owners and good faith purchasers of objects confiscated or sold under duress during the Holocaust;[51] (iv) national ownership laws and restrictions on export and import of certain classes of cultural property;[52] (v) national restrictions on the ownership or transfer of certain classes of materials;[53] and (vi) international agreements restricting the transfer of certain classes of materials.[54] Transactions in art are evaluated in a variety of ways and scrutinized differently than was frequently true in past practice.

[49] *See, e.g.*, Kunstsammlungen zu Weimar v. Elicofon, 678 F.2d 1150 (2d Cir. 1982) (cause of action does not accrue and statute of limitations does not begin to run until original owner demands return of object from current possessor and return is refused (demand and refusal rule)); Solomon R. Guggenheim Foundation v. Lubell, 569 N.E.2d 426 (N.Y. 1991); *but see* O'Keeffe v. Snyder, 416 A.2d 862 (N.J. 1980) (cause of action accrues and statute of limitations begins to run from the date when original owner discovers or should have discovered the theft/missing object; requires due diligence on the part of the original owner [discovery rule]).

[50] While a good faith purchaser may be able to acquire good title to stolen work in certain circumstances under the laws of some jurisdictions, under United States law a thief cannot transfer good title; therefore, if a work's chain of title includes the theft of that work, even the claim of a good faith purchaser is vulnerable. *See, e.g.*, Autocephalous Greek-Orthodox Church of Cyprus and the Republic of Cyprus v. Goldberg & Feldman Fine Arts, Inc., 717 F.Supp. 1374 (S.D. Ind. 1989).

[51] *See e.g.*, Republic of Austria v. Altmann, 541 U.S. 677 (2004); Vineberg v. Bissonette, 529 F. Supp.2d 300 (D.R.I. 2007); Cassirer v. Kingdom of Spain, 616 F.3d 1019 (9th Cir. 2010).

[52] U.S. v. McClain, 545 F.2d 988 (5th Cir. 1977); U.S. v. An Antique Platter of Gold, known as a Gold Phiale Mesomphalos c. 400 B.C., 184 F.3d 131 (2d Cir. 1999); U.S. v. Schulz, 333 F.3d 393 (2d Cir. 2003).

[53] Bald Eagle Protection Act of 1940, 16 U.S.C. §§ 668–668d; Migratory Bird Treaty Act, 16 U.S.C. § 703; Endangered Species Act, 16 U.S.C. §§ 1531-43; Native American Graves Protection and Repatriation Act, 25 U.S.C. §§ 3001–3013 (2006).

[54] Convention on International Trade in Endangered Species of Wild Fauna and Flora, 27 UST 1087; TIAS 8249; 993 U.N.T.S. 243 (1973) ("CITES") (which places limitations on international trade in specimens of wild animals and plants); Convention on the Means of Prohibiting and Preventing the Illicit Import, Export and Transfer of Ownership of Cultural Property, Nov. 14, 1970, 823 U.N.T.S. 231 (1972), reprinted in 10 I.L.M. 289 (1970) (the "UNESCO Convention"); Convention for the Protection of Cultural Property in the Event of Armed Conflict, May 14, 1954, 249 U.N.T.S. 240 (1954) (the "Hague Convention"); UNIDROIT Convention on Stolen or Illegally Exported Cultural Objects, June 24, 1995 (the "UNIDROIT Convention"); Convention on the Protection of the Underwater Cultural Heritage, Nov. 2, 2001, 41 Int'l Legal Materials 40 (2002) (the "Underwater Cultural Property Convention"); Convention Concerning the Protection of World Cultural and Natural Heritage, Nov. 16, 1972, 1037 U.N.T.S. 151 (1972) (the "World Heritage Convention").

1. Sales of Art under UCC Article 2

In the United States, commercial sale transactions are governed by UCC Article 2, which "applies to transactions in goods."[55] Under UCC § 2-106(1), a "sale" "consists in the passing of title from the seller to the buyer for a price."[56] Section 2-106 cross-references Section 2-401, which states that "title to goods passes from the seller to the buyer in any manner and on any conditions explicitly agreed on by the parties."[57] Section 2-401(2) states that "[u]nless otherwise explicitly agreed title passes to the buyer at the time and place at which the seller completes performance with reference to the delivery of goods, despite any reservation of a security interest and even though a document of title is to be delivered at a different time or place; and in particular and despite any reservation of a security interest by the bill of lading [under conditions specified in UCC § 2-401(2)(a) to (b)]."[58]

In an art sale transaction, passage of title is frequently provided for either in a sale agreement[59] or, for consigned goods, in the applicable consignment agreement.[60] However, sale agreements and consignment agreements do not always address when title to the goods will pass. When a sale or consignment agreement governed by UCC Article 2 is silent as to passage of title, "title passes to the buyer at the time and place at which the seller completes his performance with reference to the delivery of goods."[61]

2. Scope of Contract and Contract Formation

The United States and a number of other common law countries continue to observe the Statute of Frauds, codified (in United States law) in UCC Section 2-201. Under § 2-201(1), generally, "a contract for the sale of goods for the price of $500 or more is not enforceable by way of action or

---

55 UCC § 2-102.

56 UCC § 2-106(1).

57 UCC § 2-401(1).

58 UCC § 2-401(2).

59 *See, e.g.*, Andrew Crispo Gallery, Inc. v. Maroney, 187 A.D.2d 251 (1sr Dept. 1992) (where written sales agreement between buyer and seller stated title remained with seller until artwork fully paid for, which plaintiff failed to do; seller not obligated to buyer for profits from resale of painting under UCC 2-706(6)).

60 Matter for Miller, 545 F.2d 916 (5th Cir. 1977) (consignment of paintings to dealer under written consignment agreement gave dealer "full power . . . to convey title to each of the paintings to third parties.").

61 UCC § 2-401(2).

defense unless there is some writing sufficient to indicate that a contract for sale has been made between the parties and signed by the party against whom enforcement is sought or by his authorized agent or broker."[62] There are, however, exceptions. Section 201(2) provides that "[b]etween merchants if within a reasonable time a writing in confirmation of the contract and sufficient against the sender is received and the party receiving it has reason to know its contents, it satisfies the requirements of subsection (1) against such party unless written notice of objection to its contents is given within 10 days after it is received."[63] Under UCC Article 2, in the absence of a writing documenting passage of title in a purchase and sale transaction, claims that fraud or lack of consideration undermined passage of title ordinarily will not survive.[64]

The CISG's concept of contract is broader than what we find under UCC Article 2. Specifically, the CISG does not observe the Statute of Frauds. Rather, under CISG, art. 11, "[a] contract of sale need not be concluded in or evidenced by writing and is not subject to any other requirement as to form. It may be proved by any means, including witnesses."[65] While the CISG's approach provides parties with considerable flexibility, it also presents the risk that a party may find itself bound to offers in the form of oral or nonverbal communications.[66] This does not, however, mean that under the CISG parties can inadvertently enter into agreements without there being an intention to enter into a contract.

While under the UCC, once there is a final written agreement, the parol evidence rule will generally prohibit the consideration of extrinsic materials or prior agreements that contradict the agreement, but the CISG allows consideration of evidence of terms and conditions negotiated prior to execution of the written contract.[67] Under the CISG, contracts are interpreted by looking first to the subjective intent of the parties at the

---

[62] UCC § 2-201(1).

[63] UCC § 2-201(2).

[64] Zurich American Ins. Co. v. Felipe Grimberg Fine Art, 2008 WL 394808 (S.D.N.Y. 2008), judgment aff'd, 2009 WL 1269439 (2d Cir. 2009) (seller assumed risk of nonpayment through informal dealings with buyer by not requiring written contracts or documentation of certificates of ownership).

[65] CISG, art. 11.

[66] *See* JACK GRAVES, THE ABCS OF THE CISG 39 (2013)("Article 11 may. . . present a potential trap for an unwary U.S. business party who wrongly assumes that he or she will not be bound to a sizable sale of goods contract without seeing something in writing. . . . [A] party may find itself bound to an oral offer without any ability to revoke the offer until it expires on its own terms.").

[67] *See* CISG, art. 8, generally.

time the contract was concluded.[68] Where the parties' subjective intent is not in accord, the contract will be interpreted by an objective standard, "according to the understanding that a reasonable person of the same kind as the other party would have had in the same circumstances."[69] Unlike the UCC's parol evidence rule, the CISG allows "due consideration to be given to all relevant circumstances of the case including the negotiations, any practices which the parties have established between themselves, usages and any subsequent conduct of the parties."[70]

3. Seller's Obligation to Deliver Conforming Goods

UCC Article 2 and the CISG treat the question of a seller's obligation to deliver to a buyer goods that conform to the terms of the sale contract in conceptually different ways. Under UCC Article 2, a seller's sale of goods gives rise to certain express and implied warranties, some of which the seller may disclaim in advance. The CISG does not provide for seller warranties. Rather, the concepts underlying Article 2's express and implied warranties find broad analogues in the CISG's elements of the definition of "conforming goods."

In art sale transactions, the applicable warranties are (i) express warranties,[71] (ii) implied warranty of merchantability,[72] and (iii) implied warranty of fitness for a particular purpose.[73] These warranties find their CISG analogues in the presumptions set forth in CISG art. 35(2) concerning what qualifies as conforming goods.

a. Express Warranties

In art sale transactions, the most frequently litigated warranty is the express warranty, which may arise by (i) affirmation of a fact or promise of

---

68 CISG, art. 8(1) ("For purposes of this Convention statements made by and other conduct of a party are to be interpreted according to his intent where the other party knew or could not have been unaware what the intent was.").

69 CISG, art. 8(2).

70 CISG, art. 8(3).

71 UCC § 2-313 (a promise or description of the goods that becomes the basis of the bargain creates an express warranty).

72 UCC § 2-314 (a warranty that goods are merchantable is implied in the sale of goods by a merchant with respect to goods of that kind).

73 UCC § 2-315 (a buyer's reliance on a seller's particular skill or judgment to select or furnish suitable goods for a particular purpose will give rise to an implied warranty).

the seller,[74] (ii) the seller's description of the goods,[75] or (iii) the seller's statements of opinion.[76] The foundation of the express-warranty provision codified at UCC § 2-313 is twofold: (i) the core description of the goods,[77] and (ii) statements of the seller that become "part of the basis of the bargain."[78] An express warranty arises on "any affirmation of fact or promise made by the seller[79] to the buyer which relates to the goods and becomes part of the basis of the bargain."[80] If the goods do not conform to the affirmation or promise made, the warranty is breached, and an action may be brought, regardless of the seller's good-faith or malicious intentions in making the false statement.

Under the UCC and common law, disclaimers of a seller's express warranties are strongly disfavored and are viewed as contradicting the warranties.[81] However, where a buyer elects to examine the goods prior to purchase, the buyer may be estopped to later claim reliance upon the express warranty, where the defect is apparent and within the ability of the buyer to observe it.[82]

Under CISG art. 35(2)(c), goods are conforming only where they "possess the qualities of goods which the seller has held out to the buyer as a sample or model." Commentators have noted that the challenge in interpreting Article 35(2)(c) lies in determining what the relevant and necessary elements of the sample or model are with respect to the transaction and the intentions of the parties. "Certain aspects of a sample or

---

74 *See, e.g.*, Tunick v. Kornfeld, 838 F.Supp. 848 (S.D.N.Y. 1993) (sale of signed Picasso print where print was authentic but signature proved to be forged breached seller's express warranty).

75 *See, e.g.*, Weber v. Peck, Case No. 97 Civ. 7625(JSM), 1999 WL 493383 (S.D.N.Y. July 8, 1999) (where bill of sale included a description of a painting's provenance and it was later impossible to confirm that provenance, seller's express warranty as to the painting's provenance was breached).

76 *See, e.g.*, Levin v. Gallery 63 Antiques Corp., No. 04 CV 1504 KMK, 2006 WL 2802008 (S.D.N.Y. Sept. 28, 2006)(denying defendant gallery's motion for summary judgment where seller-provided statements and certificates of authenticity stated that sculpture were originals by and signed by specific artists and later analysis revealed the sculptures to be multiples produced in the artists' ateliers).

77 UCC § 2-313, cmt. 1, 4.

78 UCC § 2-313, cmt. 8.

79 *See* Rogath v. Siebenmann, 129 F.3d 261 (2nd Cir. 1997)(In a dispute arising between two dealers, a seller and a buyer, concerning the authenticity of a Francis Bacon self-portrait, the court held that only a seller's own statements to the buyer were relevant to whether an express warranty existed; information provided to the buyer by third parties did not give rise to an express warranty by the seller).

80 UCC § 2-313.

81 *See* Ralph E. Lerner & Judith Bresler, Art Law: The Guide for Collectors, Investors, Dealers, & Artists 96 (4th ed. 2012).

82 *See id.*

model may be absolutely crucial" to the parties' intention, "while others may be completely irrelevant."[83]

b. Implied Warranties

Generally, for art sale transactions, implied warranties are less often relevant, although disputes concerning implied warranties do sometimes arise. The most commonly applicable implied warranties for cultural property transactions are (i) the implied warranty of merchantability, and (ii) the implied warranty of fitness for a particular purpose.

i. Warranty of Merchantability

The implied warranty of merchantability has come to mean that goods must be capable of passing under the description specified in the agreement of sale and must be reasonably fit for the ordinary uses to which such goods are put.[84] Unless disclaimed, that warranty is implied in a contract for the sale of goods by a merchant dealer. For art sale transactions, goods will be deemed to be merchantable if they (i) pass without objection in the trade under the contract description, (ii) are fit for the ordinary purposes for which such goods are used, and (iii) conform to the promises or affirmations of fact made on the container or label, if any.[85] The implied warranty of merchantability tends to have limited applicability in the art trade, particularly where objects have traded in the market over time without a lack of authenticity being discovered.

The CISG addresses the analogous requirements in Article 35(2)(a) (requiring that goods be "fit for the purpose for which goods of the same description would ordinarily be used")[86] and Article 35(2)(d) (requiring that goods be "contained or packaged in the manner usual for such goods or, where there is no such manner, in a manner that is adequate to preserve and protect the goods").[87]

A seller may seek to disclaim an implied warranty of merchantability. Under UCC § 2-316(2), for a disclaimer of the implied warranty of merchantability to be effective, it must include the word "merchantability,"

---

[83] JACK GRAVES, THE ABCS OF THE CISG 66 (2013).

[84] UCC § 2-314.

[85] *See* UCC § 2-314(2)(a), (c), and (f). *See also* RALPH E. LERNER & JUDITH BRESLER, ART LAW: THE GUIDE FOR COLLECTORS, INVESTORS, DEALERS, & ARTISTS 99 (4th ed. 2012).

[86] CISG, art. 35(2)(a).

[87] CISG, art. 35(2)(d).

be "conspicuous," and be in writing.[88] Under the CISG, the requirements for goods to be deemed to be conforming goods are presumptions; they are not "warranties," nor are they "implied." Consequently, attempts to disclaim these presumptions may not be effective.

ii. Warranty of Fitness for a Particular Purpose

An implied warranty of fitness for a particular purpose may arise if (i) the seller knows of the buyer's particular purpose, (ii) the seller has actual or constructive knowledge that the buyer is relying on the seller's expertise or skill, and (iii) the buyer actually relies on the seller.[89] CISG art. 35(2) presumes that the goods "are fit for the purpose for which goods of the same description would ordinarily be used" and are "fit for any particular purpose expressly or impliedly made known to the seller at the time of the conclusion of the contract."[90]

As with the implied warranty of merchantability, a seller's disclaimer of the implied warranty of fitness for a particular purpose must be both conspicuous and in writing. As noted above, the CISG's requirements for goods to be deemed to be conforming goods are presumptions, not "warranties" (implied or otherwise). Attempts to disclaim the presumptions may not be effective. However, since most provisions of the CISG may be modified by the parties, the parties have considerable flexibility to determine what will constitute "conforming goods."

iii. Issues Concerning Breach

UCC Article 2 requires that a seller make "perfect tender" with respect to the terms of the contracts. Under Section 2-601, a buyer has a right to terminate the contract when the seller has breached a "condition" of the sale, no matter how minor.[91] The CISG, however, is considerably more seller-friendly on this point. Acknowledging that in international sales transactions, parties may be separated by distances, cultures, and languages, and goods may be transported across great distances, the CISG affords a seller who fails to perform on time, or who delivers nonconforming goods, an opportunity to correct its performance, provided that such cure does not cause the buyer an unreasonable delay or inconvenience.[92]

---

[88] UCC § 2-316(2).

[89] UCC § 2-315.

[90] CISG, art. 35(2)(b).

[91] UCC § 2-601.

[92] *See* CISG, art. 48(1).

Under the CISG, a buyer may sue for breach of contract, but the right to terminate the contract and reject the goods is limited.[93] The buyer may reject goods and require delivery of substitute goods if the contract has been "fundamentally breached." Under CISG art. 46(2), a breach is fundamental "if it results in such detriment to the other party as substantially to deprive him of what he is entitled to expect under the contract."[94] In addition, the buyer can also avoid the contract if, after demanding that the seller perform the contract within a reasonable time, the seller refuses to do so.[95]

However, in art transactions, where the goods are often rare and sometimes unique, a seller's right to cure by tendering conforming goods may be limited if not impossible. In the *Tunick* case discussed above, a seller's tender of a signed Picasso print was found to be nonconforming goods, because although the print itself was authentic, the artist's signature was forged.[96] The seller offered to replace the print with another print by Picasso, from the same series. The buyer rejected the offer and brought suit against the seller. The seller moved for summary judgment, arguing that his offer to exchange the print for another was an exercise of his right under UCC § 2-508(2) to substitute conforming goods for allegedly nonconforming goods. The court noted that the question of whether UCC § 2-508 applied to artworks was a matter of first impression—i.e., whether a nonconforming tender of a work of art can be cured by an offer of a different but similar work. The court held that two prints by the same artist and even from the same plates are nevertheless not interchangeable, and that UCC § 2-508 "does not, as a matter of law, obligate a buyer to accept in lieu of a nonconforming print, a substitute print from the same series of prints."[97]

Under both the UCC and CISG, a buyer must give notice of a breach within a reasonable time, but CISG provides an outer time limit on when notice must be given. Under CISG art. 39(2), a buyer will lose "the right to rely on a lack of conformity of the goods if he does not give the seller notice thereof within a period of two years from the date on which the goods were actually handed over to the buyer," absent any contractual agreement to the contrary.[98]

---

[93] *See* CISG, art. 45.
[94] CISG, art. 46(2).
[95] CISG, art. 49(b).
[96] *See* Tunick v. Kornfeld, 838 F.Supp. 848 (S.D.N.Y. 1993).
[97] *Id.*
[98] CISG, art. 39(2).

Two recent German decisions involving stolen property may also have implications for art transactions governed by CISG. Under CISG art. 41, a seller is required "to deliver goods which are free from any right or claim of a third party." In a 2006 case,[99] car dealers with places of business in different contracting states entered into a contract for the sale of a used car, which was later identified as having been stolen and was seized by authorities. Two months after the seizure, the buyer demanded repayment from the seller and initiated an action in Germany for termination of the contract and for damages. Though the buyer argued that the seller had breached the contract by failing to deliver conforming goods pursuant to Article 41, the court determined that the buyer lost the right to rely on Article 41 because he had failed to provide timely notice to the seller of the third party's claim as required under Article 43.

But, in a 2008 case,[100] dealers from different Contracting States entered into a contract for a sale of a used car, which was later discovered to have been stolen. The court found that CISG applied to the formation of the contract, but did not apply to the effect of the transfer of the property (i.e., whether the good-faith purchaser had acquired good title), and that German law governed the issue of title.

4. Limitation Periods

In transactions involving cultural property, statutes of limitations and limitation periods for bringing actions have been significant points of contention in many recent cases. The CISG does not itself address limitation periods. Prior to the negotiation and approval of the CISG, UNCITRAL drafted and the United Nations approved a separate convention specifically addressing limitations periods for actions involving contracts for the international sale of goods, the United Nations Convention on the Limitation Period in the International Sale of Goods (LPISG),[101] which was amended by a protocol approved in connection with the

---

[99] [Parties not listed], Bundesgerichtshof (Germany, 2006), abstract *available at* http://www.unilex.info/case.cfm?pid=1&do=case&id=1098&step=Abstract.

[100] [Parties not listed], Oberlandesgericht München (Germany, 2008), abstract *available at* http://www.unilex.info/case.cfm?pid=1&do=case&id=1342&step=Abstract.

[101] United Nations Convention on the Limitation Period in the International Sale of Goods, June 14, 1974, and Protocol Amending the Convention on the Limitation Period in the International Sale of Goods, Apr. 11, 1980, S. Treaty Doc. No. 103-10 (1993) (entered into force on Dec. 1, 1994), *available at* http://www.uncitral.org/pdf/english/texts/sales/limit/limit_conv_E_Ebook.pdf.

approval of the CISG. Currently, 29 countries have ratified the LPISG, 22 of which have ratified the amending protocol.[102]

Like the CISG, the LPISG applies to contracts for the sale of goods between contracting parties whose places of business are in different signatory nations. The LPISG sets the limitation period within which parties must assert claims regarding such contracts. The LPISG does not apply to purely United States domestic transactions; sales of goods bought for personal, family, or household use; or sales by auctions.[103] Under UCC § 2-725, the statute of limitations for "an action for breach of any contract for sale" is four years from the date the cause of action accrues.[104] The limitation period under the LPISG is also four years.[105] Under the LPISG, a claim for breach of contract accrues "on the date on which such breach occurs."[106] Likewise, for claims arising from a defect or lack of conformity, accrual is "on the date on which the goods are actually handed over to, or their tender is refused by, the buyer." But, for claims of fraud, accrual is "on the date on which the fraud was or reasonably could have been discovered." Unlike LPISG, the UCC does not have a separate provision regarding the statute of limitations for fraud.

The LPISG provides that the limitation period may be tolled or extended under certain circumstances, including during bankruptcy or liquidation proceedings, by written acknowledgment of the obligation of the debtor to the creditor, or by payment of the interest or partial performance.[107] However, the total limitation period may not exceed 10 years from the date the claim accrued.[108]

While still largely unacknowledged, the CISG is applicable to many current art sale transactions, and as the trade's globalizing trend continues and expands, its applicability—and its utility—will become increasingly apparent. In a trade that historically has been loosely and informally structured, and whose trade practices vary greatly among its participants, the CISG, as an international legal tool, offers parties to art sale

102 *See* United Nations Commission on International Trade Law, *Status, Convention on the Limitation Period in the International Sale of Goods* (New York, 1974), *available at* http://www.uncitral.org/uncitral/en/uncitral_texts/sale_goods/1974Convention_status.html.

103 *See* LPISG, Article 4.

104 UCC § 2-725.

105 LPISG, art. 8.

106 LPISG, art. 10.

107 *See* LPISG, arts. 13 to 21.

108 *See* LPISG, art. 23.

transactions an opportunity to structure their deals in a more tailored fashion than is frequently possible under national sales regimes. Whether they choose to utilize it or exclude it, parties to art sales transactions need to understand when transactions are within the CISG's scope, in order to address its applicability directly.

CHAPTER 9

Secured Transactions

A. Overview

Secured transactions are those in which property is given to serve as collateral (security) for the satisfaction of an obligation. In art transactions, secured transactions increasingly take the form of art-secured loans (as well as more conventional consignments and entrustments). There are two types of art-secured loans: "collector" loans and "gallery" loans. A collector loan is made to a collector or investor (who may be an individual, a group of individuals, or a special-purpose entity) to enable that borrower to purchase new/additional art or to leverage currently owned art. The collector loan's terms will vary chiefly depending on the net worth of the collector. A further variable is the type of lender—a private bank/ private client lender, a boutique art lender,[1] or a commercial asset-based lender.[2] A gallery loan is a business loan to a gallery or other art merchant, which is secured by, among other things, the gallery's inventory.

[1] There are several types of boutique art lenders, and they have different orientations and objectives. Some are traditional lenders while others are more like private equity investors. Each type of lender's terms and relationship to the borrower and the collateral will be quite different.

[2] *See, e.g.*, CLARE MCANDREW, FINE ART AND HIGH FINANCE: EXPERT ADVICE ON THE ECONOMICS OF OWNERSHIP 121 (2010) (adding that "Loans structured within banking institutions house the majority of art financing by value at present . . . however, there are also a number of boutique lenders and auction houses that carry out art financing activities."). Some auction houses may also provide loans to consignors (and sometimes to purchasers) of cultural property objects. Kate Taylor, *Borrowing with Fine Art as Collateral*, NEW YORK SUN (July 22, 2008), *available at* http://www.nysun.com/arts/borrowing-with-fine-art-as-collateral/82333/ (visited February 19, 2014) (noting that "Christie's will typically advance between 30% and 50% of the low estimate of a consignment," and "Sotheby's will typically advance between 50% and 60% of the low estimate, depending on the amount of risk involved.").

1. Underwriting

As with any secured loan, a lender's underwriting for an art-secured loan requires an analysis of the loan risk and an evaluation of the lender's collateral position. In most collector loans, the collector will be able to select which objects will serve as collateral (in consultation with the lender), and the maximum amount of the loan will be a percentage (often up to 50 percent) of the collateral's appraised value. In both collector loans and gallery loans, the art collateral may be augmented by guaranties. Art-secured loans will generally require that the collateral be reappraised annually, and may provide for upward adjustments to the maximum principal loan amount if supported by increasing market values.

2. Perfection

As with any secured loan, perfection of the lender's security interest is a key element, and this is one area in which art-secured loans require great care. For art-secured loans made in the United States and where the art is located in the United States, a lender has the rights and options provided under Article 9 of the UCC. Under Article 9, art constitutes "goods,"[3] particularly in collector loans. For gallery loans, art will instead usually be "inventory."[4]

For a collector loan, a security interest in art may be perfected by either the lender taking possession of the art (usually, having the art moved to a secure and climate-controlled art warehouse, pursuant to a tri-party agreement among the collector, the lender, and the warehouse), or by filing a financing statement describing the art as collateral in the appropriate filing office. For a gallery loan, where the art is inventory, perfection by possession will rarely be feasible, and perfection by filing is the norm. In describing art collateral in a financing statement, the best practice is to itemize each artwork and to promptly revise the financing statement whenever art is added to or removed from the collateral pool. Since financing statements are public documents, such itemization of artworks may raise concerns (security or other disclosure-related concerns) for some collectors. It is possible to address these concerns either

---

[3] "Goods" means all things that are movable at the time the security interest attaches. UCC § 9-102(a)(44).

[4] "Inventory" means, generally, goods held by a person for sale or lease, or consisting of raw materials, work in process, or materials consumed in business. UCC § 9-102(a)(48).

by using a more generic collateral description (which presents risks for the lender, and is not advisable) or by the collector holding the art through a special purpose entity, which is the identified debtor in the financing statement.

Perfecting a security interest in art held outside the United States is more challenging and variable. While under Article 9, the form of the transaction is irrelevant and the economic reality of the transaction is what governs, [5] and while it is also irrelevant whether title to the collateral is in the name of the debtor or the secured party,[6] this is not true in many countries, which retain a more fragmented concept of "security interest." In the United Kingdom, for instance, a collector loan where the art is owned by an individual can only be perfected by the lender taking possession of the art, but if the art is owned by an entity, a lender's security interest in that art may be perfected by filing.[7] A similar approach obtains under the laws of Germany[8] and Austria.[9] Interestingly, France[10] and Belgium[11] have enacted reforms in their secured transactions laws that now permit nonpossessory security interests in goods owned by individuals.[12] The mechanics of art-secured transactions are discussed in greater depth in Section D below.

---

5 UCC §§ 1-201(b) and 9-109(a)(1).

6 UCC § 9-202.

7 *See, e.g.*, N. Orkun Aksell, International Secured Transactions Law: Facilitation of Credit and International Conventions and Instruments 24 (2012); Michael Bridge and Robert Stevens, Cross-border Security and Insolvency 17–24 (2001).

8 *See, e.g.*, Michael Bridge and Robert Stevens, Cross-Border Security and Insolvency 91–94 (2001).

9 *See* Arnold S. Rosenberg, *Where to File Against Non-U.S. Debtors: Applying UCC § 9-307(c) [Rev] to Foreign Filing, Recording, and Registration Systems*, 39 No. 2 UCC L.J. ART 1, *17 (Fall 2006).

10 *See* Muriel Renaudin, *The Modernisation of French Secured Credit Law: Law as a Competitive Tool in Global Markets*, 24(11) I.C.C.L.R. 385–387 (2013).

11 *See* Arnold S. Rosenberg, *Where to File Against Non-U.S. Debtors: Applying UCC § 9-307(c) [Rev] to Foreign Filing, Recording, and Registration Systems*, 39 No. 2 UCC L.J. ART 1, *20 (Fall 2006).

12 As international trade has grown, there have been efforts to harmonize secured transactions laws. These efforts have been strongly influenced by the principles, and to some extent the practices, of Article 9. The United National Commission on International Trade Law ("UNCITRAL"), the European Bank for Reconstruction and Development ("EBRD"), the Organization of American States ("OAS"), and the Organization for the Harmonization of Business Law in Africa ("OHADA") have all promulgated model secured transactions laws drawing upon Article 9's guiding principles. At the national level, Albania, Australia, Bosnia-Herzegovina, Canada, the Federated States of Micronesia, Kosovo, the Marshall Islands, New Guinea, New Zealand, Palau, Papua, the Solomon Islands, Tonga, and Vanuatu have enacted secured transactions laws that strongly resemble or have been influenced by Article 9. However, harmonization efforts are far from uniform or complete. *See* Louis F. Del Duca, Marie T. Reilly, Edwin E. Smith, and Peter Winship, Secured Transactions Under the Uniform Commercial Code and International Commerce 223–224 (2nd ed. 2011); Spiros V. Bazinas, *Law Applicable to Security Rights in Movable Assets Under the UNCITRAL Legislative Guide on Secured Transactions*, 30 No. 6 Banking & Fin. Services Pol'y Rep. 7, 12–13 (June 2011); and Boris Kozolchyk, *Implementation of the OAS Model Law in Latin America: Current Status*, 28 Ariz. J. Int'l & Comp. L. 1, 13 (Spring 2011).

3. Questions of Title

If a borrower lacks clear title to an object, the value of a lender's collateral pool is doubtful. Particularly when that collateral is art that, at least in the past, has changed hands and crossed borders often with minimal documentation, the risk that someone may come forward claiming to be the rightful owner (or the heir of such owner) of a work is substantial. As part of their due diligence on a prospective art-secured loan, lenders should search at least one of the stolen-art databases that are now available online. But a lender should recognize that while an object's appearance on a stolen-art list is strong evidence that there are claims to the object, the fact that an object does not appear on such a list does not mean that there is no risk that a claim will be made. The stolen-art databases are incomplete. Each has its own limitations, and they can only address works that have been reported as having been stolen or are known to have been stolen. Many objects have not been reported. This is particularly true of art lost during periods of great catastrophe and disruption, such as the vast seizures and forced sales of art during the Second World War.

Title to art often requires intricate analysis. The first step is to examine the object (gallery labels and other markings, generally on the back of a work or otherwise out of sight, can provide important information about its history) and to conduct a thorough search of the object's provenance (bills of sale; gallery, dealer, and auction records; records of restoration; wills; and other legal documents offer evidence of the work's past ownership). In the case of antiquities, this may also include when and from where the object was excavated and when it was removed from its country of origin (the country in which it was discovered/excavated in modern times). This is the object's provenience (which is distinct from its provenance). For all types of art, special attention should be given to the provenance of objects that were present in continental Europe during the period 1933–1945, particularly if they changed hands or if there is a gap in provenance records. Many art objects during this period were confiscated by the Nazis, acquired in forced sales, or expropriated or pillaged by conquering troops or others during the war's upheaval.

As described in greater detail in Chapter 8, for stolen property, the difference between common law and civil law can be decisive. In common law countries (including the United States), a thief can never convey good title to a stolen object, even to a good faith purchaser. Therefore, if an object was stolen, it is irrelevant that the current possessor had no knowledge of the theft. The original possessor's legal right is superior (although the right to bring the claim may be limited by statutes of limitations or the doctrine of laches).[13] Civil law countries, by contrast, frequently allow a good-faith purchaser to acquire title to a stolen work after a period of possession.[14]

B. The Uniqueness of Art and Cultural Property in Secured Transactions

Knowledge cannot immunize a party from having its position and expectations unsettled or unwound, but a lack of knowledge and lack of appropriate inquiry is almost certainly an invitation to disappointment and frustration. Just as factual due diligence is necessary to know and understand the nature, authenticity, and value of art, legal due diligence into the often fluid state of national and international legal and regulatory regimes that apply to security interests in such objects is no less crucial. The rules for taking, perfecting, and enforcing security interests in cultural property can be just as movable as cultural property itself.

It is important for parties to art-secured transactions to recognize that their collateral presents specific risks. Because a security interest is limited by and dependent upon the debtor's rights in the collateral, parties must understand the circumstances under which a debtor's right in art collateral may be vulnerable or impaired, including (1) possible claims by prior owners of the work if the chain of title is unclear or doubtful, (2) possible charitable or donative restrictions or limitations, and (3) any applicable export restrictions and national preemptive rights. If the chain of title to a proposed collateral work is unclear, a secured party may be

---

13 *See* Solomon R. Guggenheim Found. v. Lubell, 569 N.E.2d 426, 431 (N.Y. 1991); Bakalar v. Vavra, 819 F. Supp. 2d 293, 304 (S.D.N.Y. 2011), *aff'd*, 500 Fed.Appx. 6 (2nd Cir. Oct. 11, 2012) (holding that laches barred the claims of heirs of a rightful owner of a drawing although the heirs had such notice before they knew of the drawing's specific whereabouts).

14 *See* Deborah A. DeMott, *Artful Good Faith: An Essay on Law, Custom, and Intermediaries in Art Markets*, 62 DUKE L. J. 607, 632 (2012) (*citing* Alan Schwartz & Robert E. Scott, *Rethinking the Laws of Good Faith Purchase,* 111 COLUM. L. REV. 1332, 1337 (2011)).

well advised to consider obtaining title insurance as a condition of the transaction. Where there is a possibility that a collateral work may be subject to uncertain export license procedures, and even moreso if there exists a possibility that it would be subject to acquisition in an exercise of national preemptive rights, a secured party may wish to address such possibilities contractually, including by requiring the delivery of replacement collateral of equal value, the issuance of a standby letter of credit, or a pledge of any judgment award.

When entering into an art-secured loan—whether as debtor or as lender—the parties need to be clear what the parties' intentions and goals are at the outset of the transaction. A formal term sheet should be prepared, detailing the terms of the proposed loan, negotiated and agreed upon by both parties. A debtor particularly must be cognizant of the risk that the art collateral will be forfeited to the secured party if the debtor defaults on its obligations. Clarity in what actions will constitute defaults is essential. Similarly, a secured party must understand whether the debtor has understood and agreed to the terms as the secured party understands them, particularly if the loan transaction is structured to give the secured party agency, liquidation, or auction rights with respect to all or part of the collateral (and what events or circumstances will trigger those rights).

In a consignment or entrustment arrangement, the consignor or entrustor (or a secured lender to either) must understand and recognize that secured parties and consignors in art-secured transactions may be subject to differing levels of protection of their interests. While the UCC consignment and entrustment rules may apply generally, artist consignment statutes may override those rules in particular circumstances and may both provide specific protections for artist consignors with respect to consignments of their own works (and the artist's estate, heirs, and representatives). However, an artist consigning work other than the artist's own created work does not enjoy that heightened level of protection, and so is subject to the same requirements as other owners, collectors, and dealers. Conversely, consignees accepting artists' created work on consignment need to understand the heightened requirements—segregating sales proceeds from operating accounts, providing accountings of sales, and timely paying over consignment proceeds. Indeed, criminal penalties may attach to a consignee's failure to understand the distinction and comply with the rules.

When a secured party[15] takes (and a debtor[16] grants) a security interest[17] in one or more movable works of art whether as the transaction's primary purpose or as a tag-along element of a broader collateral[18] package, the nature of the collateral means that the secured transaction[19] presents higher risks for the parties than if ordinary commodities were at stake. The due diligence required of both the debtor and the secured party in evaluating and preparing for an art-secured transaction will entail highly specific and otherwise uncommon considerations.

1. Secured Party Considerations

A secured party's typical concerns include whether the proposed collateral is authentic, whether it will support the collateral value needed for the transaction,[20] whether the debtor has rights in the collateral, whether any party other than the debtor has rights in the collateral, whether there are restrictions limiting or prohibiting security interests in the collateral or use of the collateral, whether the proposed language of the security

---

15 A "secured party" generally is a person in whose favor a security interest is created or provided for under a security agreement, whether or not any obligation to be secured is outstanding; or a consignor. UCC § 9-102(a)(73).

16 "Debtor" refers to the person or entity that has the security or other interest in the personal property in which the security interest is created. "Debtor" also includes a consignee. UCC § 9-102(a)(28).

17 A "security interest" is "an interest in personal property or fixtures which secures payment or performance of an obligation," and includes "any interest of a consignor." UCC § 1-201(b)(35).

18 "Collateral" means property that is subject to a security interest. Collateral includes proceeds to which a security interest attaches, accounts, chattel paper, payment intangibles, and promissory notes that have been sold, and goods that are the subject of a consignment. UCC § 9-102(a)(12).

19 A "secured transaction" is a "business arrangement by which a buyer or borrower gives collateral to the seller or lender to guarantee payment of an obligation." BLACK'S LAW DICTIONARY (9th ed. 2009).

20 Art-collateralized loans typically are loans to individuals (for the purchase of art or to leverage existing owned art) or to galleries or other art merchants. In making its underwriting decisions, a lender in an art-collateralized loan evaluates the risk of nonpayment, and that risk will determine the amount of the loan, the interest rate that will apply, and various other terms of the loan. The purpose of a lender taking collateral to secure a loan is to reduce the lender's risk and provide an asset that the lender can look to as a source of repayment if the borrower defaults. Part of the lender's risk assessment when underwriting an art-secured loan includes determining what ratio it will accept between the value of the collateral and the amount of the loan. The lender will obtain an appraisal of the proposed collateral, and the amount of the loan will be a fraction of that appraised value. CLARE MCANDREW, FINE ART AND HIGH FINANCE: EXPERT ADVICE ON THE ECONOMICS OF OWNERSHIP 121 (2010) (adding that "Loans structured within banking institutions house the majority of art financing by value at present . . . however, there are also a number of boutique lenders and auction houses that carry out art financing activities."). Some auction houses may also provide loans to consignors (and sometimes to purchasers) of art. Kate Taylor, *Borrowing with Fine Art as Collateral*, NEW YORK SUN (July 22, 2008), *available at* http://www.nysun.com/arts/borrowing-with-fine-art-as-collateral/82333/ (visited February 19, 2014) (noting that "Christie's will typically advance between 30% and 50% of the low estimate of a consignment," and "Sotheby's will typically advance between 50% and 60% of the low estimate, depending on the amount of risk involved.").

agreement[21] sufficiently describes the collateral and the nature of the transaction, what steps will be necessary to "perfect"[22] its security interest, and what provisions are necessary to enable the secured party to realize on the collateral in the event of a default. But in an art-secured transaction, these considerations have different weights and risks. This is because art objects are nonfungible and are often unique. Social and cultural significance may be attributed to certain art objects (or even to the class of "art" or "cultural property" more generally), which, while contributing to monetary values, may be distinct and distinguishable from those monetary values. Art is also frequently subject to national or international legal and regulatory regimes. Finally, the nature of the art trade itself contributes to the challenges in art-secured transactions, since the trade has traditionally relied more on relationships and reputations than on negotiated legal documentation. Because of the increased availability of art-secured loans and broader domestic and cross-border regulation, this is changing.

2. Debtor Considerations

For a debtor, the conceptual need is similar—clarity and certainty in the nature, purpose, and terms of the transaction. If the transaction is a loan, the principal and interest amounts are key considerations, but perhaps more important are the default and collateral provisions. Will the debtor be able to retain possession of the collateral or will the secured party take possession of the collateral for the term of the loan? What defaults will give the secured party the right to foreclose on the collateral? Because the debtor faces the possibility of losing the collateral if the transaction fails, it is essential that the debtor clearly understand this risk at the outset. Dispossession and loss of art are also risks that must be understood and managed in entrustment and consignment transactions.

---

21 "Security agreement" refers to "an agreement that creates or provides for a security interest." UCC § 9-102(a)(73).

22 "Perfection" of a security interest is the process whereby a secured party makes its security interest in the debtor's collateral enforceable against third parties (for instance, the debtor's other creditors). WILLIAM H. LAWRENCE, WILLIAM H. HENNING & R. WILSON FREYERMUTH, UNDERSTANDING SECURED TRANSACTIONS 115–116 (4th ed. 2007). Perfection and its relation to the enforceability and priority of a security interest are discussed in greater detail later in this paper.

3. Considerations Arising from the Art Trade

While the statement may be repetitive, it is nevertheless important to remember that the trade in art is global.[23] When an art-secured transaction has a cross-border character, it may be impacted by the secured transactions laws of the country in which the collateral, debtor, or secured party is located; the export or import laws or regulations of the countries involved (including any laws providing national museums or agencies with a preemptive right to acquire certain designated art objects); the property laws (including law providing for national ownership of certain categories of art), not only of the state in which the debtor or the secured party is located, but potentially of any state from which the collateral has been removed or into which it has been imported; and national laws or international agreements relating to the collateral or any of its constituent parts.

C. Forms of Art-Secured Transactions

Most art-secured transactions will fall into one of two broad categories: (1) consignments (and entrustments) or (2) secured loans. However, since, in the art trade, roles and relationships frequently overlap, any given situation may have aspects of each category.

1. Consignments

In an art consignment, a consignor may be an artist consigning the artist's own work; an artist's heirs or estate consigning work; a collector consigning work; a dealer consigning work to another dealer; or even a dealer who is a

[23] TEFAF ART MARKET REPORT 2014, 26 (2014) (stating "Apart from its rapidly increasing size, the art market has undergone an intense period of globalization since the turn of the century. The distribution of sales has changed fundamentally over the last ten years, with significant changes in the size and distribution of world wealth, leading to the emergence of new markets and buyers. New collectors from Asia, Latin America, the Middle East and elsewhere have increased global buying in the traditional art hubs of London and New York, while also helping to support some thriving local markets. China has been the most dominant of all these newer markets, both as an important buyer of art globally, and as one of the largest markets in the world for domestic sales."). *But see* Melanie Gerlis, *Is the Global Art Market a Myth? The Academic Olav Venthuis Argues That the Business of Art Isn't As International As It Seems,* THE ART NEWSPAPER (April 25, 2014), *available at* http://www.theartnewspaper.com/articles/Is-the-global-art-market-a-myth/32400 (stating Velthuis "has found that the majority of businesses are organised 'extremely locally,' despite aspiring to the borderless ideals of international artists who command global demand—which he said has been 'vastly exaggerated.'").

consignee with respect to a work sub-consigning the work to another dealer. In each such instance, the consignor retains a security interest in the work and in the proceeds from the sale or exchange of the work. However, a consignor must either have a statutory priority in the work or comply with applicable rules for perfecting the consignment. A consignor's unperfected security interest risks being lost or subordinated to the consignee's creditors.

We typically believe that if we entrust our property to someone else to sell it, the property remains ours until it is sold. However, this may not always be true. If the party into whose hands property has been entrusted files for bankruptcy, the entrusted property may be deemed to be property of the debtor's bankruptcy estate, the bankruptcy trustee may have the right to sell the property, and the debtor's secured creditors and judgment creditors may even have a higher priority to receive distribution of proceeds from the property's sale.

This type of transaction is a "consignment," which the UCC defines as "a transaction . . . in which a person delivers goods to a merchant for the purpose of sale." UCC § 9-102(a)(20). To qualify as a consignment, the consigned artwork must have a value of not less than $1,000 and must not be "consumer goods." UCC § 9-102(a)(20)(B). "Consumer goods" are those which are "used or bought for use primarily for personal, family, or household purposes." UCC § 9-102(a)(23). Although many artworks will be considered consumer goods, particularly those consigned by art collectors, artworks that are held for investment purposes or which are consigned by art dealers, corporate entities (i.e., corporate collections), or museums are not consumer goods. Also, the party to whom the artwork is consigned (the "consignee") must deal in artwork of that kind, must not be an auctioneer, and must not be generally known to sell artworks owned by others. UCC § 9-102(a)(20)(A).

If the transaction qualifies as a consignment, the UCC provides important protections for the owner (the "consignor"). The consignor's right in the consigned artwork is deemed to be a purchase money security interest, which gives the consignor a superpriority right to it, superior to the rights of other creditors. UCC § 9-103(d). However, this protection does not arise automatically. The consignor must perfect its consignment interest by (i) filing a UCC-1 financing statement describing the artwork before delivering the artwork to the gallery, and (ii) sending a notice to the art gallery's secured creditors describing the artwork and stating the consignor's intention to retain a consignment interest. UCC § 9-324(b). Since a debtor's bankruptcy estate may have no legal or equitable interest in an artwork that is subject to a perfected consignment interest, the artwork will likely be abandoned and turned over to the consignor. However, an unperfected consignment interest is subordinate to the interests of the art gallery–debtor's bankruptcy trustee, secured creditors, and judgment creditors. The consignor will have only an unsecured claim.

However, if the consignor is the artist of the consigned artworks, or the artist's heirs, estate, or representative, the UCC requirements may not apply. A number of states have enacted artist consignment statutes designed to protect artists in their dealings with art merchants. Thirty-four states (including California, Illinois, New York, and Michigan) have enacted such artist consignment statutes, which override the UCC consignment rules and give artists consigning their works to an art merchant an automatically perfected purchase money security interest in the consigned work. Such statutes generally provide that consigned works are held in trust by the art merchant for the consigning artist, as are the proceeds from the sale of consigned works.

2. Secured Loans

With an art-secured loan, a lender ("Lender A") may have made a loan to an artist or collector and received a security interest in a specific work or a group of works. If the lender has perfected its security interest, that security interest will attach to the work and its proceeds when the work is in the hands of the artist or collector; when it is sold or transferred to a third party (provided that the artist or collector is not known to be a dealer in such goods); when it is in the hands of a storage facility or other third party bailee (provided the third party is aware of the lender's security interest and is not known to be a dealer in such goods); or when it is consigned to a dealer (but the dealer, if known to be a dealer in such goods, can convey the work to a buyer in the ordinary course). Another lender ("Lender B") may have made a loan to a dealer, an art warehouse or storage facility, or other party in whose possession the work that serves as collateral for Lender A's loan. Lender B may have received, as security for its loan, a security interest in all of the art merchant's or art warehouse's or storage facility's assets, including its inventory. The same work of art may serve as collateral for multiple secured parties, securing the very different obligations of separate debtors.

If a secured party has provided acquisition financing for its debtor to purchase the work, that secured party may have a purchase money security interest in the work and its proceeds, which would have priority over any other security interests in the work. Moreover, ownership of the work may not reside in a single person or entity. It may be shared, fractionally, by agreement. Ownership of a work (or group of works) may be securitized and sold off as interests in an art fund. In some contexts, art and cultural property is an asset class in which investments are made.

With the dramatic increase in art auction prices, particularly for post-war and contemporary art, lenders are being asked to make more and larger loans secured by art and other cultural property.[24] However, as an asset class,[25] art and cultural property presents issues that lenders do not commonly encounter and which require both particular knowledge to identify and specific forms of due diligence to address.

D. Fundamentals of Secured Transactions

The role of secured transactions, generally, is to facilitate the extension of credit and to lower barriers to extending and obtaining credit. Without security, a party making a loan or providing goods or services has only the debtor's naked promise to repay the loan or perform the obligation. If the debtor fails to perform, the creditor will need to obtain a judgment, identify enough of the debtor's assets to satisfy the debt, and execute the judgment against those assets, all under applicable local laws and procedures. The creditor will have to expend funds and effort in this process, and the time

---

[24] The European Fine Art Foundation ("TEFAF") has estimated that global art sales (public auctions, private gallery sales, and dealer sales) in 2013 were roughly £47.4 billion (ca. $63.9 billion), an increase of 8% over the previous year, and an increase of 150% from a decade before. TEFAF ART MARKET REPORT 2014, 24 (2014). In 2014 and 2015, TEFAF estimated art sales at US$68.2 billion and US$63.8 billion, respectively. TEFAF ART MARKET REPORT 2016, 15 (2016). The "current size of the art lending market is estimated at £6 billion ($9.6 billion) a year." Kathryn Tully, *How Easy Is It to Get an Art-Backed Loan?* FORBES (Oct. 27, 2014), *available at* http://www.forbes.com/sites/kathryntully/2014/10/27/how-easy-is-it-to-get-an-art-backed-loan/. Deloitte Luxembourg and ArtTactic report that 36% of private banks now offer art-secured lending services. Deloitte Luxembourg and ArtTactic, ART & FINANCE REPORT 2014, 16 (2014).

[25] Analysts disagree as to whether art should be regarded as a distinct asset class for purposes of financial planning and investment. *See, e.g.*, Kathryn Tully, *Could Fine Art and Collectibles Become a New Asset Class?* FORBES (Nov. 26, 2012), *available at* http://www.forbes.com/sites/kathryntully/2012/11/26/could-fine-art-and-collectibles-become-a-new-asset-class/; James B. Stewart, *With Art, Investing in Genius*, THE NEW YORK TIMES (Nov. 28, 2014), *available at* http://www.nytimes.com/2014/11/29/business/with-art-investing-in-genius.html?_r=0; *but see* Arthur Korteweg, Roman Kräussl & Patrick Verwijmeren, *Research: Is Art a Good Investment?* INSIGHTS BY STANFORD BUSINESS (Oct. 21, 2013), *available at* http://www.gsb.stanford.edu/insights/research-art-good-investment.

period from default to judgment and enforcement may be many months, if not longer.[26] Taking a security interest in certain of the debtor's assets facilitates extensions of credit (and sales of goods or services on credit) because it provides the creditor with not only an identifiable source of repayment, but also, importantly, an expedited, frequently nonjudicial procedure for execution on the collateral.[27] Taking security can also protect a secured creditor's interest if the debtor becomes insolvent.[28]

In the United States, secured transactions are governed by Article 9 ("Article 9") of the UCC.[29] Article 9 marked a departure from a prior, fragmented concept of a security interest.[30] Previous United States practice held that specific types of security interests applied to specific categories of collateral, and each separate type of security interest was subject to its own distinct rules, unrelated to the rules governing other types of security interests.[31] In Article 9, the form of the transaction or the label that parties place on it is irrelevant. Article 9 instead looks to the economic reality of the transaction.[32] It is also irrelevant whether title to the collateral is in the name of the debtor or the secured party.[33] A more fragmentary concept of security interest remains the norm in many countries, including many that have traditionally been significant market countries

---

26 William H. Lawrence, William H. Henning & R. Wilson Freyermuth, Understanding Secured Transactions 3 (4th ed. 2007) ("Absent security, a borrower's mere promise to repay money, albeit legally enforceable, might not suffice to induce a prospective lender to proceed with a transaction—and even if the lender agreed to proceed, the interest rate would inevitably reflect the level of risk. Similarly, a seller might be reluctant to give a prospective buyer current possession of property based solely on the buyer's promise to make installment payments.").

27 *Id.* (If the debtor defaults, "the creditor can proceed directly against the security without having first to reduce its claim to judgment. Secured creditors thus can reduce significantly the costs and delays associated with enforcement of their rights.").

28 Ian Fletcher, *"L'Enfer, C'Est Les Autres": Evolving Approaches to the Treatment of Security Rights in Cross-Border Insolvency*, 46 Tex. Int'l L.J. 489, 490 (Summer 2011).

29 The UCC is a model law drafted as a joint project of the National Conference of Commissioners on Uniform State Laws and the American Law Institute, and is designed to harmonize the commercial laws of the United States. It was first published in 1952 and has been amended numerous times. The UCC has been enacted by all 50 U.S. states with some (mostly minor) variations. William H. Lawrence, William H. Henning & R. Wilson Freyermuth, Understanding Secured Transactions 4–5 (4th ed. 2007).

30 The UCC moved away from prior United States practice (which is still the practice in a majority of foreign states), which maintained "a fragmentary conception of security interest, which is variable for different types of collateral, and where perfection of the security interest was accomplished with reference to the *lex situs*—where the collateral was physically located—to a more unified security interest that is taken in much the same manner over most forms of collateral and which is perfected by notice filing in the location where the debtor is organized." Arnold S. Rosenberg, *Where to File Against Non-U.S. Debtors: Applying UCC § 9-307(c) [Rev] to Foreign Filing, Recording, and Registration Systems*, 39 No. 2 UCC L.J. Art 1, *4 (Fall 2006).

31 *Id.*

32 UCC §§ 1-201(b) and 9-109(a)(1).

33 UCC § 9-202.

in the cultural property trade. This includes England,[34] Germany,[35] Austria,[36] Belgium,[37] and France.[38]

---

34 English law has no general concept of a security interest, but distinguishes between forms of possessory and nonpossessory security interests. *See* N. ORKUN AKSELL, INTERNATIONAL SECURED TRANSACTIONS LAW: FACILITATION OF CREDIT AND INTERNATIONAL CONVENTIONS AND INSTRUMENTS 24 (2012). English law has three principal types of security interest: a pledge, a mortgage, and a charge. *See* MICHAEL BRIDGE & ROBERT STEVENS, CROSS-BORDER SECURITY AND INSOLVENCY 17 (2001). A pledge is a possessory security interest in, generally, movable tangible personal property. *Id.* at 18. English law recognizes two forms of mortgage over personal property—a legal mortgage, in which the legal title to the property is transferred to the secured party and then retransferred back to the debtor once the debt has been paid; and an equitable mortgage, in which the secured party receives only the beneficial title to the property, with the legal title remaining in the debtor. *Id.* at 20. What distinguishes a mortgage from an outright transfer of title is that the mortgage secures a liability and the debtor retains residual rights in the property. In the case of a legal mortgage, the debtor has the right, on payment of the secured liability, to have the property retransferred into its name. This is not merely a personal right against the creditor; it is a proprietary right, frequently referred to as an "equity of redemption." While the mortgage subsists, there are therefore two proprietary interests in the asset, the creditor having a legal interest in the asset to secure the debt and the debtor having a residual equitable interest. In the case of an equitable mortgage, the creditor has the beneficial interest in the asset and the debtor retains bare legal title and the residual equitable interest. Possession of the asset almost invariably remains with the debtor. *Id.* at 20–21. Finally, English law recognizes two forms of charge—the fixed charge (over specifically identified collateral) and the floating charge (similar to Article 9's "all assets" security interest). With a charge, the secured party obtains an equitable proprietary interest in the collateral, but does not obtain possession of the collateral or receive title to the collateral. Once the debt has been paid, the secured party's rights under the charge are automatically released. *Id.* at 23. With a fixed charge, the debtor is prohibited from transferring the collateral without the secured party's prior written consent. In contrast, with a floating charge, a debtor may sell or transfer collateral in the ordinary course of its business, with the floating charge attaching to proceeds and to new inventory or assets as they are acquired. *Id.* at 24.

35 German secured transactions law recognizes a variety of forms of security interests, including (i) Charges on Property (*Grundpfrandrechte*), (ii) the Pledge over Goods and Rights (*Pfandrecht an Sachen unter Rechten*), (iii) Transfer of Title for Security Purposes (*Sicherungsubereignung*), and (iv) a Security Assignment of Receivables (Sicherungsabtretung). See MICHAEL BRIDGE & ROBERT STEVENS, CROSS-BORDER SECURITY AND INSOLVENCY 91–92 (2001). Charges on property and Pledges over Goods and Rights are deemed to forms of Accessory Security, meaning that the security interest is dependent upon the existence of the secured debt; when the debt has been satisfied, the security interest automatically ceases to exist. *Id.* By contrast, the Transfer of Title for Security Purposes and the Security Assignment of Receivables are regarded as forms of Abstract Security, in which the debt and the security interest are independent elements. *Id.* Under German law, a Pledge over Goods is a possessory security interest, requiring the secured party to take and retain possession of the collateral until the debt has been satisfied. Once the debt is satisfied, the Pledge ceases to exist and the secured party must return the collateral to the debtor. German law does not provide for the registration of security interests. *Id.* at 94.

36 Austrian law with respect to secured transactions generally follows the forms of German secured transactions law. For tangible property, Austria does not have a nonpossessory form of security interest. Rather, the primary form of security interest in Austria is the *Pfandrecht*, which is a possessory pledge that requires that the secured party take possession of the collateral. *See* Arnold S. Rosenberg, *Where to File Against Non-U.S. Debtors: Applying UCC § 9-307(c) [Rev] to Foreign Filing, Recording, and Registration Systems*, 39 No. 2 UCC L.J. ART 1, *17 (Fall 2006). Austria similarly has no registration system for security interests in movable tangible personal property. *Id.*

37 Belgian law recognizes possessory pledges of movable tangible property. Such pledges are known as gages, and they require dispossession of the debtor. A possessory pledge of goods by a pledgor who does not own them is effective in favor of a pledgee who received the goods in good faith. Belgian law presumes that possession of movable property is a title for ownership. Therefore, the original owner who has been dispossessed of property cannot make a proprietary claim against the possessor in good faith unless the original owner can show that the goods were stolen, and even then the claim must be brought within three years after dispossession. *Id.* at 20.

38 French secured transactions law has been significantly changed in the last decade, simplifying many of the forms of security interests, with more frequent use of nonpossessory forms. *See*

Secured transactions exist in most countries and cultures,[39] although the forms of secured transactions vary greatly. As international trade has grown, there have been efforts to harmonize secured transactions laws. These efforts have been strongly influenced by the principles, and to some extent the practices, of Article 9.[40] The United Nations Commission on International Trade Law (UNCITRAL),[41] the European Bank for Reconstruction and Development (EBRD),[42] the Organization of American States (OAS),[43] and the Organization for the Harmonization of Business

---

Muriel Renaudin, *The Modernisation of French Secured Credit Law: Law as a Competitive Tool in Global Markets*, 24(11) I.C.C.L.R. 385 (2013). The most common French form of security interest is the *gage*, which is generally used for security interests in tangible, movable personal property, was formerly a possessory security interest, but may now be either possessory or nonpossessory. When possessory, the *gage* is perfected by the secured party dispossessing the debtor of the collateral. Whereas, when it is nonpossessory, the *gage* is perfected by registering the gage with the Commercial Tribunal. Under French law, a valid possessory *gage* provides the secured party with a *droit de retention*, which authorizes the secured party to retain the collateral until the debt is satisfied. If the debt matures and is not repaid, the secured party may sell the collateral and receive priority in payment from the proceeds. A secured party with a nonpossessory *gage* is considered to have a fictitious *droit de retention*, and is entitled to receive priority in payment upon sale of the collateral. *Id.* at 387. For intangibles, French law employs the *nantissement*. *Id.* However, French secured transactions law retains certain special regimes with respect to specific types of assets. Special regimes exist for the charge created in (i) films, (ii) software, and (iii) business components (client lists, trademarks, and other intellectual property assets associated with a business)(*nantissement de fonds de commerce*). *Id.* at 388.

39 Mehnaz Safavian, Heywood Fleisig & Jevgenijis Steinbuks, *Unlocking Dead Capital: How Reforming Collateral Laws Improves Access to Finance*, 307 WORLD BANK PUB. POL'Y J., Mar. 2006, *available at* http://rru.worldbank.org/documents/publicpolicyjournal/307Safavian_Fleisig_Steinbuks.pdf (stating that "Collateralized loans are the most common lending contract in the formal financial sector. In low- and middle-income countries 70–80 percent of loans require some form of collateral. The same holds true in high-income countries: in the United States, for example, 70 percent of loans are secured by collateral. This makes sense from a lender's perspective: loan contracts can be more easily enforced when secured by property.").

40 Article 9's departure from prior secured transactions practice advances a set of basic principles: (1) a single set of rules should govern all security interests, regardless of the form of the transaction; (2) security interests should be available to all types of creditors, and not be restricted to only certain types (such as licensed banks); (3) rules should recognize and provide for nonpossessory security interests; (4) collateral should not be required to specifically itemized, but should be able to be validly described by general descriptive category (i.e., "all goods," "all equipment"); (5) parties should be able to grant and take security interests in property acquired by the Debtor in the future; (6) perfection and priority rules should be based upon notice filing; (7) purchase money security interests should receive "super-priority status"; (8) a security interest should attach automatically to the proceeds of Collateral when it is sold, and the security interest should have the same priority as in the original Collateral; (9) the secured transactions system should include clear rules for enforcing security interests; and (10) there should be clear conflict of law rules to determine which jurisdiction governs security interests. *See* LOUIS F. DEL DUCA, MARIE T. REILLY, EDWIN E. SMITH, & PETER WINSHIP, SECURED TRANSACTIONS UNDER THE UNIFORM COMMERCIAL CODE AND INTERNATIONAL COMMERCE 223–224 (2nd ed. 2011).

41 *Id.* at 225; Spiros V. Bazinas, *Law Applicable to Security Rights in Movable Assets Under the UNCITRAL Legislative Guide on Secured Transactions*, 30 No. 6 BANKING & FIN. SERVICES POL'Y REP. 7, 12–13 (June 2011).

42 *Id.* at 226.

43 Boris Kozolchyk, *Implementation of the OAS Model Law in Latin America: Current Status*, 28 ARIZ. J. INT'L & COMP. L. 1, 13 (Spring 2011).

Law in Africa (OHADA)[44] have all promulgated model secured transactions laws drawing upon Article 9's guiding principles. At the national level, Albania, Australia, Bosnia-Herzegovina, Canada, the Federated States of Micronesia, Kosovo, the Marshall Islands, New Guinea, New Zealand, Palau, Papua, the Solomon Islands, Tonga, and Vanuatu have enacted secured transactions laws that strongly resemble or have been influenced by Article 9.[45] However, harmonization efforts are far from uniform or complete. Taking, perfecting, and enforcing security interests in cross-border transactions continues to be both challenging and imperfect.

1. Taking a Security Interest in Art

In creating and enforcing security interests in art, the critical concepts are "attachment," "perfection," and "priority." Each of these elements will be influenced by the nature of the collateral itself—what category of object it is. A security interest can be created in essentially any interest that a debtor has in property, and Article 9 will apply to such security interests in personal property and fixtures and which secure the payment or other performance of an obligation.[46] For purposes of security interests, personal property can be either tangible or intangible. Tangible personal property includes goods,[47] inventory,[48] and equipment.[49] Intangible personal property includes accounts,[50] software,[51] and general intangibles.[52] Security interests in art typically relate to tangible personal property, in

---

[44] Bazinas, *Law Applicable to Security Rights in Movable Assets Under the UNCITRAL Legislative Guide on Secured Transactions*, 30 No. 6 BANKING & FIN. SERVICES POL'Y REP. 7, 8 (June 2011).

[45] *Id.*; LOUIS F. DEL DUCA, MARIE T. REILLY, EDWIN E. SMITH & PETER WINSHIP, SECURED TRANSACTIONS UNDER THE UNIFORM COMMERCIAL CODE AND INTERNATIONAL COMMERCE 223–224 (2nd ed. 2011).

[46] UCC § 9-109(a)(1).

[47] "Goods" means all things that are movable at the time the security interest attaches. UCC § 9-102(a)(44).

[48] "Inventory" means, generally, goods held by a person for sale or lease, or consisting of raw materials, work in process, or materials consumed in business. UCC § 9-102(a)(48).

[49] "Equipment" means goods other than inventory, farm products, or consumer goods. UCC § 9-102(a)(33).

[50] "Account" means a right to payment for goods or services rendered. UCC § 9-102(a)(2).

[51] "Software" means a computer program and includes related supporting information. UCC § 9-102(a)(76). Depending on the manner in which it is embodied, software may be either goods or an intangible. Software embedded in goods is considered as part of the goods if the software is customarily viewed as a part of the goods or if, by becoming the owner of the goods, a person acquires a right to use the software with the goods.

[52] "General Intangibles" is a residual category for intangible property, and includes any personal property other than goods, accounts, chattel paper, documents, instruments, investment property, letter-of-credit rights, commercial tort claims, deposit accounts, and money. UCC § 9-102(a)(42).

the categories of "goods" and (particularly for art dealers or other art merchants) "inventory."

2. Attachment of Security Interests in Art

The first step in creating a security interest in art is for the security interest to "attach" to the object. "Attachment" is the moment at which a security interest becomes enforceable against the debtor,[53] and it has several elements: (1) value must have been given; (2) the debtor must have rights in the collateral (or the power to transfer rights); and (3) the debtor must have authenticated (i.e., executed) a security agreement[54] that sets out a description of the collateral.[55] The most important and challenging of these elements for secured transactions involving art is the debtor's rights in and ability to transfer rights to art.

A debtor can only grant a security interest in whatever ownership or other right the debtor has. Similarly, a secured party cannot obtain greater rights in the collateral than the debtor itself holds.[56] Article 9 codifies the common law principle of *nemo dat quod non habet* (discussed in Chapter 6)—under which no one can give what one does not have—which means that a thief cannot convey good title, even when stolen property passes through the hands of an intermediary to a good faith purchaser.[57] For art and cultural property, which has often passed through many hands over long periods of time, frequently with little or no surviving documentation, knowing that a party has "good title" to an object can be difficult indeed. However, to create a security interest, a debtor's mere power to transfer the object may be enough to satisfy the requirement that the debtor have "rights in the collateral."[58] What this means is that a consignee (say, an art dealer) may have the power to transfer rights in consigned goods (like a painting) even against the express wishes of the consignor.[59] This happens all too often, in a variety of circumstances. A debtor may have rights in collateral either by owning the collateral prior to the secured transaction or by purchasing the collateral as part of a secured transaction. When a debtor already owns property, it should

[53] UCC § 9-203(a).
[54] Under UCC § 9-102(a)(74), "security agreement" means an agreement that creates or provides for a security interest.
[55] UCC § 9-203(b).
[56] UCC § 9-203(b); see Official Comment 6 to § 9-203.
[57] See the more detailed discussion in Chapter 8.
[58] UCC § 9-203(b)(2).
[59] UCC § 9-319.

be clear that the debtor has rights in it and can use it as collateral. In other cases, a debtor will buy items (materials, inventory, and so on) on credit and will want to use those same items as collateral. In that case, the debtor will sign a conditional sales contract (which is also considered a security agreement), which under the UCC will give the debtor the necessary rights in the purchased items to use them as collateral.[60]

With art collateral, a debtor's rights may be contingent upon (1) claims of original owners for return of the object, if it has been stolen; (2) charitable or donor restrictions or limitations; or (3) export restrictions and preemptive rights in favor of national retention.[61] A consideration of each of these is instructive.

As discussed in greater detail in Chapter 6, in the United States, the United Kingdom, and other common law jurisdictions, a thief cannot convey good title to a stolen object. As a result of this, a debtor who may have acquired a work as a good faith purchaser and without any knowledge or suspicion that it was stolen, perhaps even many years after the theft, may find that its rights in the work are subject to the rights of the original owner.[62] Such situations arise with some frequency, particularly in recent years, with art that was confiscated by the Nazis or acquired in forced-sale circumstances. When the chain of title for a work includes theft, the original owner will generally have a superior right to the work than a subsequent possessor.[63] However, the original owner's ability to bring a claim to re-

---

[60] AKSELL, INTERNATIONAL SECURED TRANSACTIONS LAW at 25 ("[I]n order to create a security interest, ownership of the property that serves as collateral is crucial and must be acquired either before the creation or the attachment of the security-interest.").

[61] Additionally, a debtor's rights in art collateral may be affected by (i) international agreements, national ownership laws, and restrictions on the importation of certain classes of art; and (ii) national restrictions on the ownership or transfer of certain classes of materials. The potential impact of these issues on art-secured transactions, while important, are beyond the scope of this paper.

[62] Not all purchases of stolen works without knowledge of the theft are made in good faith. In fact, whether the purchase was actually made in good faith, or whether the purchaser did have or should have had reason to question the sale, is dependent upon the circumstances. *See* Kunstsammlungen zu Weimar v. Elicofon (KZW), 678 F.2d 1150 (2nd Cir. 1982) (current possessor purchased two works by Albrecht Durer from a former American serviceman in 1946, but did not realize their worth or that they had been stolen during the war until 1966). In *Elicofon*, the court applied New York law (whether the current possessor purchased the works) rather than German law (where the theft had occurred). As a result, the current possessor could not obtain good title to the works. Had German law applied, the doctrine of *Ersitzung* (discussed below) would have dictated a different result. For another example of an unsuccessful effort to persuade a court to apply the law of a civil-law jurisdiction (Switzerland) to insulate a purchaser of stolen art, *see* Autocephalous Greek-Orthodox Church of Cyprus v. Goldberg & Feldman Fine Arts, Inc., 717 F. Supp. 1374, 1394 (S.D. Ind. 1989), *aff'd*, 917 F.2d 278 (7th Cir. 1990), which found under an Indiana state-law analysis that any connection of stolen art to Switzerland was not strong enough to justify applying Swiss law.

[63] *See* Solomon R. Guggenheim Found. v. Lubell, 569 N.E.2d 426, 431 (N.Y. 1991).

cover the work may be limited by applicable statutes of limitations[64] or by the doctrine of laches.[65]

In an international context, however, the result may well be different, since some jurisdictions allow a good-faith purchaser to acquire title to a stolen work.[66] Under German law (the doctrine of *Ersitzung*), a possessor of a stolen work may obtain good title after ten years of good-faith possession.[67] Under Swiss law, a good-faith purchaser may acquire good title to stolen property after holding the property for five years.[68] Under French law, even a party who acquires possession of a work in bad faith will have good title to the work after the passage of thirty years.[69] Both French and Swiss law require that an original owner recovering a stolen work from a good-faith purchaser compensate that purchaser for the purchase price of the work.[70]

These differences in national legal rules not only require diligence on the part of parties to secured transactions, but they also, at times, have enabled parties to leverage those differences in ways that support a subsequent purchaser's rights and impair or defeat the claims of original owners.[71]

3. Perfection and Priority of Security Interests in Art

Perfection of security interests in art and the relative priority of security interests in art are both critically important for secured parties, and perfection and priority work hand-in hand.

---

64 *Id.*

65 *See* Bakalar v. Vavra, 819 F. Supp. 2d 293, 304 (S.D.N.Y. 2011), *aff'd*, 500 Fed.Appx. 6 (2nd Cir. Oct. 11, 2012) (holding that laches barred the claims of heirs of a rightful owner of a drawing although the heirs had such notice before they knew of the drawing's specific whereabouts.

66 *See* Deborah A. DeMott, *Artful Good Faith: An Essay on Law, Custom, and Intermediaries in Art Markets*, 62 Duke L. J. 607, 632 (2012) (citing Alan Schwartz & Robert E. Scott, *Rethinking the Laws of Good Faith Purchase*, 111 Colum. L. Rev. 1332, 1337 (2011).

67 *Id.* at 636 (citing to BüRgerliches Gesetzbuch [BGB] [Civil Code], 2011, Bundesgesetzblatt [BGBI] §§ 937–945 [Ger.]).

68 *Id.* (citing to Bakalar v. Vavra, 619 F.3d 136, 140 [2nd Cir. 2010], and noting that Swiss "law also presumes that the purchaser acted in good faith and imposes on a party seeking to reclaim stolen property the burden of establishing the purchaser's lack of good faith.").

69 *Id.* (citing to Warin v. Wildenstein & Co., 846 N.Y.S.2d 153, 155 [App. Div. 2007] [discussing Article 2262 of the French Civil Code], aff'g 824 N.Y.S.2d 759 [Sup. Ct. 2006]).

70 *Id.* (citing to Code Civil [C. Civ.] arts. 2277 [Fr.]; Schweizerisches Zivilgesetzbuch [ZGB] [Civil Code] Dec. 10, 1907, SR 210, arts. 641, 934 [Switz.]).

71 *See Id.* at 633, note 140 (quoting A.J.G. Tijhuis, *The Trafficking Problem: A Criminological Perspective*, in Crime in the Art and Antiquities World: Illegal Trafficking in Cultural Property, 92–94 (2011) ("[An art dealer] smuggled the objects from Russia to the Netherlands and was able to funnel the illicit art into the legitimate market . . . . The differences between the Netherlands and Russia further enabled the successful traffic: the absence of specific legislation in the Netherlands, as well as the lack of effective international registries of stolen and smuggled art, combined with the lack of efficiency in communications between law enforcement agencies across international borders.").

a. Perfection of Security Interests in Art

To be enforceable against other parties (whether the debtor's creditors or a bankruptcy trustee), a security interest must be "perfected."[72] While there are multiple ways in which security interests in various categories of collateral can be perfected, for art collateral (which typically is movable, tangible personal property in the form of goods or inventory), two methods of perfection have the greatest relevance: (1) perfecting a security interest by filing a financing statement;[73] and (2) perfecting a security interest by taking possession of the collateral.[74]

i. Perfection by Filing

Security interests in goods and inventory (and most other types of collateral) can be perfected by filing a financing statement. Filing a financing statement (which is filed with a public office, such as the Secretary of State) puts the public on notice of the secured party's security interest in the collateral. In the United States, this is the most common method of perfecting a security interest. A significant benefit of perfection by filing is that it allows the debtor to retain possession of the collateral. In art-secured transactions, this is often a primary concern for the borrower wishing to monetize art while retaining the use and enjoyment of it. For art-secured transactions, perfection by filing is critical when the debtor is an art dealer obtaining financing secured by art that the debtor maintains as inventory. For a transaction where the debtor is an individual, retaining possession of the collateral may be important (particularly when the financing is to enable the debtor to acquire one or more works). However, when the secured financing is leveraging a debtor's existing holdings (whether to acquire additional works or for other purposes), a debtor may not need to retain possession of all or part of the collateral (and the lender may require that the lender take possession of certain pieces of the collateral).

ii. Perfection by Possession

Alternatively, a security interest may be perfected by possession—which means that the secured party (or a third party for the secured party's

---

[72] UCC § 9-308(a).

[73] UCC §§ 9-102(a)(39) (defining "financing statement") and 9-310(a). A form of UCC-1 financing statement is *available at* http://www.dos.ny.gov/forms/corporations/UCC1.pdf.

[74] UCC §§ 9-310(a), 9-312(a) and 9-313.

benefit) takes possession of the collateral.[75] In many jurisdictions outside of the United States, perfection by possession of the collateral (sometimes described as dispossession of the debtor) is the norm. Even within the United States, perfection by possession is common for some types of art-secured transactions. For a secured party, significantly, a security interest perfected by possession has priority over security interests perfected by any other means, including filing, even if the filing was prior in time to the perfection by possession. This is critical for security interests in art, where movable objects with a high market value may be at stake. While a security interest in art can be perfected by filing,[76] it presents a greater risk for the secured party, who may not want the debtor to remain in possession where the collateral can be damaged or removed without the secured party's knowledge.

An alternative to either the debtor or the secured party maintaining possession of art is for the collateral to be stored (generally at the debtor's expense) in an art warehouse or other specialized storage facility. While a security interest in goods held by a third party may be perfected without filing a financing statement,[77] when art collateral is held in a storage facility, a secured party is well-advised to file a financing statement. Prior to the collateral being delivered to any such third party or storage facility, the secured party and the third party should enter into a written agreement in which the third party acknowledges that it is aware of the secured party's security interest in the collateral, is holding the collateral for the secured party's benefit, and that the third party agrees to provide exclusive control to the secured party to the portion of the facility where the collateral is housed. The secured party should also retain all receipts issued by the third party.

When the debtor is a gallery or dealer engaged in the business of selling goods of the same type as the collateral, the secured party should insist on taking possession of the collateral, since under the UCC a buyer in the ordinary course of business can acquire goods free from the security interest granted by the debtor. This is true even when the buyer is aware of the security interest.[78]

There may also be circumstances in which a debtor may choose to grant a security interest in collateral that has been delivered for sale to a

[75] UCC § 9-313(1).
[76] UCC § 9-310(2)(e).
[77] UCC §§ 9-312(3) and 9-312(4).
[78] UCC § 9-320(1).

gallery or dealer or that is on exhibit at a museum. In such circumstances, prior to delivering the collateral to the third party, the secured party should enter into a written agreement with the third party that provides (1) the secured party with access to the collateral; (2) that the third party acknowledges the secured party's security interest in the collateral and agrees to hold the collateral for the secured party's benefit; and (3) the third party agrees that the collateral will not be moved without the secured party's prior written consent. When collateral is being held for sale by a dealer or gallery, the secured party should obtain an irrevocable direction from the debtor to the dealer or gallery instructing the dealer or gallery to remit any sale proceeds immediately to the secured party. Consideration should also be given in those circumstances to requiring the dealer or gallery to segregate the collateral from its own inventory and to designate the collateral as being held on consignment and subject to the secured party's security interest.

If a secured party wishes to take a security interest in collateral by possession but the collateral is actually in the possession of a third-party Article 9 requires the third party (the bailee) acknowledge in a written agreement that it is holding the collateral for the secured party.[79] For this method of perfection to be effective, the third party bailee cannot be the debtor or a lessee of the debtor.[80] A lender that perfects a security interest by taking possession of collateral does not lose or relinquish that perfected status simply by virtue of delivering the collateral to a potential purchaser where the delivery is made exclusively for inspection and return.[81]

b. Priority

i. General Unsecured Creditors

A secured party's perfected security interest in collateral has priority over the claims of the debtor's general unsecured creditors.[82] Importantly, even an unperfected security interest will have priority over the debtor's unsecured creditors, at least with respect to the secured party's specific

---

[79] UCC § 9-313(c)(1). For an excellent general summary of issues of priority (and secured transactions generally), see Stephen L. Sepinuk, Practice Under Article 9 of the Uniform Commercial Code (2nd ed. 2008).

[80] UCC § 9-313(c).

[81] UCC § 9-313(h).

[82] UCC §§ 9-201(a) and 9-317(a).

collateral.[83] It should be noted, however, that this may not always hold true in a debtor's bankruptcy case.

ii. Lien Creditors

A party becomes a "lien creditor" when that party obtains a judgment against the debtor and the judgment gives rise to a lien against the debtor's property.[84] A trustee in a debtor's bankruptcy case is deemed to be a lien creditor (what is termed in the Bankruptcy Code a "hypothetical lien creditor"). A secured party with a perfected security interest has priority over a lien creditor, provided that the secured party's security interest is perfected at or before the time the judgment lien attaches.[85] However, a lien creditor will have priority over a security interest unless, before the time that the judgment lien arises, the secured party has filed a financing statement, the debtor has executed a security agreement, or the secured party has taken possession of (or has control over) the collateral.[86]

iii. Purchase-Money Security Interests

A "purchase-money security interest" (a "PMSI"), that is, a security interest in collateral that is either acquired from the secured party or is acquired with funds provided by the secured party,[87] is accorded a higher priority than a general security interest, irrespective of whether another secured party has perfected a security interest in that specific collateral. A holder of a perfected PMSI achieves super priority, i.e., its security interest in the purchase-money collateral will rank ahead of any security interest which would otherwise be entitled to priority under the first-to-file-or-perfect rule. If two secured parties, one being a supplier and the other being a lender, each claim PMSI priority over the same collateral, the supplier's PMSI prevails over that of the lender.[88] The situation for a supplier of collateral who has not been paid differs depending on whether the supplier has delivered the goods (in which case, the supplier does not receive a PMSI, and another perfected secured party may have priority) or still retains the goods (in which case,

---

83 UCC § 9-201(a).

84 UCC § 9-102(a)(52). *See also* 11 U.S.C. § 544 (concerning a bankruptcy trustee's hypothetical lien creditor status).

85 UCC § 9-317(a)(2)(A).

86 UCC § 9-317(a)(2)(B). *See also* Sepinuk, Practice Under Article 9 of the Uniform Commercial Code, 46 (2nd ed. 2008).

87 UCC § 9-103.

88 UCC § 9-324(g)(1).

the supplier receives a PMSI and will have priority over other perfected security interests.[89]

iv. Conflicting Security Interests

In cases where there is more than one secured party claiming a security interest in the same collateral, the first secured party to file a financing statement or perfect its security interest has priority.[90] A perfected security interest in collateral will prevail over an unperfected security interest in the collateral.[91] As between two unperfected security interests, the first security interest to attach to the collateral will prevail.[92]

4. Conflicts in Art-Secured Transactions

Art-secured transactions are vulnerable to the same sources of conflict and misunderstanding that may arise in any commercial secured transaction—differing expectations among the parties with respect to the purpose or scope of the relationship, as well as conflicts between competing or overlapping interests. Art transactions, though, frequently have a different tone, at least at the outset. They frequently occur in a more informal, less business-like context, with the parties relying to a greater degree than many other kinds of transactions on reputations and personal relationships. That tone, however, does not always remain so pleasant, as the following examples show.

a. Expectations of the Parties and Debtor Risk of Forfeiture

i. *M.L. Private Finance v. Minor*

In a common art lending transaction, an art collector borrows funds from a lender, whether to acquire additional artworks or for other purposes, and the loan is collateralized by the art the collector owns. When the loan is paid off, the collateral is released. However, loans are not always paid off. Halsey Minor, a well-known collector, borrowed $20 million from M.L. Private Finance, LLC, a specialty lender.[93] The loan was secured by "a continuing first-priority lien and security interest" in certain of Mr. Minor's

---

[89] UCC § 9-110.
[90] UCC § 9-322(a)(1).
[91] UCC § 9-322(a)(2).
[92] UCC § 9-322(a)(3).
[93] M.L. Private Finance LLC v. Minor, No. 08-Civ. 11187(SHS), 2011 WL 1900613 (S.D.N.Y. May 19, 2011).

owned artwork. The loan agreement provided that the collateral would serve as security for the loan until Mr. Minor's obligations under the loan agreement and other loan documents had "indefeasibly been paid and performed in full."[94]

When the borrower subsequently defaulted under the loan, the lender sought and obtained a monetary judgment in the amount of $21,502,907.60, plus payment of costs and fees of collection. The court appointed a receiver, whom the court directed to sell the collateral art and pay over the proceeds to the lender to satisfy the judgment. After enough of the art had been sold to satisfy the judgment, and such payment to the lender had been made, Mr. Minor petitioned the court for release of the lender's liens on the remaining art. The lender objected, arguing that although the judgment had been repaid, the borrower's "obligations" under the loan agreement continued in force and effect, since there remained contingent obligations that had not been satisfied, such as costs of an appeal (which had not yet been filed).[95] The court held that the lender's liens should be released, observing that the lender's interpretation of the term "obligations" in the loan agreement "admits of no limiting principle."[96]

ii. *Resolution Trust Corp. v. Johnson*

Sometimes, though, the question may be whether the art or cultural property collateral was intended to serve as collateral at all. Unlike Mr. Minor's deliberate pledge of his art, in some circumstances art or cultural property may become collateral securing an obligation by virtue of the nature and breadth of the security interest granted. In *Resolution Trust Corp. v. Johnson (In re Johnson)*,[97] a commercial real estate developer borrowed $12 million to construct and develop a hotel. As security, the borrower gave the lender a mortgage lien on the real property on which the hotel would be built, together with the hotel itself, and also gave the lender a security interest in respect to fixtures and personal property, which included the hotel's furnishings.

When the developer defaulted, the lender foreclosed on the hotel. The court held that paintings that hung in the hotel prior to the lender's foreclosure were collateral securing the borrower's obligations, stating that

---

94 *Id.* at *1.

95 *Id.* at *5.

96 *Id.*

97 Resolution Trust Corp. v. Johnson (*In re* Johnson), 139 B.R. 208 (Bankr. D. Minn. 1992).

the "artwork clearly was 'furnishings,' under the common understanding of that term, and within the meaning of the mortgage instrument. In any event, it was 'personal property;' the parties' specific intent to give a broad sweep to that general category is prominently evidenced by the provision in Granting Clause B which makes its lengthy enumeration of categories nonexclusive as to the types of assets to which the security interest would attach."[98]

iii. *Citibank NA v. Ercole Ltd., Guido Carieri*

A borrower's conception of his relationship with his art lender, especially when the lender also provides art advisory services, can be at odds with the lender's understanding of the relationship. In 1990, Citibank was in the practice of lending to its clients to purchase works of art, and to provide its Art Advisory Services (AAS) to advise the clients on what to buy and sell. Guido Carieri, an Italian businessman and art collector based in Palermo, answered a Citibank ad in an Italian newspaper offering the services of AAS.[99] Citibank expressed its willingness to lend Mr. Carieri funds to expand his art collection, on the basis, first, that part of his existing collection would be used as collateral and placed in what was known as 'the collateral pool' and, second, that the amount of the loan would be limited to 50 percent of the value of the works included in the collateral pool. Citibank appraised that portion of Mr. Carieri's collection that would be included in the collateral pool in October 1991 at over US$3 million.

The Carieris formed Ercole Ltd., a Jersey company, to serve as borrower and pledgor for the loan. Citibank loaned Ercole up to $2 million with a maturity date of November 19, 1996. Ercole executed a chattel mortgage in favor of Citibank with respect to the works held in the collateral pool. The value of the works in the collateral pool were required to maintain a value of not less than 200 percent of the advances under the loan. Mr. and Mrs. Carieri guaranteed Ercole's repayment obligations under the loan. The principal amount of the loan was subsequently increased to $3.5 million, with additional works added to the collateral pool. Mr. and Mrs. Carieri drew down the full amount of the loan. In June 1996, Citibank valued the works in the collateral pool at $7 million. Although

[98] *Id.* at 213.

[99] Citibank NA v. Ercole Ltd., Guido Carieri, Vivia Carieri, No. HQ 9901546, 2001 WL 1751176 (High Court of Justice, Queen's Bench Div. 1 March 2001).

Mr. and Mrs. Carieri made period principal and interest payments on the loan during the term, they did not repay the outstanding balance of the loan on the maturity date. In February 1998, Citibank began selling the works in the collateral pool; however, the amount realized from such sales was only $1.3 million, significantly lower than the outstanding balance of the loan, and very much lower than Citibank's prior valuations of the collateral. In July 1999, Citibank brought suit against Ercole and the Carieri's, seeking repayment of the deficiency amount.

The defendants filed counterclaims, asserting claims (i) that Carieri purchased artworks based upon negligent valuation advice given by Citibank's AAS staff, and (ii) Citibank disposed of the collateral artwork at less than their true value. The Queen's Bench Master gave judgment for Citibank. On appeal, the High Court of Justice affirmed the Master's judgment.

b. The Power to Convey Title to Art

Secured transactions, consignments, and entrustments, while legally distinct relationships, nevertheless share certain characteristics, including the risk that one will involuntarily be dispossessed of property. Consignment and entrustment figure prominently in the art trade, with artists, owners, and dealers consigning and entrusting works to third parties with the expectation (or naked hope) that such party will serve as a dutiful and responsible agent. That expectation or hope is not always warranted.

i. Co-ownership and Fractional Interests

Title to the collateral is only one form of interest that a debtor may have that is sufficient to form a basis for a security interest.[100] A security interest may be created in a debtor's interest in property—(i) currently owned property; (ii) property to be acquired in connection with the transaction in which the security interest is granted; (iii) fractional interests in property (including securitizations); (iv) property that is to be transferred to the debtor by the secured party (retention of title); (v) property that is entrusted to the debtor; and (vi) property that is consigned to the

100 *Id.* at p. 23 (stating that "While a debtor does not need title to goods to have rights in the goods to convey a security interest, title is one means of establishing such rights in the collateral."); *see also* Hong Kong and Shanghai Banking Corp., Ltd. v. HFH USA Corporation, 805 F.Supp. 133, 142 (W.D.N.Y. 1992) ("title to goods is indicative of certain rights that the debtor has to dispose of the goods.").

debtor.[101] Artworks and many other forms of cultural property, like other forms of property interests, frequently serve as collateral in a variety of secured transactions.[102]

It is not uncommon for multiple parties to have fractional ownership interests in an artwork. Fractional ownership, though, frequently has an underlying investment purpose, particularly when the fractional owners are either art merchants or art investors. However, the informal, gentlemen's agreement approach that is common in the art trade means that key elements of the parties' relationship go written, and perhaps undiscussed.

In 1987, the Love Gallery sold a painting to Altman Fine Arts, a New York dealer, and Andre Lopoukhine, a Boston dealer.[103] Each of the two co-purchasers contributed half of the purchase price. Each, in return, received an undivided 50 percent interest in the painting. In January 1989, Altman sold its interest to Morgold, Inc. (although Lopoukhine disputed whether Morgold purchased Altman's interest). In July of that year, Lopoukhine consigned the painting to the Vose Gallery. Morgold learned of the consignment and objected. Eventually, Morgold and Lopoukhine entered into an agreement, setting out their respective rights in the painting, and they agreed to withdraw the painting from consignment with Vose.

Despite the parties' disagreement about the Vose consignment, Lopoukhine retained possession of the painting and later sold the painting, without Morgold's knowledge or consent, to Grossman, a nondealer businessman and collector, in exchange for forgiveness of a debt that Lopoukhine owed to Grossman. Grossman later sold the painting to

---

[101] Spiros v. Bazinas, *Law Applicable to Security Rights in Movable Assets Under the UNCITRAL Legislative Guide on Secured Transactions*, 30 No. 6 BANKING & FIN. SERVICES POL'Y REP. 7, 12–13 (June 2011) ("Under the law recommended in the Guide, the term 'security right' means 'a property right in a movable asset that is created by agreement and secures payment or other performance of an obligation, regardless of whether the parties have denominated it as a security right.'. . . The term includes both acquisition security rights and non-acquisition security rights (if a State follows a unitary approach to acquisition financing, categorizing all rights securing the performance of an obligation, including retention-of-title and financial lease rights, as security rights.").

[102] Jennifer Anglim Kreder and Benjamin Bauer, *Protecting Rights and Unleashing Capital in Art*, 2011 UTAH L. REV. 881, 886 (2011) (stating that "Art is frequently collateralized."); Thomas J. Hall and Chet A. Kronenberg, *AB Recur Finans v. Andersson - Artwork Is Just Another "Good" Under the UCC*, 13-WTR ENT. & SPORTS LAW. 15, at *1 (Winter 1996) (stating that "artwork is just another 'good' under the law, as defined in the Uniform Commercial Code. . . . Accordingly, the UCC governs the sale of artwork and many of the legal issues that arise therefrom, including passage of title, defects in title, stolen goods, risk of loss, enforceability of security interests, priority of security interests, warranties, payment, delivery, transit, sale of goods by dealers, sale of goods at auction, and many others.").

[103] Morgold, Inc. v. Keeler, 891 F.Supp. 1361 (N.D. Cal. 1995).

Adler, who was a dealer in paintings, who in turn sold it to Keeler. Learning of the sales, Morgold filed a replevin action against Keeler, seeking return of the painting. The court denied Morgold's request, holding that Lopoukhine, as co-owner of the painting, had the power to pass title to the painting to Grossman. Morgold had no right to the painting, but only a claim against Lopoukhine.[104]

ii. Consignment and Entrustment

In a consignment, the consignor retains title to goods delivered to the consignee. Title passes to the consignee upon the consignee's use or sale of the goods. The consignor usually issues an invoice after the consignee's reported sale or use of the goods, and the consignee can return used or unused goods to the consignor. Article 9 treats all consignments as purchase-money security interests and requires consignors to comply with Article 9 rules applicable to purchase-money secured parties in order to obtain priority.[105]

In a consignment arrangement involving cultural property, the consignor (or the secured party) may be (i) an artist consigning his or her own work to a dealer, (ii) an artist's heirs or representatives consigning an artist's work to a dealer, (iii) an owner who is not the artist of the work (or the artist's heirs or representatives) consigning works to a dealer, (iv) another dealer or art merchant consigning work to the dealer, or (v) the dealer's secured lender. When a consignment transaction involves multiple levels of art merchants consigning works to other dealers, there may be a waterfall of security interests at play, as the secured lenders of each of those art merchants may have security interests in their debtor's interests in the work. The consignee may be a dealer taking works on consignment from an artist or artist's estate, a collector (whether an individual or an entity), or another dealer.

Nonartist owners of consigned works must file a financing statement to perfect their consignment interest. An unperfected consignment interest is nevertheless enforceable against the consignee (although it may not be enforceable against in the consignee's bankruptcy case). However, a third party with a perfected security interest in the work, including secured creditors of the consignee, may have priority over the unperfected

---

[104] *Id.* at 1367.

[105] UCC §§ 1-201(b) (defining a consignment as a security interest) and 9-103(d).

consignor's consignment interest in both the consigned work and any proceeds from its sale.

A number of states have enacted artist consignment statutes designed to protect artists in their dealings with art merchants. Thirty-one states (including California, Illinois, New York, and Michigan) have enacted such artist consignment statutes,[106] which override the UCC consignment rules and give artists consigning their works to an art merchant an automatically perfected purchase money security interest in the consigned work. Such statutes generally provide that consigned works are held in trust by the art merchant for the consigning artist, as are the proceeds from the sale of consigned works. However, most artist consignment statutes have not until recently included express enforcement mechanisms or criminal penalties for violations of an art merchant's duties.

(A) *Lindholm v. Brant*

Under UCC § 2-403(2), "[a]ny entrusting of possession in goods to a merchant who deals in goods of that kind gives him power to transfer all rights of the entruster to a buyer in the ordinary course of business."[107] A buyer in the ordinary course of business "buys goods in good faith, without knowledge that the sale violates the rights of another person in the good, and in the ordinary course from a person . . . in the business of selling goods of that kind."[108]

When a buyer, acting in good faith, acquires an object from an art dealer (or other merchant in goods of the kind), the buyer's right to possess the object is that of the person who entrusted it to the dealer, notwithstanding any breach of duties owed by the dealer to the entruster. That the dealer cheated the owner or sold the object or sold the object in disregard of the owner's instructions would breach the dealer's duties as the owner's agent, but would not defeat a good-faith purchaser's right to possession.

In *Lindholm v. Brant*,[109] Lindholm entrusted a number of paintings to a Swedish dealer, Anders Malmberg.[110] Lindholm's arrangement with Malmberg was for him to sell certain of the paintings. However, Warhol's

---

[106] *See* TAD CRAWFORD & SUSAN MELLON, THE ARTIST-GALLERY PARTNERSHIP: A PRACTICAL GUIDE TO CONSIGNING ART (Rev. ed. 2008); *see also* Mark Marcone, *The UCC and Consignment: Making the Code Safe for Artists and Other "Little Fellow,"* 12 CARDOZO ARTS & ENT. L.J. 579, 580–581 (1994).

[107] UCC § 2-403(2).

[108] UCC § 1-201(b)(9).

[109] Lindholm v. Brant, 925 A.2d 2048 (Conn. 2007).

[110] *Id.* at 1050.

"Red Elvis" was not among the paintings to be sold. Rather, Malmberg was solely to arrange for "Red Elvis" to be included in a traveling exhibition organized by the Guggenheim Museum. After seeing the painting in the exhibition, Brant contacted Malmberg and expressed an interest in acquiring the Warhol. Malmberg's representation to Brant was that Malmberg owned the painting, having purchased it from Lindholm.[111] Malmberg sold the painting to Brant for a purchase price of $2.9 million, $900,000 of which was paid as a deposit, and the remainder to be paid upon the delivery of the painting in Denmark.[112]

Believing the painting was still on loan for museum exhibition, Lindholm attempted to sell the painting for $4.6 million,[113] only to discover that it had been conveyed to another purchaser, Brant. Lindholm brought suit against Brant, alleging conversion of the painting, and seeking its return.[114] In considering whether Brant was a good-faith purchaser, the court looked to whether he had observed "usual or customary practices and observed reasonable commercial standards of fair dealing in the art industry."[115]

The court found that the informality of the transaction showed that Brant had no reason to expect any frailty in Malmberg's right to convey title to the painting, with the sale being "completed on a handshake and an exchange of an invoice."[116] Where the trade practice was generally informal, the court reasoned, a buyer would not be expected to require confirmation of a dealer's authority to transfer title to a work. Rather, a buyer would typically rely on the dealer's statements and reputation.[117] Trade practice also typically protected the anonymity of sellers, where desired, and this fact did not, for the court, raise questions as to the propriety of Brant's failure to question Malmberg's claims.[118]

(B) Salander O'Reilly Galleries, LLC

Recent years have seen the collapse of several major art galleries, some from financial conflicts with lenders or other parties, others from shady business practices and outright fraud. Perhaps the most spectacular

---

111 *Id.* at 1051–52.

112 *Id.* at 1052.

113 *Id.* at 1053–54.

114 *Id.* at 1054 & n.8.

115 *Id.* at 1056.

116 *Id.* at 1056–57 (quoting Lindholm v. Brant, 2005 WL 2364884, at *13 (Conn. Super. Ct. Aug. 29, 2005), aff'd, 925 A.2d 1048 (Conn. 2007)) (internal quotation mark omitted).

117 *Id.*

118 *Id.* at 1058.

was the collapse of Salander O'Reilly Galleries, LLC (SOG). In 2007, facing numerous lawsuits alleging the SOG and its founder and principal Larry Salander ("Salander") had sold works, double-pledged works, and failed to pay consignors proceeds from sales, SOG filed a petition for relief under chapter 11 of the bankruptcy code. As of the petition date, SOG had in its possession more than 4,000 works, some owned in whole or in part by SOG, others consigned by artists, artists' estates, collectors, or other dealers.[119] The SOG case presents, in microcosm, almost every possible way in which a secured transaction, consignment, or entrustment of cultural property can go awry, and it spurred strengthening amendments to New York's artist consignment statute.

(1) Earl Davis

Stuart Davis was an American modernist painter, known for jazz-influenced, proto pop art paintings in the 1940s and 1950s. After Davis's death, his son, Earl Davis, consigned more than 90 of his father's works to SOG for sale.[120] As of the petition date, many of the works were unaccounted for, and Earl Davis had not received distribution of proceeds from any sold works (nor had Salander or SOG given Davis an accounting). With SOG's commingling of sales proceeds, failure to provide consignors with accountings, and failure to pay over consignment proceeds, the Davis consignment, together with the DeNiro consignment described below, highlighted the limitations inherent in New York's artist consignment statute as it then stood.

(2) Robert DeNiro, Jr.

Robert DeNiro, Sr., was a prominent American 20th-century painter, who blended abstraction and representation. After his father's death, the artist's son, the actor Robert DeNiro, Jr., inherited his father's remaining paintings. DeNiro consigned 12 of these paintings to SOG. However, SOG instead delivered the paintings to an Italian gallery, Benucci S.r.l., along with other works, in satisfaction of an existing SOG debt to that gallery. DeNiro was ultimately able to retrieve 6 of the consigned paintings from the SOG bankruptcy estate, but only after he paid $14,000 for them.[121]

---

119 James Panero, *An Old Master in Ruins*, New York Magazine (Mar. 24, 2008), *available at* http://nymag.com/news/features/45324/.

120 Eileen Kinsella, *Untangling the Salander Mess*, ArtNews (July 1, 2010), *available at* http://www.artnews.com/2010/07/01/untangling-the-salander-mess/.

121 *Id.*

(3) John McEnroe

SOG and Salander not only took work on consignment, but also acquired works, including fractional and co-ownership arrangements. The gallery's business practices with co-owners was as duplicitous as its dealings with consignors. In 2004, Salander and tennis player John McEnroe agreed to co-purchase two paintings by Arshile Gorky. The purchase price was $4 million. McEnroe advanced the entire amount of the purchase price. Without McEnroe's knowledge or consent, Salander arranged to deliver one of the paintings, *Pirate II*, to a third party in exchange for a different work.[122] McEnroe retained possession of *Pirate I*. But establishing his rights with respect to *Pirate II* required legal action. Ultimately, in 2013, a court awarded McEnroe co-ownership of the painting. The other co-owner is the third-party foundation to which Salander had delivered the work.[123]

(4) Kraken Investments Ltd. v. Jacobs

One of the most dramatic and best-publicized losses suffered in the SOG case was that of Kraken Investments, Ltd. In *Kraken Investments Ltd. v. Jacobs (In re Salander O'Reilly Galleries, LLC)*,[124] Kraken, as the consignor of the Botticelli painting, nearly found its interest in the painting trumped by the security interest of the gallery's working capital lender. What is frequently lost in discussions of Kraken's situation, though, is that the fundamental issue—Kraken's failure to file a financing statement to perfect its consignment interest—is not a unique or surprising legal rule, nor an unusual result dictated by the complexities of bankruptcy law. Rather, the requirement that a consignor file a financing statement to publicize its consignment interest and perfect it against competing rights of third parties has been required by consignment law for many years. It only comes as a surprise within the informal, relationship-based cultural property trade.

In May 2006, Kraken and SOG entered into a consignment agreement, pursuant to which Kraken consigned a painting by Sandro Botticelli (*Madonna and Child* [1485]) to SOG for a term of one year after

---

122 *Id.*

123 Julia Marsh, *Judge Rules McEnroe the Rightful Owner to $2M Artworks*, New York Post (Aug. 27, 2013), *available at* http://nypost.com/2013/08/27/judge-rules-mcenroe-the-rightful-owner-to-2m-artworks/.

124 Kraken Investments Ltd. v. Jacobs (*In re* Salander O'Reilly Galleries, LLC), 475 B.R. 9 (S.D.N.Y. 2012).

SOG's receipt of the painting. Under the consignment agreement, SOG would feature the painting in an exhibition and would use its best efforts to sell the painting for a price of at least $9.5 million, of which Kraken would receive not less than $8.5 million. Kraken delivered the painting to SOG on May 11, 2006. Kraken did not file a UCC-1 financing statement with respect to its consignment interest in the painting. The consignment period terminated on May 11, 2007. SOG requested an extension of the consignment period, and Kraken granted that request. Subsequently, Kraken requested the return of the painting, but SOG failed to return it.[125]

At the same time, in April 2006, First Republic Bank made a revolving line of credit available to SOG, in a maximum principal amount of $26 million. The loan was secured by a continuing security interest in "all personal and fixture property of every kind and nature including all goods (including inventory, equipment and any accessions thereto)" of SOG.[126] The bank perfected its security interest by filing a UCC-1 financing statement with the appropriate filing office.

SOG's bankruptcy case intervened, and Kraken filed a motion in the bankruptcy court for relief from the automatic stay and authorization to arbitrate its dispute with SOG's bankruptcy trustee (the "Trustee") under Jersey law, as the consignment agreement required. The bankruptcy court denied Kraken's motion, noting that neither the Trustee nor the lender was a party to the consignment agreement, and so they were not bound by its choice of law provision.[127] On appeal, the U.S. District Court for the Southern District of New York upheld the bankruptcy court's decision, concluding that:

> The Court well understands why Kraken is perturbed, even outraged, by the idea that SOG's creditors may enjoy proceeds from the sale of a valuable painting concededly owned by Kraken. The law of the state in which Kraken consigned the painting, however, allows for such an outcome where the consignor does not protect itself by filing a financing statement giving notice of the consignment to the consignee's creditors. Whether that result will obtain here remains to be seen. But while Kraken may have thought it was protecting itself vis-à-vis SOG by the

---

[125] *Id.* at *16.

[126] *Id.* at 15.

[127] *See In re* Salander O'Reilly Galleries, 453 B.R. 106, 132 (Bankr. S.D.N.Y. 2011).

> arbitration and choice-of-law clauses in the Consignment Agreement, it did not protect itself via those clauses when it came to SOG's creditors.[128]

The district court's decision was not a final disposition of the fate of the painting, but Kraken's chances of getting the painting back looked dark.

Both the Trustee and Kraken filed motions for summary judgment, the trustee arguing that the "transactions between Kraken and the Debtor fall squarely within the definition of a consignment," while Kraken argued that the lender did not obtain a lien on the Botticelli and Kraken's consignment agreement with SOG had terminated prior to SOG's bankruptcy filing.[129] In support of its contention that the consignment had terminated prior to the bankruptcy filing, Kraken asserted that not only had the consignment agreement terminated by its terms, but that Kraken's agents had removed the Botticelli from SOG's premises, and then returned it merely as a loan for purposes of an exhibition. The Trustee disputed that the painting had been removed from SOG's premises. The bankruptcy court denied both motions to dismiss, reasoning that "[a]t the summary judgment stage, the Court cannot resolve this disputed issue of fact."[130]

Bankruptcy Code § 544 provides that a bankruptcy trustee has the rights of a lien creditor and is empowered to avoid unperfected liens.[131] This allowed the Trustee to have priority over Kraken's unperfected consignment interest in the Botticelli. The Trustee additionally stood in the shoes of SOG's secured lender, whose loan to SOG was secured by a security interest in substantially all of SOG's assets. The lender had assigned its lien to the Trustee.

Kraken filed both an art claim (pursuant to the bankruptcy court's art claims protocol), asserting its ownership claim to the Botticelli, and a proof of claim, asserting its $9.5 million claim for consigned artwork. In January 2013, the Trustee filed an objection to both claims. Both Kraken and the Trustee filed motions seeking summary judgment, but the

---

128 *See* Kraken Investments Ltd. v. Jacobs (*In re* Salander O'Reilly Galleries, LLC), 475 B.R. 9, 32 (S.D.N.Y. 2012).

129 Jacobs v. Kraken Investments Ltd. (*In re* Salander-O'Reilly Galleries, LLC), Case No. 13-09004 (Bankr. S.D.N.Y. Mar. 21, 2014).

130 *Id.* at *20.

131 11 U.S.C. § 544.

bankruptcy court denied both motions.[132] Two elements of the parties' cross-motions and the bankruptcy court's decision denying took on significance in the ultimate resolution of this dispute. For his part, the Trustee sought summary judgment solely based upon his role as assignee of the secured lender's rights, and expressly disclaimed that he was seeking to assert any lien creditor rights under Bankruptcy Code § 544(a).[133] The Trustee asserted, and the bankruptcy court agreed, that the lender's loan agreement gave it a security interest in all of SOG's property, including consigned property.[134] Kraken, for its part, argued instead that the loan agreement excluded consigned works from the lender's pool of collateral. On appeal to the district court, this became the decisive issue.

On November 25, 2014, more than seven years after the SOG bankruptcy case began, and nearly eight-and-a-half years after Kraken consigned the Botticelli to SOG, the district court reversed the bankruptcy court's denial of Kraken's motion for summary judgment, stating that:

> [t]he Court disagrees with the bankruptcy court's interpretation of the Loan Agreement. Although the Court agrees the Loan Agreement can mean only one thing, what it plainly means is that the Bank was given a broad security interest in inventory owned by the Debtor. As such, the Loan Agreement unambiguously does not grant the Bank a lien on consigned artwork.[135]

The district court remanded the matter to the bankruptcy court with instructions to enter summary judgment in favor of Kraken. In the end, what for a time appeared to be one of the most dramatic and best-publi-

---

[132] *See* Jacobs v. Kraken investments Ltd. (*In re* Salander O'Reilly Galleries, LLC), 506 B.R. 600 (Bankr. S.D.N.Y. 2014).

[133] *See id.* at 612. Kraken had argued that the consignment agreement with SOG had terminated pre-petition, and pointed to the decision of the United States Bankruptcy Court for the District of Delaware in *In re Valley Media, Inc.*, 279 B.R. 105, 123 (Bankr. D. Del. 2002), in which that court had stated that nothing in the Uniform Commercial code "affected the ownership rights of the consignor in relation to the consignee." The bankruptcy court acknowledged that "As between the Debtor and Kraken, the Court agrees that Kraken owns the Botticelli. . . . However, the claims made by the Trustee in this adversary proceeding are based on provisions of the Uniform Commercial Code that allow creditors of a consignee such as the Debtor to obtain rights in consigned goods that are superior to those of the actual owner of the goods if the owner fails to take steps to perfect its interest." Jacobs v. Kraken investments Ltd., 506 B.R. at 607.

[134] *See id.* at 611.

[135] Kraken Investments Ltd. v. Jacobs (*In re* Salander O'Reilly, LLC), Case No. 14-cv-3544 (S.D.N.Y. Nov. 25, 2014).

cized losses suffered in the SOG case turned on a question of contract interpretation.

However, the lesson of the Kraken Botticelli is not that art consignors should hope that their galleries either do not end up in bankruptcy or that the galleries' secured lenders' collateral only extends to artworks actually owned by the galleries. Rather, it is that consignors need to protect themselves against the entirely forseeable and wholly unnecessary risk that Kraken took in failing to file a financing statement to perfect its consignment. Art consignors should not be lulled into complacency by the informal, relationship-based norms of art transactions. They need to be aware of (and comply with) the rules that are in place to protect them, just as they would in any other type of business transaction. Had SOG's loan agreement read differently, Kraken's Botticelli might not have come home.

(5) Aftermath

Following SOG's collapse, New York amended its artist consignment statute. The amendment (i) requires dealers and art galleries to maintain artist sale proceeds in segregated accounts, separate from the dealer's/gallery's operating accounts, (ii) an artist's own work consigned to a dealer or gallery and the proceeds from the sale of such works are insulated from attachment by the dealer's/gallery's creditors, (iii) the statute now provides for criminal penalties for dealers or galleries that fail to comply with their statutory obligations, and (iv) the statute now includes fee-shifting provisions, entitling artists to receive attorneys fees in actions to enforce their rights under the statute.[136]

---

136 Arts & Cultural Affairs Law, N.Y. Arts & Cult. Aff. Law §12.01(2012).

CHAPTER 10

International Trade in Art and Cultural Property

A. Export Controls

1. Export Restrictions and Preemptive Rights

A common form of regulation of the movement of art is restriction on the export of art determined to be part of a country's national treasure or national patrimony. More than 150 countries currently have export restrictions on cultural property, including the United Kingdom, but, notably, not the United States.[1] National export regimes generally employ multiple export regulation mechanisms, which can operate together. Among the forms of export restrictions of particular interest to parties to art-secured transactions are export licensing and preemptive rights.[2]

A recent example from the United Kingdom is typical of export licensing/preemptive rights cases. In December 2009, a private collector sold Hoare of Bath's 1733 portrait of Ayuba Suleiman Diallo[3] at Christie's for £541,250. The buyer was the Qatar Museums Authority (QMA). The portrait is the earliest known portrait by a British artist of a freed slave. The United Kingdom Export of Cultural Interest (Control) Order of 2003 (the "Order") requires a license for the export of "[a]ny objects of

1 Clare McAndrew, Fine Art and High Finance: Export Advice on the Economics of Ownership 169–170 (2010).

2 "Preemptive rights" are "rights associated with export licensing and give public museums or other institutions the first right to purchase the work of art to be exported at either a competitive market price or one set or agreed through negotiation. License application is initially needed to defer export and allows time for potential domestic purchasers to mobilize the necessary funds." *Id.*

3 Anne Laure Bandle, Raphael Contel & Marc-André Renold, *Case Ayuba Suleiman Diallo—Qatar Museums Authority and the United Kingdom, available at* http://unige.ch/art-adr.

cultural interest manufactured or produced more than 50 years before the date of exportation."[4] Under the Order, evaluation of whether an object sought to be exported qualifies as a national treasure is vested in the Reviewing Committee on the Export of Works of Art & Objects of Cultural Interest (RCEWA) under three criteria, which are known as the Waverly Criteria. The Waverly Criteria to be considered in such an evaluation are: (1) Connection of the object to the history and national life of the United Kingdom in such a way, that "its departure would be a misfortune for our history and national life;" (2) An object of "outstanding aesthetic importance;" and (3) Outstanding significance of the object for research purposes (for "a wide number of disciplines e.g. art history, archaeology, ethnography, anthropology, paleontology (subject to definition of 'fossils') science, engineering, architecture or literature, etc."[5] If the RCEWA concludes that one or more of the Waverly Criteria is satisfied, it recommends that a decision on the export license request be deferred while interested British museums have an opportunity to present the owner with an offer to purchase the object. If a public source makes an offer and the owner declines that offer, the Ministry of Culture, Media and Sport generally denies the request for an export license, and any new export permit request must wait at least 10 years.[6]

As required, the QMA submitted a request for an export license. In March 2010, the United Kingdom exercised its preemptive rights and temporarily barred export of the painting to allow British museums the opportunity to acquire it. With respect to the portrait of Diallo, the RCEWA found that it satisfied Waverly Criteria 1 and 3.[7] The RCEWA noted that "the subject of the portrait, Ayuba Suleiman Diallo, is an important figure in the history of the early transatlantic slave trade, and Britain's engagement in that trade."[8] The National Portrait Gallery made an offer to acquire the painting from the QMA, but that offer was declined. Ultimately, the United Kingdom and the QMA reached an agreement under which the QMA agreed to loan the painting to the National Portrait Gallery for a 5-year period. The National Portrait Gallery

[4] *Id.* at 3.
[5] RCEWA Guidelines No. 12.
[6] RCEWA Guidelines No. 21.
[7] Reviewing Committee on the Export of Works of Art and Objects of Cultural Interest: Note of case hearing on 3 March 2010: Portrait of Ayuba Suleiman Diallo, called Job ben Solomon, by William Hoare of Bath (Case 22, 2009-10), *available at* http://www.artscouncil.org.uk/media/uploads/pdf/Note_of_case_hearing_case_14_09-10.ashx.pdf. (visited Mar. 26, 2014).
[8] *Id.*

committed to organize a program of research, conservation, and interpretation of the painting, which would be funded by the QMA. The painting was permitted to be exhibited in Doha in 2013, but was then required to be returned to the U.K. The Diallo matter was able to be addressed as an opportunity for inter-governmental cultural exchange. However, when private parties are involved, a country's exercise of preemptive rights may not be resolved in so mutually beneficial a manner.

In *Beyeler v. Italy,*[9] the Italian government issued an order determining that Vincent Van Gogh's Portrait of a Young Peasant (1889) was "a work of historical and artistic interest within the meaning of Section 3 of Law no. 1089 of 1 June 1939,"[10] and served the owner of the painting, Verusio, a citizen of Italy living in Rome, with a copy of the order. Under Law no. 1089 of 1939, notice of any sale of the painting must be given to the Italian Ministry of Cultural Heritage, which has a right of preemption to acquire the painting. In 1977, Verusio sold the painting to Beyeler, a Swiss art collector and art dealer, through Pierangeli, an art dealer. Verusio submitted a notice of the sale to the Ministry of Cultural Heritage, identifying himself as the seller and Pierangeli as agent, but not indicating the buyer.

After the two-month preemption period lapsed, Pierangeli, on behalf of Beyeler, submitted a request for an export license to send the painting to London. The painting was placed in temporary custody with the Italian authorities, pending a determination on the export license request. Under Law no. 1089 of 1939, in addition to having a preemption right to acquire the painting upon a sale, the Italian government also had a preemption right to acquire it upon request for an export license. The Ministry advised Pierangeli that it did not intend to purchase the painting. Nevertheless, the Italian government denied the request for an export license "on the ground that it would be seriously detrimental to the national cultural heritage for the painting to be exported."[11] Had things ended there, the matter of the Van Gogh might have been similar to the matter of Diallo.

In 1983, the Peggy Guggenheim Collection in Venice made an offer to buy the painting for a purchase price of US$2,100,000. Pierangeli at this time informed the Ministry that Beyeler was the buyer of the

[9] Beleyer v. Italy, 33202/96 Eur. Ct. H. R. (2000).
[10] *Id.* at 4.
[11] *Id.* at 5.

painting in the 1977 sale. In February 1988, after years of discussions between Beyeler and the government concerning requests to move the painting to Venice so that it could be evaluated by the Peggy Guggenheim Collection and disputes over Beyeler's rights in the painting, the Ministry informed Beyeler that it was interested in acquiring the painting. Beyeler notifed the Ministry that he was willing to sell the painting for US$11 million, but the Ministry did not respond to Beyeler's offer. In May 1988, Beyeler delivered notice to the Ministry that he had sold the painting to the Peggy Guggenheim Collection for a purchase price of US$8.5 million. In November 1988, the Ministry exercised its right of preemption, justifying the untimely exercise on the grounds that the true identity of the contracting parties had been uncertain. The notice stated that the purchase price the Ministry would pay to Beyeler for the painting was the original purchase price he had paid Verusio in 1977. From 1989 until 1996, Beyeler litigated the exercise of preemptive rights in the Italian courts, and ultimately, in 1996, he applied to the European Court of Human Rights, arguing, among other things, that Italy's exercise of its preemptive rights with respect to the painting had violated Article 1 of Protocol No. 1 of the European Convention for the Protection of Human Rights and Fundamental Freedoms.[12]

In its decision of January 5, 2000, the court observed that the Italian government had "failed to give a convincing explanation as to why the Italian authorities had not acted at the beginning of 1984 in the same manner as they acted in 1988."[13] The court held that the Italian government's actions, taken as a whole, presented a violation of Article 1 of Protocol No. 1. The authorities' actions between 1983 and 1988, the court stated, "allowed the Ministry of Cultural Heritage to acquire the painting in 1988 at well below its market value. Having regard to the conduct of the authorities between December 1983 and November 1988, the Court considers that they derived an unjust enrichment from the uncertainty that existed during that period and to which they had largely

[12] Article 1 of Protocol No. 1 provides that "Every natural or legal person is entitled to the peaceful enjoyment of his possessions. No one shall be deprived of his possessions except in the public interest and subject to the conditions provided for by law and by the general principles of international law. The preceding provisions shall not, however, in any way impair the right of a State to enforce such laws as it deems necessary to control the use of property in accordance with the general interest or to secure the payment of taxes or other contributions or penalties." Council of Europe, *European Convention for the Protection of Human Rights and Fundamental Freedoms, as amended by Protocols Nos. 11 and 14*, 4 November 1950, ETS 5, *available at*: http://www.refworld.org/docid/3ae6b3b04.html [accessed 28 April 2014] (the "Convention).

[13] Beleyer v. Italy, 33202/96 at 23.

contributed. . . . The Court concludes that [Beyeler] had to bear a disproportionate and excessive burden."[14] The court ordered the government of Italy to pay to Beyeler the amount offered by the Peggy Guggenheim Collection (US$8.5 million minus the amount paid to him by the Italian government at the time of the exercise of its preemption right, plus interest from November 24, 1988, in the amount of US$3,934,142.90, plus Beyeler's costs in the amount of 912,025.60 Swiss francs.[15]

Although neither *Diallo* nor *Beyeler* directly involved, for instance, secured transactions, either could certainly have done so. As a dealer as well as a collector (a not uncommon overlapping of roles in the art trade), Beyeler could well have had inventory or operational financing. To simplify the legal paradigm, if we assume that either QMA or Beyeler, in their respective transactions, either had secured financing or wished to create security interests in the works they were acquiring, the secured party's expectation in each instance would have been that the acquired paintings would serve as the secured party's collateral.[16]

In *Diallo*, QMA's secured lender's security interest would still attach and could still be perfected, even where the painting itself is maintained and displayed at the National Gallery, provided that the National Gallery executed an agreement acknowledging the secured lender's interest. The inability to export the painting from the United Kingdom *may* have some impact on the painting's value, but it would not divest QMA of title to the work, nor would it divest QMA's secured lender of its security interest in it. The limitation on export and the government's expression of interest in the painting do not prohibit QMA from selling the work (and the secured lender being repaid from proceeds of that sale), although they may have the effect of chilling interest by potential purchasers.

---

[14] *Id.* at 23–24.

[15] *Id.* at 25. In a subsequent judgment on an issue the court had reserved as not yet ripe for decision, in 2002 the court further held that Italy's actions with respect to the Beyeler matter also violated Article 41 of the Convention, which allows the court to "afford just satisfaction to the injured party" when the internal law of the State "allows only partial reparation to be made." Beyeler v. Italy, 33202/96, 2 Eur. Ct. H. R. (2000). The court required the Italian government to pay to Beyeler €1.3 million "in compensation for the damage, including ancillary costs and costs incurred before the domestic courts" and €55,000 "for costs and expenses incurred before the Convention institutions." *Id.* at 7.

[16] As discussed in greater detail below, secured parties face particular issues and challenges in perfecting security interests in cultural property, particularly when the cultural property is located outside of the United States.

The impact on a secured lender of a *Beyeler* scenario, however, would be considerably more severe. The Italian government's exercise of its preemption right divests Beyeler of his rights in the painting, and thereby divests the lender of its security interest in the painting. The lender's security interest would, however, attach to the proceeds of the sale.[17] Unfortunately, in *Beyeler* the sale proceeds were limited to the original 1977 purchase price, so if Beyeler's secured lender had advanced funds based upon underwriting of a loan using a 1988 value of the painting, it would be significantly under-secured by the sale proceeds. Although Beyeler himself ultimately prevailed in the European Court of Human Rights, the monies awarded to him in the court's judgments would not generally constitute sale proceeds. In most circumstances, the secured lender would need to obtain a judgment against Beyeler, and execute on that judgment against such of Beyeler's assets as it would be able to attach through normal judicial means.

The United Kingdom's export permit process is more liberal than its continental European counterparts, since after an object has been declared to be of interest to the national heritage, a brief waiting period is imposed on issuance of an export permit while opportunity is given to national institutions to match the purchase price. Under most European export permit regimes, the designation of an object as being a part of the national heritage in itself deprives the owner of the right to export an object. In this manner, a country's export laws restricting the export of art can impact not only individual transactions, but the art market itself. At the 2014 Frieze art fair in London, Italian mid-20th-century work moved briskly. Sotheby's Italian and Contemporary sales broke records, including the highest price ever paid for the work of Piero Manzoni, whose *Achrome* sold for £12.6 million.[18] Several galleries focusing on Italian art of the 1950s and 1960s opened in London and Paris.[19] Some suggested that the

---

[17] Proceeds are whatever is received upon the sale, exchange, or other disposition or collection of collateral. UCC § 9-102(a)(64). Upon the sale, exchange, or other disposition or collection of collateral, a secured party's security interest continues in any identifiable proceeds. UCC §§ 9-203(f) and 9-315(a)(2). A secured party's priority as to its security interest in proceeds will usually date from the time of the secured party's priority as to its security interest in the original collateral. UCC § 9-322(b)(1).

[18] *See* Sotheby's, *Record-Breaking Italian Sale Leads Sotheby's Strongest Ever Frieze Week Auctions, available at* http://www.sothebys.com/en/news-video/videos/2014/10/record-breaking-italian-contemporary-sale-frieze.html.

[19] *See* Georgina Adam, *Modern Italian Art Falls Under an Export Ban*, THE FINANCIAL TIMES (October 10, 2014), *available at* http://www.ft.com/cms/s/0/3809db72-4982-11e4-8d68-00144feab7de.html#axzz3HZxttX8j.

rising amount of sales activity in Italian mid-century work was driven, at least in part, by pressure exerted by Italian laws restricting the export of art. *The Art Newspaper* reported that "[d]ealers and collectors are rushing to export works from Italy before they fall under the restrictions. . . . The number of works by *Arte Povera* artists (such as Alberto Burri, Alighiero Boetti, Mario Merz and Michelangelo Pistoletto) sold at auction has grown from 35 in 1997 to nearly 300 in 2013."[20] Of course, increased auction sales reflect changing tastes and collector interests, but the looming effect of export restriction cast a long shadow over the *Arte Povera* works held in public and private collections in Italy.

A common form of regulation of the movement of art is restriction on the export of art determined to be part of a country's national treasure or national patrimony. More than 150 countries currently have export restrictions on art.[21] National export regimes generally employ multiple export regulation mechanisms, which can operate together. Among the forms of export restrictions of particular interest to parties to art-secured transactions are export licensing and preemptive rights.[22]

Under the Italian Code of Cultural Heritage and Landscape (ICCHL), works by living artists or works created less than 50 years ago do not require an export license, but works older than 50 years do.[23] ICCHL restrictions apply to all artworks that are located in Italy, whether created there or not. *The Art Newspaper* noted that "[u]nlike most European countries, Italy has no lower price limit for works that need an export licence." Export restrictions can have a material impact on works' value, since "[o]nce they are designated as national heritage, works lose, on average, 70% to 80% of their value, because they can no longer leave Italy, reducing their appeal to foreign buyers."[24]

A group of galleries, dealers, and auction houses have lobbied the Italian government for reform of the ICCHL. *The Art Newspaper* reported that "the group seeks to bring Italy closer in line with France and the U.K.,

---

20 The Art Newspaper, October 2014, *available at* http://www.cbmlaw.it/media/News-Arte-Povera.pdf.

21 Clare McAndrew, Fine Art and High Finance: Export Advice on the Economics of Ownership 169–170 (2010).

22 "Preemptive rights" are "rights associated with export licensing and give public museums or other institutions the first right to purchase the work of art to be exported at either a competitive market price or one set or agreed through negotiation. License application is initially needed to defer export and allows time for potential domestic purchasers to mobilize the necessary funds." *Id.*

23 Bruno Boesch & Massimo Sterpi, The Art Collecting Legal Handbook 184 (2013).

24 The Art Newspaper, October 2014, *available at* http://www.cbmlaw.it/media/News-Arte-Povera.pdf.

extend the age limit on works from 50 to 75 years and introduce a minimum value for works requiring an export licence."[25] Such liberalization of art export permit processes does not appear to be the current trend.

On July 8, 2016, the German Bundesrat—the legislative body that represents Germany's sixteen states at the national level—approved an amendment to its Cultural Property Protection Law ("Kulturgutschutzgesetz" or "KGSG"), tightening the country's regulation of the sale and export of art and antiquities. An earlier version of the KGSG was proposed more than a year previously and was widely criticized by collectors, dealers, and museum directors. The KGSG was revised in response to the criticism, but both criticism of and confusion about it continues.

Outside of the antiquities and coin trade, the most important provisions of the KGSG are those that increase the documentation requirements for the sale of antiquities (archäologisches Kulturgut). However, these provisions are the ones that have received the least attention. Any antiquity imported into or sold in Germany must now be accompanied by evidence of it having been removed from its country of origin licitly, and most notably, with an appropriate export permit from that country. Collectors and antiquities and coin dealers have argued that for many objects such documentation does not exist, and that the KGSG treats objects as illicit until proven otherwise.

Yet most of the criticism of the KGSG, particularly of the original proposal, has focused on its export permit requirements. Since 1993, European Union law has mandated that EU countries, including Germany, require export permits for all artworks being exported to non-EU countries (like Switzerland or the United States) when the artwork is more than 50 years old and has a value of at least €150,000 (the value amount is for paintings; different value thresholds apply to other media). The KGSG now imposes a similar export permit requirement for artworks exported from Germany to other EU countries. As originally proposed, the KGSG would have enforced the same terms (50 years or older, €150,000 or greater) for export within the EU. This raised protests from the German art community, with artists Georg Baselitz, Gerhard Richter, and others speaking out strongly against the requirement. Following this outcry, the revised KGSG requires intra-EU export permits only for artworks

---

[25] THE ART NEWSPAPER, October 2014, *available at* http://www.cbmlaw.it/media/News-Arte-Povera.pdf.

of 70 years or older and valued at €300,000. Additionally, the export permit requirement does not apply to exports by artists of their own works.

Under the KGSG's export permit plan, each of Germany's 16 federal states (Länder) bears the responsibility for issuing permits. Each Länder also bears the responsibility for maintaining a list of artworks and other cultural property that are determined to be of national significance and thus would constitute Germany's national heritage. For objects designated as such, no export permit may be issued and objects in this category may not be exported from Germany. For purposes of "national heritage" designation, an object need not have been produced in Germany or by a German national. Rather, the determination is that the presence of that object in Germany has national significance of its own.

B. Freeports

The globalization of the art trade has given new importance to freeports. A freeport is a multifunctional, customs-privileged facility, often specially constructed to provide secure and confidential storage for art, as well as other high-value collectibles, such as wine, previous metals, jewels, and classic cars. Typically located proximate to international airports, freeports are effectively regarded as "outside" the customs zone of the host countries in which they are located, for customs and tax purposes.[26] Consequently, objects imported into a freeport are not subject to customs duties or value added taxes. Objects may be stored in the freeport for an indefinite period of time. They may even be loaned out to local museums for temporary exhibition without invalidating the tax benefits to the owner.[27] Once an object leaves the freeport and enters a country, it must clear customs, and customs duties and taxes must be paid at that time.

An important feature of the freeport arrangement is that objects may be bought and sold without leaving the freeport itself, with the result that such sales are exempt from sales, VAT, or other transaction taxes. This does not, however, mean that the owners of such objects are free from

[26] Susan Tiefenbrun, *U.S. Foreign Trade Zones, Tax-Free Trade Zones of the World, and Their Impact on the U.S. Economy*, 12 J. INT'L BUS. & L. 149, 158 (2013).

[27] *See Uber-Warehouses for the Ultra-Rich*, THE ECONOMIST (Nov. 23, 2013), *available at* http://www.economist.com/news/briefing/21590353-ever-more-wealth-being-parked-fancy-storage-facilities-some-customers-they-are.

capital-gains or other income taxes. Those taxes remain payable as they normally are, based on the owner's tax residency and local tax laws. It is also important to note that objects stored in a freeport remain subject to the host country's laws, and so attention must be paid to the local laws governing bailment and entrustment of property to third parties, as well as damage and loss. It is advisable for parties to transactions where art may be stored in a freeport to become familiar with applicable local law, and, where possible, to augment such protections as local law may provide with contractual arrangements with the freeport itself.

For decades, the most prominent art storage freeports have been located in Switzerland,[28] of which the Geneva freeport[29] is the best-known. However, similar freeports exist in Chiasso[30] and Zurich. A new 20,000-square-meter freeport facility specially designed for the storage of art and valuables was opened in Luxembourg in 2014.[31] The Luxembourg freeport's website succinctly describes the tax benefits of the freeport, noting that it

> operates under a regime of suspension of customs duties and VAT covering incoming goods and services rendered with respect of the goods while in storage at LE FREEPORT Luxembourg. VAT applies and is due when and by the last owner who removes the goods from the suspension regime to introduce them into an EU member country. Goods that leave LE FREEPORT Luxembourg for a Non-EU country do not suffer VAT and the suspension of VAT becomes final. Goods that change hands at LE FREEPORT Luxembourg are not subject to VAT nor is a withholding tax collected on the capital gain (which may of course be reportable and/or taxable in the country of the residence of the vendor).

Prominent freeports for art and collectibles storage have also been constructed in Singapore, Hong Kong, and Beijing.[32]

An important consideration for art transactions involving objects stored in freeports is the availability of adequate insurance. The concentration of high-value objects of art and other collectibles in freeports

[28] *See, e.g.*, David Segal, *Swiss Freeports Are Home for a Growing Treasury of Art*, THE NEW YORK TIMES (July 21, 2012), *available at* http://www.nytimes.com/2012/07/22/business/swiss-freeports-are-home-for-a-growing-treasury-of-art.html?_r=1.

[29] *See* http://geneva-freeports.ch/en/.

[30] *See* http://www.puntofranco.com/Chiasso.html.

[31] *See* http://www.lefreeport.lu/site/.

[32] Antony Dapiran, *Freeports*, 81 ART ASIA PACIFIC MAGAZINE (Nov./Dec. 2012).

presents challenges for insurers, and that challenge in turn impacts owners and other parties to transactions who need to insure those objects. Although freeports are typically quite secure, the risk that raises problems for insurance is the fact of concentration of so many objects of great value in a single location. If a freeport were to suffer a catastrophic event, the losses could be overwhelming for the art insurance industry. As a result, insurers increasingly have specific requirements and limitations on policies for objects located in freeports.

Insurers frequently require "specific declarations from clients that include detailed description, valuation and provenance details, sum insured and in addition the exact building, floor and room the art is stored in. This allows insurers to monitor their exposure and produce more accurate Probable Maximum Loss calculations. Each insurer will set its own limits on maximum aggregate sums insured that they can accept, some by location, some by building, some by floor."[33] Parties requiring insurance for objects that are or that may be located in a freeport should consult their insurer early in the process and may need to structure the transaction, at least in part, to address insurer requirements.

---

[33] Richard Northcott, *Freeport Storage of Fine Art: Plan Insurance in Advance* (June 16, 2015), *available at* http://www.ironshore.com/blog/freeport-storage-of-fine-art--plan-insurance-in-advance.

CONCLUSION

Art and cultural property transactions present tremendous opportunities and unique challenges. A trade whose transactions have relied on personal relationships, reputations and trust is undergoing significant transformation. These changes are being driven by developments in international law that are directed at protecting art and cultural property, deterring looting and destruction, protecting endangered species, preventing illicit trafficking, and preserving the common heritage of humankind. At the same time, changes to art and cultural property transactions and the art trade are driven by changes in global wealth and wealth distribution, and by the demands of global trade, commercial transactions, and finance. While the changes to the art trade to date have been significant, the process continues, and by some measures is accelerating.

APPENDIX A

Legal Restrictions Applicable to Art and Cultural Property

Nature of Restriction	Legal Source of Restriction	Categories of Objects to Which Restrictions Potentially Apply
Liens/security interests	**The Uniform Commercial Code,** as enacted by the various states. *See* Uniform Law Commission website, available at http://www.uniformlawcommission.com. **State artists' statutes and art consignment statutes** (ca. 34 states). For a list and brief description of state art consignment statutes, with links to state laws, see Volunteer Lawyers and Accountants for the Arts, available at http://www.vlaa.org/?view=Artist-Gallery-Consignment-Statutes.	All—Contemporary Art; Postwar and Contemporary (1945-present); Modern; Impressionist and Post-Impressionist; Old Masters; Medieval; Antiquities; Pre-Columbian; Archaeological or ethnographic materials.
Export restrictions	**National laws and regulations.**	Potentially all, but principally objects older than 50 years—Postwar (1945 and more recent); Modern; Impressionist and Post-Impressionist; Old Masters; Medieval; Antiquities; Pre-Columbian; Archaeological or ethnographic materials.
Import restrictions	**National laws and regulations.**	Potentially all, but principally objects older than 50 years—Postwar (1945 and more recent); Modern; Impressionist and Post-Impressionist; Old Masters; Medieval; Antiquities; Pre-Columbian; Archaeological or ethnographic materials.
VAT/duties	**National laws and regulations.**	All—Contemporary Art; Postwar and Contemporary (1945-present); Modern; Impressionist and Post-Impressionist; Old Masters; Medieval; Antiquities; Pre-Columbian; Archaeological or ethnographic materials.

Nature of Restriction	Legal Source of Restriction	Categories of Objects to Which Restrictions Potentially Apply
Intellectual property rights (copyright, VARA, etc.)	**United States Constitution, Article I, Section 8** ("The Congress shall have Power . . . To promote the Progress of Science and useful Arts, by securing for limited Times to Authors and Inventors the exclusive Right to their respective Writings and Discoveries."). **Copyright Act**, 17 U.S.C. 101, et seq. (1976, as amended), available at http://www.copyright.gov/title17/. **Visual Artists Rights Act**, 17 U.S.C. 106A et seq. (1990, as amended), available at http://www.law.cornell.edu/uscode/text/17/106A. In other countries, often referred to as *Droit Morale* or Moral Rights. **Berne Convention for the Protection of Literary and Artistic Works** (1886, as amended), available at http://www.wipo.int/treaties/en/ip/berne/. **Artist's Resale Right or *Droit de Suite*.**	Contemporary; Postwar and Contemporary (1945-present); Modern
Restrictions on materials (ivory, coral, tortoise shell, other species, etc.)	**The Convention on International Trade in Endangered Species of Wild Fauna and Flora** ("CITES") (1973, entered into force 1975), 27 UST 1087; TIAS 8249; 993 UNTS 243, available at http://www.cites.org/eng/disc/text.php (Established a system of import/export regulations to prevent the over-exploitation of certain specified plants and animals. Different levels of trade regulations are provided depending on the status of the listed species and the contribution trade makes to decline of the species). **The Endangered Species Act**, 16 U.S.C. 1531-1544 (1973, as amended), available at http://www.epw.senate.gov/esa73.pdf (among other things, authorizes the determination and listing of species as endangered and threatened; and prohibits unauthorized taking, possession, sale, and transport of endangered species; authorizes the assessment of civil and criminal penalties for violating the Act or regulations).	All—Contemporary Art; Postwar and Contemporary (1945-present); Modern; Impressionist and Post-Impressionist; Old Masters; Medieval; Antiquities; Pre-Columbian; Archaeological or ethnographic materials.

Nature of Restriction	Legal Source of Restriction	Categories of Objects to Which Restrictions Potentially Apply
	The Bald and Golden Eagle Protection Act,16 U.S.C. 668-668c (1940, as amended), available at http://www.fws.gov/permits/ltr/ltr.html (prohibits, except under certain specified conditions, the taking, possession, and commerce of bald eagles and golden eagles).	
Stolen art	**National Stolen Property Act, 18 U.S.C. § 2311 and 18 U.S.C. §§ 2314–2315, et seq.** (1948, as amended), available at http://uscode.regstoday.com/18USC_CHAPTER113.aspx#18USC2314. **National Ownership Laws.** **Resources:** • **Federal Bureau of Investigation National Stolen Art File**, available at http://www.fbi.gov/news/stories/2010/december/national-stolen-art-file/national-stolen-art-file. • **Interpol Stolen Art Database**, available at http://www.interpol.int/Crime-areas/Works-of-art/Works-of-art. • **The Art Loss Register**, available at http://www.artloss.com/en. • **Cultural Plunder by the Einsatzstab Reichsleiter Rosenberg: Database of Art Objects at the Jew de Paume**, available at http://www.errproject.org/jeudepaume/. • **The Central Registry of Information on Looted Cultural Property 1933-1945**, available at http://www.lootedart.com. • **The Lost Art Internet Database**, available at http://www.lostart.de/Webs/EN/Start/Index.html. • **Stolen Art Listing Belgium**, available at http://www.stolenart.be. • **International League of Antiquarian Booksellers, Stolen Book Database**, available at http://www.stolen-book.org.	All—Contemporary Art; Postwar and Contemporary (1945–present); Modern; Impressionist and Post-Impressionist; Old Masters; Medieval; Antiquities; Pre-Columbian; Archaeological or ethnographic materials.

Nature of Restriction	Legal Source of Restriction	Categories of Objects to Which Restrictions Potentially Apply
	• **Smithsonian Institution, Provenance in the World War II Era, 1933–1945**, available at http://provenance.si.edu/jsp/lost_art_databases.aspx (An excellent resource, with links to many national stolen art registries). • **The Getty Research Institute, German Sales Catalogues, 1930–1945**, available at http://www.getty.edu/research/tools/provenance/german_sales.html (A tremendously valuable resource, providing online, searchable German sales catalogues from the Nazi period).	
Authenticity	**Resources:** • **The Getty Research Institute, Collecting and Provenance Research**, available at http://www.getty.edu/research/tools/provenance/index.html. • **The Getty Research Institute, The Getty Provenance Index Databases**, available at http://piprod.getty.edu/starweb/pi/servlet.starweb?path=pi/pi.web.	All—Contemporary Art; Postwar and Contemporary (1945-present); Modern; Impressionist and Post-Impressionist; Old Masters; Medieval; Antiquities; Pre-Columbian; Archaeological or ethnographic materials.
Warranties	**The Uniform Commercial Code**, as enacted by the various states. See Uniform Law Commission, available at http://www.uniformlaws.org/Default.aspx. **United Nations Convention on Contracts for the International Sale of Goods** ("CISG") (1980), available at http://www.uncitral.org/uncitral/en/uncitral_texts/sale_goods.html.	All—Contemporary Art; Postwar and Contemporary (1945-present); Modern; Impressionist and Post-Impressionist; Old Masters; Medieval; Antiquities; Pre-Columbian; Archaeological or ethnographic materials.
Provenance	**Resources:** • **International Foundation for Art Research ("IFAR"), Provenance Guide**, available at http://www.ifar.org/provenance_guide.php.	Potentially all, but less commonly an issue with studio sales. Principally applies to secondary market sales of Contemporary Art; Postwar and Contemporary (1945-present); Modern; Impressionist and Post-Impressionist; Old Masters; Medieval; Antiquities; Pre-Columbian; Archaeological or ethnographic materials.

Nature of Restriction	Legal Source of Restriction	Categories of Objects to Which Restrictions Potentially Apply
Nazi-era confiscated and stolen art	**No U.S. federal law explicitly authorizing actions with respect to Nazi-era confiscated or stolen art.** **Cal. Code Civ. Pro. Code § 338(3)(a)(2010)** (authorizes persons to file actions against museums, galleries, auctioneers, or dealers for recovery of art taken or stolen by means of fraud or duress within the past 100 years, provided such actions are filed prior to Dec. 21, 2017). [NOTE: Cal. Civ. Pro. Code § 354.3 previously provided for an express Nazi-era cause of action, but was held to be an unconstitutional infringement of the federal government's exclusive foreign policy power] **Soft Law:** • **Commission for Looted Art in Europe**, website (with helpful links to other resources) available at http://www.lootedartcommission.com/home. • **Inter-Allied Declaration against Acts of Dispossession committed in Territories under Enemy Occupation and Control** (1943), available at http://www.lootedartcommission.com/inter-allied-declaration. • **Washington Conference Principles on Nazi-Confiscated Art** (1998), available at http://www.lootedartcommission.com/Washington-principles. • **International Council of Museums Recommendations concerning the Return of Works of Art Belonging to Jewish Owners** (1999), available at http://www.lootedartcommission.com/OXSHQE36019. • **Resolution 1205 of the Council of Europe** (1999), available at http://www.lootedartcommission.com/council-of-europe.	Modern and earlier (specifically, any objects that may have been located within continental Europe during the period 1933–1945).

Nature of Restriction	Legal Source of Restriction	Categories of Objects to Which Restrictions Potentially Apply
	• **Vilnius Forum Declaration** (2000), available at http://www.lootedart-commission.com/vilnius-forum. • **European Parliament Resolution and Report of Committee on Legal Affairs and the Internal Market** (2003), available at http://www.lootedartcommission.com/european-union. • **Joint Declaration of the European Commission and the Czech EU Presidency 29 June 2009**, available at http://www.lootedartcommission.com/NPNLJV15496. • **Terezin Declaration** (2009), available at http://www.lootedartcommission.com/NPNMG484641. • **Draft UNESCO Declaration of Principles Relating to Cultural Objects Displaced in Connection with the Second World War** (2009), available at http://www.lootedartcommission.com/OVNKN480270. • **Conference on Jewish Material Claims against Germany report, Holocaust-Era Looted Art: A Current World-Wide Overview** (Sept. 10, 2014) (Providing a 50-country survey of restitution efforts), available at http://www.claimscon.org/2014/09/looted-art-update/.	
Illicit Trade	**National Ownership Laws:** • **UNESCO Database of National Cultural Heritage Laws**, available at http://www.unesco.org/new/en/culture/themes/illicit-trafficking-of-cultural-property/unesco-database-of-national-cultural-heritage-laws/. **Civil forfeiture:** • **19 U.S.C. § 1595a(c)** (authorizing U.S. customs officials to seize merchandise introduced or attempted to be introduced into the U.S. contrary to law—the merchandise shall be seized and forfeited if it is "stolen, smuggled, or clandestinely imported or introduced" into the U.S.).	All—Contemporary Art; Postwar and Contemporary (1945-present); Modern; Impressionist and Post-Impressionist; Old Masters; Medieval; Antiquities; Pre-Columbian; Archaeological or ethnographic materials.

Nature of Restriction	Legal Source of Restriction	Categories of Objects to Which Restrictions Potentially Apply
	Criminal forfeiture: • **18 U.S.C. § 545** (providing for forfeiture of objects brought into the United States "contrary to law"). • **18 U.S.C. § 542** (any person who makes a false declaration is subject to criminal liability). • **National Stolen Property Act, 18 U.S.C. § 2311 and 18 U.S.C. §§ 2314–2315, et seq.** (1948, as amended)("NSPA"), available at http://uscode.regstoday.com/18USC_CHAPTER113.aspx#18USC2314 (Makes it an offence to trade in stolen goods, knowing them to be stolen, of the value of $5,000 or more, when they are moving in interstate or foreign commerce). • **Convention for the Protection of Cultural Property in the Event of Armed Conflict** (The "Hague Convention")(1954), available at http://portal.unesco.org/en/ev.php-URL_ID=13637&URL_DO=DO_TOPIC&URL_SECTION=201.html. • **Convention on the Means of Prohibiting and Preventing the Illicit Import, Export and Transfer of Ownership of Cultural Property** (1970), available at http://www.unesco.org/new/en/culture/themes/illicit-trafficking-of-cultural-property/1970-convention/. • **Convention on Cultural Property Implementation Act, 19 U.S. Code § 2601 et seq.** (1983), available at http://eca.state.gov/cultural-heritage-center/cultural-property-protection/process-and-purpose/background.	

Nature of Restriction	Legal Source of Restriction	Categories of Objects to Which Restrictions Potentially Apply
	• **Country-specific bilateral Memoranda of Understanding pursuant to the CPIA**. For a complete, updated list and information about these MOUs, see United States Department of State Bureau of Educational and Cultural Affairs website, available at http://eca.state.gov/cultural-heritage-center/cultural-property-protection/bilateral-agreements. For a chart showing current U.S. cultural property import restrictions, see http://eca.state.gov/files/bureau/chart-of-import-restrictions.pdf. • **UNESCO Convention for the Protection of the World Cultural and Natural Heritage** (1972), available at http://portal.unesco.org/en/ev.php-URL_ID=13055&URL_DO=DO_TOPIC&URL_SECTION=201.html (Establishes framework for international cooperation in conservation of world heritage sites, primarily with monuments, buildings, and archaeological sites.) For a current list of states' parties to this convention, see http://portal.unesco.org/la/convention.asp?KO=13055&language=E&order=alpha. For a current list of World Heritage Sites, see http://whc.unesco.org/pg.cfm?cid=31&l=en&&&mode=table. • **European Union Directive on the Return of Cultural Objects** (1993), available at http://eur-lex.europa.eu/LexUriServ/LexUriServ.do?uri=CELEX:31993L0007:EN:HTML (Guides the return of national treasures of artistic, historic, or archaeological value that have been unlawfully removed from the territory of a Member State of the European Union.). • **European Union Regulation (#3911/92) on the Export of Cultural Goods** (1992), available at http://eca.state.gov/files/bureau/eu3911.pdf (Ensures that exports of cultural goods are subject to uniform controls at the community's external borders.).	

Nature of Restriction	Legal Source of Restriction	Categories of Objects to Which Restrictions Potentially Apply
	• **UNIDROIT Convention on Stolen or Illegally Exported Cultural Objects** (1995), available at http://www.unidroit.org/english/conventions/1995culturalproperty/main.htm (Establishes common legal rules for the restitution and return of cultural objects between State Parties to the convention.) For a current list of states' parties to this convention, see http://www.unidroit.org/english/conventions/1995culturalproperty/main.htm (The U.S. is not a party to this convention). • **UNESCO Convention on the Protection of Underwater Cultural Heritage** (2001), available at http://portal.unesco.org/en/ev.php-URL_ID=13520&URL_DO=DO_TOPIC&URL_SECTION=201.html (The U.S. is not a party to this convention). • **Archaeological Resources Protection Act,** 16 U.S.C. § 470aa-470mm (1979, as amended) (ARPA), available at http://www.law.cornell.edu/uscode/text/16/chapter-1B (Places restrictions on archaeological resources which have been excavated or removed from federal lands or Indian lands or which have been excavated, removed, sold, purchased, exchanged, transported, or received contrary to state or local law (ARPA, §§ 470ee(b),(c)). "Archaeological resources" is defined as any material remains of past human life or activities which are of archaeological interest and includes pottery, basketry, bottles, weapons, weapon projectiles, tools, structures or portions of structures, pit houses, rock paintings, rock carvings, intaglios, graves, human skeletal materials or parts of any of these items. All items have to be at least 100 years old (ARPA, § 470bb)).	

Nature of Restriction	Legal Source of Restriction	Categories of Objects to Which Restrictions Potentially Apply
	• **The Native American Graves Protection and Repatriation Act**, 25 U.S.C. 3001-3013 (1990, as amended) (NAGPRA), available at http://indian-affairs.org/programs/aaia_repatriation_nagpra.htm. • **The Indian Arts and Crafts Act** (1990), available at http://www.iacb.doi.gov/act.html (Makes it illegal to offer or display for sale, or sell any art or craft product in a manner that falsely suggests it is Indian produced, an Indian product, or the product of a particular Indian or Indian Tribe or Indian arts and crafts organization, resident within the United States). • **Pre-Columbian Monumental and Architectural Sculpture and Murals Statute** (1973) (Public Law 92-587). (Applies to any monumental or architectural sculpture or mural or fragment thereof from a Pre-Columbian Indian culture imported into the United States from Belize, Bolivia, Colombia, Costa Rica, Dominican Republic, Ecuador, El Salvador, Guatemala, Honduras, Mexico, Panama, Peru, Venezuela. Restricts imports of these materials into the U.S. without authorization from the country of origin), available at http://eca.state.gov/cultural-heritage-center/international-cultural-property-protection/process-and-purpose/laws#sthash.LS8Ampj5.dpuf. • **Treaty of Cooperation Between the United States of America and the United Mexican States Providing for the Recovery and Return of Stolen Archaeological, Historical and Cultural Properties** (1970), available at http://eca.state.gov/cultural-heritage-center/international-cultural-property-protection/process-and-purpose/laws#sthash.LS8Ampj5.dpuf.	

Nature of Restriction	Legal Source of Restriction	Categories of Objects to Which Restrictions Potentially Apply
	• **Iraqi Sanctions Regulations, Title 31 Part 575 of the U.S. Code of Federal Regulations** (May 23, 2003), available at http://eca.state.gov/cultural-heritage-center/international-cultural-property-protection/process-and-purpose/laws#sthash.LS8Ampj5.dpuf. (The Office of Foreign Assets Control [OFAC] issued a General License lifting most of the sanctions against Iraq. Restrictions were retained on any transactions involving Iraqi cultural property since August 6, 1990. Any trade in or transfer of such items remains prohibited by subpart B of 31 CFR part 575.). See also the UN Security Council Resolution 1483, regarding Iraq, published 22 May 2003, available at http://eca.state.gov/files/bureau/unsc1483.pdf. • **Agreement Between the United States of America and the Republic of Peru for the Recovery and Return of Stolen Archaeological, Historical, and Cultural Properties** (1981), available at http://eca.state.gov/files/bureau/1981usperu.pdf. • **Agreement Between the United States of America and the Republic of Guatemala for the Recovery and Return of Stolen Archaeological, Historical, and Cultural Properties** (1984), available at http://eca.state.gov/files/bureau/1981usperu.pdf. • **Organization of American States ("OAS") Convention on the Protection of the Archaeological, Historical, and Artistic Heritage of the American Nations** (1976) (Convention of San Salvador), available at http://eca.state.gov/files/bureau/oasssx.pdf (The U.S. is not a party to this convention.).	

APPENDIX B

Market Sectors for Art and Cultural Property and Applicable Legal Restrictions

Categories of Objects	Type of Sale	Applicable Restrictions
		Primary Market
Contemporary Art	Studio sales	Restrictions on materials (i.e., ivory, coral, tortoise shell, other species, etc.) Liens by artist's creditors Restrictions on export Restrictions on import VAT/duties Intellectual property rights (copyright, VARA, etc.) Native American/Indigenous objects Stolen art
	Gallery/dealer sales	Restrictions on materials (i.e., ivory, coral, tortoise shell, other species, etc.) Artist consignment statutes (34 states) (in MA, also covers nonartist consignments) Liens/security interests Restrictions on export Restrictions on import VAT/duties Intellectual property rights (copyright, VARA, etc.) Native American/indigenous objects Stolen art Warranties (title, authenticity, condition)

Categories of Objects	Type of Sale	Applicable Restrictions
		Secondary Market
Postwar and Contemporary (1945–present)	Gallery/dealer sales/auction sales	Restrictions on materials (i.e., ivory, coral, tortoise shell, other species, etc.) Artist consignment statutes (34 states) (in MA, also covers nonartist consignments) Liens/security interests Restrictions on export Restrictions on import VAT/duties Intellectual property rights (copyright, VARA, etc.) Native American/indigenous objects Warranties (title, authenticity, condition) Provenance Stolen art
Modern	Gallery/dealer sales/auction sales	Restrictions on materials (i.e., ivory, coral, tortoise shell, other species, etc.) Artist consignment statutes (MA only, which covers nonartist consignments) Liens/security interests Restrictions on export Restrictions on import VAT/duties Intellectual property rights (copyright, VARA, etc.) Warranties (title, authenticity, condition) Provenance Stolen art Nazi-era "looted" art
Impressionist and Post-Impressionist	Gallery/dealer sales/auction sales	Restrictions on materials (i.e., ivory, coral, tortoise shell, other species, etc.) Artist consignment statutes (MA only, which covers nonartist consignments) Liens/security interests Restrictions on export Restrictions on import VAT/duties Intellectual property rights (copyright, VARA, etc.)

Categories of Objects	Type of Sale	Applicable Restrictions
		Warranties (title, authenticity, condition) Provenance Stolen art Nazi-era "looted" art
Old Masters	Gallery/dealer sales/auction sales	Restrictions on materials (i.e., ivory, coral, tortoise shell, other species, etc.) Artist consignment statutes (MA only, which covers nonartist consignments) Liens/security interests Restrictions on export Restrictions on import VAT/duties Intellectual property rights (copyright, VARA, etc.) Warranties (title, authenticity, condition) Provenance Stolen art Nazi-era "looted" art
Medieval	Gallery/dealer sales/auction sales	Restrictions on materials (i.e., ivory, coral, tortoise shell, other species, etc.) Artist consignment statutes (MA only, which covers nonartist consignments) Liens/security interests Restrictions on export Restrictions on import VAT/duties Intellectual property rights (copyright, VARA, etc.) Warranties (title, authenticity, condition) Provenance Stolen art Nazi-era "looted" art

Categories of Objects	Type of Sale	Applicable Restrictions
Antiquities	Gallery/dealer sales/auction sales	Restrictions on materials (i.e., ivory, coral, tortoise shell, other species, etc.) Artist consignment statutes (MA only, which covers nonartist consignments) Liens/security interests Restrictions on export Restrictions on import VAT/duties Intellectual property rights (copyright, VARA, etc.) Warranties (title, authenticity, condition) Provenance Stolen art Nazi-era "looted" art Antiquities looting
China	Gallery/dealer sales/auction sales	Restrictions on materials (i.e., ivory, coral, tortoise shell, other species, etc.) Artist consignment statutes (MA only, which covers nonartist consignments) Liens/security interests Restrictions on export Restrictions on import VAT/duties Intellectual property rights (copyright, VARA, etc.) Warranties (title, authenticity, condition) Provenance Stolen art Nazi-era "looted" art Antiquities looting

Categories of Objects	Type of Sale	Applicable Restrictions
Asia (other than China)	Gallery/dealer sales/auction sales	Restrictions on materials (i.e., ivory, coral, tortoise shell, other species, etc.) Artist consignment statutes (MA only, which covers nonartist consignments) Liens/security interests Restrictions on export Restrictions on import VAT/duties Intellectual property rights (copyright, VARA, etc.) Native American/Indigenous Warranties (title, authenticity, condition) Provenance Stolen art Nazi-era “looted” art Antiquities looting
Mexico/Latin America	Gallery/dealer sales/auction sales	Restrictions on materials (i.e., ivory, coral, tortoise shell, other species, etc.) Artist consignment statutes (MA only, which covers nonartist consignments) Liens/security interests Restrictions on export Restrictions on import VAT/duties Intellectual property rights (copyright, VARA, etc.) Warranties (title, authenticity, condition) Provenance Stolen art Nazi-era “looted” art Antiquities looting

Categories of Objects	Type of Sale	Applicable Restrictions
Africa	Gallery/dealer sales/auction sales	Restrictions on materials (i.e., ivory, coral, tortoise shell, other species, etc.)
		Artist consignment statutes (MA only, which covers nonartist consignments)
		Liens/security interests
		Restrictions on export
		Restrictions on import
		VAT/duties
		Intellectual property rights (copyright, VARA, etc.)
		Warranties (title, authenticity, condition)
		Provenance
		Stolen art
		Nazi-era "looted" art
		Antiquities looting

INDEX

D

V

W

X

Y